Thinking Nature

Thinking Nature

An Essay in Negative Ecology

SEAN J. McGRATH

EDINBURGH
University Press

Edinburgh University Press is one of the leading university presses in the UK. We publish academic books and journals in our selected subject areas across the humanities and social sciences, combining cutting-edge scholarship with high editorial and production values to produce academic works of lasting importance. For more information visit our website: edinburghuniversitypress.com

Edinburgh University Press Ltd
The Tun – Holyrood Road, 12(2f) Jackson's Entry, Edinburgh EH8 8PJ

Typeset in Garamond and Gill Sans
by R. J. Footring Ltd, Derby, UK, and
printed and bound by CPI Group (UK) Ltd
Croydon, CR0 4YY

A CIP record for this book is available from the British Library

ISBN 978 1 4744 4926 7 (hardback)
ISBN 978 1 4744 4928 1 (webready PDF)
ISBN 978 1 4744 4929 8 (epub)

Contents

Preface

This essay uncovers and critiques the philosophical assumptions – historical, metaphysical and ethico-political – operative in the claim that 'nature', whether posited as a social construct or as reality, has 'died'. Such a claim can only mean that the concept of nature has become, in the Anthropocene, evacuated of significance. Without denying the obsolescence of a certain ancient sense of nature now popular in the re-enchantment industry (nature as an organic whole to which the human belongs as a part), in what follows I will consider the opposite claim – that the so-called death of 'nature' in the Anthropocene in fact heralds nature's re-emergence as a living symbol, an overdetermined sign the multiple senses of which are inextricably intertwined with the theological and philosophical heritage of the West. Indeed, the transformation our thinking about nature is currently undergoing speaks to the need for us to reconsider the religious heritage of the West – the ecologically ambiguous legacy of Christianity in particular.

This book is an essay in the classical sense of the term, a non-systematic, meandering meditation on a theme. An essay makes its case not through watertight argument but through suggestion and evocation of other texts and common human experiences. A philosophical treatise solves problems and closes questions, often by anticipating critics and outflanking them before they begin; an essay does not solve or settle so much as invite further thought. It welcomes the critic. Its aim is not to close a debate but to open one – to raise an issue for consideration.

The subtitle of this essay introduces the neologism 'negative ecology', which evokes the medieval tradition of negative theology. The negative theologian practises an early form of deconstruction, unsaying what has been said about God at the pinnacle of the theological quest, since everything said about God is ultimately untrue of God, drawn as it must be from a language made up of finite referents.[1] My point is not that nature is infinite and so escapes language, but rather that the new meaning of nature emerging in the Anthropocene is still inchoate, still not actual enough to be defined. The preparation for its advent requires the clearing away of concepts of nature that are no longer meaningful for us. I have in view the two principal metaphors through which nature has been conceived in the West: as organism and as mechanism, and the presupposition of both, nature as pre-established order. The death of these previously living metaphors of nature is not, I will argue, the death of the symbol of nature, but rather its transformation. Since what nature will mean in the future is still unclear – still undecided – the work of the eco-critic must be largely negative, not offering a new theory or concept but, rather, showing why some of the older concepts are no longer viable. But just as in negative theology the deconstruction need not issue in atheism, so in negative ecology the demise of familiar concepts of nature need not leave us, *pace* Bruno Latour, with an eco-politics without nature. It might leave us, rather, with an eschatological eco-politics, a politics awaiting the unveiling of the new thinking of nature now occurring in countless contexts, however unconsciously and tentatively.[2]

If there is one classic text in the history of ecology upon which this essay's meditation is built, it is Lynn White Junior's 'The Historical Roots of Our Ecological Crisis' (White 1967). White's argument, presented in the 155th volume of *Science*, has never truly been refuted. Our ecological crisis is the result, writes White, of a certain line of technological development anticipated by a certain ethico-theological attitude – an attitude not universally present in human history but proper to a specific historical form of human culture, namely Christendom, the womb of modern Europe. By assuming the human being's – the *Imago Dei*'s – right to 'subdue' and 'have dominion' over 'every living thing' on earth (Gen. 1: 28) without recourse to that oldest of human institutions, slavery (for the *Imago Dei* is never a means to an end, as Kant puts it in a later development of the same Christian anthropology[3]), the medieval European set upon the earth with unprecedented energy to transform it into an environment suitable to human flourishing. For Christendom, nature was not divine but, like us, created – designed, so to speak, to be subordinated to our needs. White reminds a world on the cusp of ecological consciousness (and at the beginning of the great acceleration) that the bind we are in today has non-rational – that is, religious – roots. In doing so, he argues that we moderns are not as secular as we might presume. A merely technical fix to the problem, White maintained in 1967, is not possible: the (now even more) widespread assumption that more technology will solve the problem of climate change, that geo-engineering or space travel or AI will lead us to greener pastures, is itself symptomatic of the attitude of mastery that must be transcended.

But what so few of those who continue to cite White's article advert to is the way White concludes his critique of Western thinking about nature. White does not argue for an unqualified rejection of the ethico-theological orientation of modernity, but rather for its internal transformation. The ecological crisis requires not a transcendence of Western religion but the West's religious transformation, which, whatever else it means, signifies a return: 'Since the roots of our trouble are so largely religious, the remedy must also be essentially religious, whether we call it that or not. We must rethink and re-feel our nature and destiny' (White 1967: 1207). It is in this context that I presume to argue in the following essay that ecology is not yet finished with Christianity; nor is Christianity yet finished with us.

I will, at the end of the essay, suggest that modernity might be re-routed through a retrieval of contemplation, the sense of surrender to the mysterious origin of all being, which underwrites the vast and increasingly forgotten literature of mystical Christianity. With the fourteenth-century Rhineland mystic Meister Eckhart, I will argue that contemplative ecology is not at odds with ecological action but ought to issue naturally into it, just as action ought to call us to contemplation. Eckhart can help us greatly here. The ethics of critique, control and calculation – the predominant attitude towards nature embraced by modernity – in short, the technological attitude – cannot be simply abandoned at this precarious moment in the history of civilisation, since we are going to need good tech to pull through; but it must be qualified by contemplative reverence for the incalculable and unfathomable origins of existence.

As the reader will discover in the pages of the essay, contemplative political ecology is under the symbol of Mercurius, the mediator, that daemon of the coincidence of opposites (*coincindentia opposituorum*) and the guiding spirit of the Renaissance who refuses to abide by conventional exclusions. In Renaissance Hermeticism, Mercurius is the symbol of that which is common to all, the water of life (*aqua viva*), the quicksilver that runs through the centre of everything. Good with the good, bad with the bad, Mercurius is the *anima naturae*, the spirit of nature, as finite as creation, if still greater than the human. S/he (for Mercurius is the Androgyne) communicates between the high and the low, the good and the bad (and, in our context, the left and the right) because s/he is exclusively neither one thing nor the other. Mercurius is retrieved here as the spirit of the Anthropocene, the patron saint of the new thinking now occurring (Leahy 1994), for s/he is the incalculable, the Lord of *chaosmos*, composed of equal parts matter and spirit, both human and non-human. S/he is the spirit of the *technosphere*, the spirit of AI, the cyborg, the hypostatic union of *techne* and *physis*: fully human and fully machine. S/he is also the genius of modernity, as any honest survey of Renaissance literature and early-modern science demonstrates. The late medievals and early moderns did not, with the ancients, worship the earth as a god, for they were, for the most part, Jews, Christians and Muslims, and stood under the First Commandment of Moses, the imperative that introduces an infinite gulf between the Creator and creation. But they nonetheless sought with ancient Hermeticism the philosopher's stone (the *lapis philosophorum*), the uncommon gold (*aurum on vulgi*), which they identified with Mercurius. They followed Mercurius wherever s/he led and dedicated themselves to understanding her/him, even if for the sake of controlling the environment. For there is nothing evil or unusual about controlling an environment per se: beavers do it, stone-age farmers did it; moderns, too – exceptionally well, perhaps too well. But a green technology is no less a technology when it is contemplatively self-limited to allow the beautiful to occur (McGrath 2003).

Some of the chapters that make up the essay have their origin elsewhere. 'Eco-Anxiety' originated in a paper I first read in Montreal in November of 2010, at the annual meeting of the International Association of Environmental Philosophy. It was delivered again later that year as a public lecture at Grenfell College, Corner Brook, and in St John's, Newfoundland, at the Ship Pub. It is published here for the first time. 'The Theology of Disenchantment' was first delivered as a paper entitled 'The Search for Environmental Holism and the Theologico-Political Trajectory of the West' at the 'A Concept of Nature for the Twenty-First Century' conference co-organised by the Institute of Philosophy and the Centre for Environmental Science at the University of Augsburg (WZU) in June 2014. It, too, is published here for the first time. Some of the new material added to that chapter was delivered in a presentation entitled 'The Future Nature Initiative' at the University of Bonn in December 2016. An earlier version of 'Dark Ecology' was published under the title 'The Question Concerning Nature' in *Interpreting Nature: The Emerging Field of Environmental Hermeneutics*, edited by Brian Treanor and Forrest Clingerman and published by Fordham University Press (McGrath 2014). This earlier version was first read publicly under the title 'Dark Ecology and the Question Concerning Nature' in November 2012, at the University of Augsburg. 'The Human Difference' has recently appeared under the title 'In Defense of the Human Difference' in a special issue of *Environmental Philosophy* dedicated to the memory of eco-philosopher Scott Cameron, whose career was cut short by illness (McGrath 2018).

I owe thanks to the University of Augsburg for having supported the work via the (ongoing) exchange that it initiated with Memorial University on the philosophy of nature and interdisciplinary ecology, and to the Social Sciences and Humanities Research Council for continuing to fund my research in interdisciplinary ecology in a variety of ways. Special thanks go to Christina Galego for her invaluable editorial assistance. I should also like to thank the staff at Edinburgh University Press – namely Carol Macdonald, Commissioning Editor for Philosophy, and Peter Gratton, my co-editor on the series in which this book appears – for taking a chance on this somewhat unconventional venture into eco-criticism. My thanks go out as well to my collaborators in 'For a New Earth' (FANE), the newest ENGO in the province of Newfoundland and Labrador, whose mission is nothing short of 'ecological conversion for everyone'. Much that is written in these pages was researched, discussed and conceived at FANE-organised events.

This is probably a good place to acknowledge also two very pleasant weeks spent reading Renaissance Hermeticism in 2008 at the Ritman Library Bibliotheca Philosophica Hermetica in Amsterdam. It is a top-notch collection in a fine facility maintained by excellent staff, to whom I extend my sincere gratitude. I would alike to thank Adam Maclean for the reproductions of the alchemical images which appear in this book – the painting of Mercurius on page xiv and the engraving from Khunrath on page 155.

Notes

1. See Coward and Foshay (1992).
2. The phrase is D. G. Leahy's. See Leahy (1994).
3. I am not denying that throughout much of its history Christendom has co-existed with slavery and has even encouraged this oldest of institutions. While the early Christian communities practised equality – 'There is neither Jew nor Greek, there is neither slave nor free, there is no male and female, for you are all one in Christ Jesus' (Gal. 3: 28; cf. Acts 4: 32–5) – Paul has frequently been taken to task for not openly objecting to slavery and for encouraging slaves to obey their masters (Eph. 6: 5). My point is that, in principle, Christianity (and before it, and to a lesser degree, Judaism) could never theoretically justify slavery, as could Aristotle or Plato, or the Ancient Hindus for that matter, since Christianity regards all human beings as equally imaging God and equally redeemed by Christ. In Christianity, by contrast to all other ancient worldviews, slavery could never be justified on the basis of putatively qualitative differences among human beings. This ontological egalitarianism impelled Christendom towards the cult of progress, the emancipation of human beings from servile labour through the design of technology and the equitable distribution of wealth. In short, Christendom produces the emancipated human being that is the modern ideal, even if modernity breaks with Christendom at decisive points. See Belloc (1912), Gauchet (1999), Grant (1987) and Berman (2008).

Man is a microcosm, or a little world, because he is an extract from all the stars and planets of the whole firmament, from the earth and the elements; and so he is their quintessence.

Paracelsus

But where the danger is, also grows the saving power.

Friedrich Hölderlin

To Terry Hewlin, fellow pilgrim

Mercurius, 1499. Anonymous.

Chapter 1

Religion is not Only the Problem, but also the Solution

We are the nature – the animal, the life – that thinks. *Thinking nature*, a passable if figurative translation of Aristotle's *zoon logon echon*, describes at once the *animal rationale* – the rational animal, the thinking animal – and the *animal symbolicum* – the symbolising animal, as Ernst Cassirer puts it – for it is only by means of symbols that thinking occurs (Cassirer 1944). On the basis of a Cassirerian analysis of symbol, we will venture a yet more figurative translation of *zoon logon echon*: contemplative life. For to symbolise is, first and foremost, to contemplate the meaning of things as they show themselves, and it is only on the basis of this original showing of sense that the objectification and manipulation of things (that is, science and technology) are possible. Thinking nature is thus the human who can conceive, represent, objectify, but also and above all contemplate and revere the nature that it is and that it depends on, and who possesses this capacity uniquely (it seems) among the earth community. 'Nature begins as unconscious and ends as conscious' (Schelling 1800: 219). We ourselves are thinking nature; that is the first sense of the title of this essay.

A second sense of the title points to the task to which we are now called, which is to think – or, rather, rethink – the meaning of nature in the Anthropocene. Overpopulation, climate change, genetic engineering, geo-engineering, the mass extinction not only of non-human species but also of indigenous human cultures and their languages: all of these dubious markers of human progress compel us to think nature anew. None of the familiar epithets applies. We must think nature in the way it is given to us to think it today. No longer is nature accessible to us as divine cosmos or eternally balanced container of human life. Traditional preconceptions of nature have come to an end in the Anthropocene. We can no longer deny the finitude of the earth; we can no longer pretend that it will remain what it is for us now, that it is invulnerable to what we do.

The Anthropocene discloses not only the fragility of what Pope Francis calls 'our common home' (Francis 2015), but the untenability of older ways of thinking about it. Bruno Latour writes:

> There is no harmony in this contingent cascade of unforeseen events and there is no nature either – at least not in this sublunary realm of ours. But to learn how to situate human actions into this geostory is not – such is the crucial lesson – to 'naturalize' humans either. No unity, no universality, no indisputability, no indefeasibility is to be invoked when humans are thrown in the turmoil of geostory. (Latour 2017: 74)

The 'order of things' has indeed dissolved in the Anthropocene. But Latour goes too far in saying that we can no longer think of the earth as natural in any sense. Nature still means, and can continue to mean, more than the 'already out there now real'.[1] Today, when the only promising prospect for the survival of humankind (which seems unable to imagine the end of the capitalist economy responsible for overheating the planet) appears to be geo-engineering – transforming the earth into a sustainable-energy storage system, a giant battery – is it still meaningful to speak of nature at all? This is the first question we must consider, then. *Is* there anything yet to be thought in the term *nature*? Is Latour right? Is nature as symbol really dead and gone? Have we finally exhausted its significance and appeal? Or is the opposite the case? Has the 'death of nature', proclaimed not only by Latour but by various environmental thinkers and journalists over the past two decades, not in fact precipitated the most heated discussion of nature we have seen since the beginning of the nineteenth century? The question concerning nature has never been more in the forefront of both public and academic discourse than it is now. The philosophy of nature has never been more relevant.

Some provisional definitions are needed. Without presuming to provide a comprehensive account of what it means to be modern, and without identifying precisely when the modern era emerges in history, we can say that modernity is uniquely characterised by *critique*, *control* and *calculation*. That we can, with some accuracy, say as much is indication enough that modernity, at least in its first iteration, is over. We know *what* we are only when we also know that we are no longer identical to it: predication is always of that which is in some basic sense the past of the subject and thereby differentiable from it.[2] We have entered a new era, and its newness is indicated by the disturbing fact that we still do not know how to name it. With the advent of 'the new thinking now occurring' (Leahy 1994: 8), with the emergence of *chaosmos* as the dominant paradigm for thinking the universe – Joyce, not Deleuze: 'Every person, place and thing in the chaosmos of Alle anyway connected' (Joyce 1939: ch. 5, para. 21) – with the emergence of quantum communication, and indeed with the Anthropocene, which denies us our fantasy of transcending the material conditions of our existence, critique has given way before the incomprehensibility of space-time (relativistic on the macro-scale, indeterminate on the micro); control has capitulated before that which is at bottom uncontrollable; and calculation has been forced to admit that, in itself, nature is incalculable because it is originally indeterminate. Nature is *meontic* – neither determinate being nor nothing, but *possibility* – as conceived in the Schellingian–Peircean tradition – in a Platonic rather than Aristotelian sense. As possibility, it is not restricted to any of its past forms or senses, but stands open, always, to the new.[3] Precisely because we have lost our early-modern bearings, because we can no longer regard nature as either organism or mechanism, precisely now, in this negative place of disorientation, acceleration and uncertainty, where 'all that is solid melts into air' (Marx), we can paint a portrait of who we *were*. We were critics, controllers and calculators, and through critique, control and calculation we transformed the earth, for better or for worse, creating a civilisation capable of hosting over 7 billion human beings (a figure more than double what it was when I was born) unparalleled in its technical achievements.

What were we, then?

Critique designates the modern turn away from traditional knowledge, which was content-oriented and negligent of the means and methods of knowing. Critique was subject-oriented and content-sceptical, a promoter of self-consciousness, a product of 'the turn to the subject', of moderns who, with Kant, first queried the conditions of understanding before accepting the truth of any claim. '*Sapere audē*', enjoins Kant in his celebrated essay 'What Is Enlightenment?' 'Have the courage to use your own intelligence' (Kant 1784: 132). Whereas the premodern mind trusted what was received or revealed by tradition, its modern counterpart was suspicious of delusion, deception, ideology. In the hands of moderns, critique was the two-edged sword that both destroys and liberates. The power of critique impelled Europe toward the revolutions in theology, science and politics that ultimately overthrew the medieval system and awakened a will to justice in societies that had for too long tolerated tyranny. Critique broke the spell of ancient knowledge on the medieval mind, making technological progress possible. But so too did it promote naïveté and ignorance of the past. Critique empowered the individual to disidentify with tradition, community and class; whereas every era prior to the modern regarded individuals as bound to the social stratum into which they were born, critique enabled social mobility. In liberating so much forward-looking movement, critique paved the way for capitalism and consumerism. In what follows I use the term 'consumer-capitalism', rather than 'capitalism', because I believe that consumerism and capitalism can, and indeed should be distinguished. Capitalism is an economic theory of wealth creation; consumerism is a modern ethos, a world-view, even a spirituality, not at all unrelated to the degeneration of modern Christianity and distorted secular Christian attitudes. It is consumerism that destroys communities, atomises individuals and plunders eco-systems, not capitalism as such (Campbell 1987; McGrath 2014c). But capitalism always needs a qualifier, such as 'social', 'distributive', 'ecological' or 'natural'. The transition from consumer capitalism to natural capitalism is, in my view, the most realistic and plausible solution on offer to the ecological crisis (Fenech et al. 2003; Foster 2003; Hawken et al. 1999). The term 'natural capital' was coined by E. F. Schumacher (Schumacher 1973: 4–6). It refers to natural resources such as rainforests, oceans, climate, etc., which classical economics fails to take into account, but which all economic growth depends upon.

Control refers, among other things, to the typically modern impetus to change the world to make it more suitable for human flourishing. While the controlling nature of modern thought is often subject to scathing criticism by those thinkers attached to more contemplative ways of thinking (above all, Heidegger), it is worth remembering, as I will illustrate elsewhere in this essay, that the modern will to control is based on the deeply theological assumption that creation, far from being complete, is, rather, advancing continually toward an end that will be different from (and perhaps better than) its beginning (Benz 1965; Löwith 1949). The modern will to control the world is not inevitably evil, nor was it originally motivated by hubristic or tyrannical fantasies of despotic rule. It is, as I will consider in greater detail, theological in origin. Moderns sought to control the world to make it more suitable for human living because they believed it to be their destiny to 'fill the earth and subdue it', to 'have dominion over the fish of the sea and over the birds of the heavens and over every living thing that moves on the earth' (Gen. 1: 28). Early-modern science was shot through with a Biblical sense that the Creator left the earth unfinished so that humankind might complete the Creator's work.[4]

Closely aligned with critique and control (and underwriting both) is the basic modern attitude toward being, which I call *calculative*. Here it is important to make a distinction between quantitative reasoning and totalising calculation. The latter is not merely quantification, but the reduction of all values to quantities, and with that levelling move, the re-description of reason as a means in service of whatever ends have been chosen – as a tool that can be applied in any way whatsoever. Calculation may well have been the secret to our success; but it may prove to be the seed of our demise. In premodern ages, reason was held to be intrinsically oriented toward the good, and thus hardly indifferent to its own applications. Modern reason, by contrast, indifferent and value-free, tells us nothing about how it should be used. Totalising calculation is the essence of what the Frankfurt school calls 'instrumental reason'. Since critique and control are both grounded by it, it is worth dwelling further, for a moment, on this phenomenon of totalising calculation. Max Horkheimer discerns two opposing elements in calculative or what he calls instrumental reason. On the one side, calculation reduces the self to 'the abstract ego emptied of all substance except its attempt to transform everything in heaven and on earth into means for its preservation'; on the other side, it reduces the earth, leaving only 'an empty nature degraded to mere material, mere stuff to be dominated, without any other purpose than that of this very domination' (Horkheimer 1947: 97). In short, the outcome of totalising calculation is the disenchanted world and its abandoned subject. Forgotten Canadian philosopher George Grant relates calculation to some of the more tyrannical features of secular society, among them the rejection of diverse views of the good, at least insofar as such values might influence public policy (a rejection Grant holds responsible for the production of 'the mass society' or 'the homogenous state'). He considers, for example, the way calculation has transformed the university – once a haven for the pursuit of knowledge for its own sake – into a training centre for the technocracy:

> What must be stressed in this connection is that reason itself is thought of simply as an instrument. It is to be used for the control of nature and the adjustment of the masses to what is required of them by the commercial society. This instrumentalist view of reason is itself one of the chief influences in making our society what it is; but, equally, our society increasingly forces on its members this view of reason. It is impossible to say which comes first, this idea of reason or the mass society. They are interdependent. Thought that does not serve the interests of the economic apparatus or some established group in society is sneered at as 'academic.' The old idea that 'the truth shall make you free,' that is, the view of reason as the way in which we discover the meaning of our lives and make that meaning our own, has almost entirely disappeared. In place of it we have substituted the idea of reason as a subjective tool, helping us in production, in the guidance of the masses, and in the maintenance of our power against rival empires. People educate themselves to get dominance over nature and over other men. (Grant 2002: 319)

Grant has described the economic and cultural situation of the West with accuracy, but that was sixty years ago, and it says something about how little we have changed since then that the description still applies; indeed, it now equally applies to most of the world and is no longer particularly Western.[5] Not even the much-hyped information revolution has had much of an observable effect on our ethico-political commitment to atomistic, self-maximising individualism. But could we not at least imagine alternatives to consumerism and the homogenous state? Or do we believe that the ecological collapse of traditional and non-human communities before industrial and economic exploitation is inevitable? The demonisation of instrumental reason is neither original nor helpful. What is most needed now is a more imaginative approach to technology, a bit of adventurous economic speculation such as the nineteenth century possessed in spades, a sense of possibility that we might continue to develop the earth in a less destructive and monotonously utilitarian fashion. Why is technological advancement so tethered to one contingent form of unsustainable politics, namely liberalism? Could we not expend some energy in speculating about alternatives to automobility, homogenisation and consumerism? Such re-visionary thinking will require a more thorough understanding of modernity in all its historical and ideological ambiguity than is presently on offer.

Only by retrieving certain aspects of the religious origins of modernity will we be able to helpfully reform our present ways of living. Anything less than a rethinking of the West's unconscious ethico-theological orientation will fail to address the roots of the ecological crisis. Such retrieval need be neither reactionary nor romantic, however. The point is not to restore theological attitudes that are correctly assumed by most critics of culture to be no longer tenable or desirable. The perennial error of conservatism has been to underestimate the difference and deflection of history. Somewhere, G. K. Chesterton refutes the progressive, whose argument he characterises as, if something has been done before, it cannot be done again. The exact opposite is true, Chesterton counters: precisely because something has been done before is it proven to be doable again. But let us not misunderstand his meaning: we are not to assume that the clock can be turned back. We can always retrieve older ways of doing things, and I will argue for such a retrieval in this essay; but such a retrieval would not be the restoration of the past of which the conservative dreams. Retrieval does not restore but recapitulates in a new key. Adults can restore their lost childhood innocence by playing with toys no more readily than a culture can return to what it was at a different stage in its maturation by experimenting with antiquated religions. No number of pilgrimages to Stonehenge or Machu Picchu will re-enchant the universe. That is not to say that we should not consider the costs of our development, nor that there is nothing to be gained by confronting the casualties of growth. At a certain point in what Henry Ellenberger calls C. G. Jung's 'creative illness' (the breakdown Jung suffered after his separation from Freud), Jung could do nothing other than sit by the lake, building castles out of stones and mud (Ellenberger 1970: 672). He was not thereby undoing his psychoanalytical training and restoring the innocence of his childhood; he was, rather, becoming a new kind of man by retrieving something lost in his past.[6] In other words, Jung had to go back to be able to move forward. Similarly, the retrieval we need today is not an attempted restoration of the past but a completion of what the modern project started – a recalibration of the habits of critique, control and calculation that have so often helped to emancipate ordinary human beings from the servility in which they have languished for most of human history. I do not want to lose the good things modernity has given us; I want to leaven, with a measure of moderation, the modern attitudes that have made them possible, and to correct thereby that totalising tendency in the modern mind that forecloses the range of our imagination, impoverishing human and non-human living alike in the process.

The path ahead proposed in these pages involves careful preservation of what is best in the modern turn – as well as necessary adjustment to our increasingly uncontrollable and incalculable planetary situation. Rather than letting chaos reign, we are called to take a much humbler approach to the preservation and production of nature in all its forms. I suggest we drop the absolutist pretensions of Promethean modernity and rethink some basic presuppositions such that we do not abandon but rather *qualify* critique, control and calculation – with the help, to start, of a medieval European cultural value that has been all too quickly forgotten in the rush of reformation and revolution. I dare to name this value with an old Latin word: *contemplatio*. This word will, no doubt, evoke Heidegger's famous 'Memorial Address', in which he contrasts 'calculative thinking', 'thinking that plans and investigates', with 'meditative thinking', 'thinking which contemplates the meaning which reigns in everything that is' (Heidegger 1959: 49). This distinction of Heidegger's has become hackneyed in the vast secondary literature that has accumulated around his ambiguous figure and more recently been derided as romantic by a number of eco-critics. It is crucial to recognise, however, that 'meditative thinking' (*besinnliches Denken*), which can also be translated as 'contemplative thinking', is not one of Heidegger's signature concepts. In taking up a central theme of medieval mystical literature, Heidegger engages the legacy of the Christian theological tradition in which he was situated.[7] In the early Middle Ages, the *vita contemplativa* was generally held in higher regard than the *vita activa*, for one single and simple reason: in the active life, we assume, at least pragmatically and performatively, that everything depends on us; in the contemplative life, we understand from experience an opposite truth, that we are not the ultimate source of meaning and order in the universe. The contemplative understands that because we have received all that we have and know, we might learn to trust a bit more in the transcendent source of existence. When we call this source 'transcendent', we are not necessarily saying anything positive about it; we are saying only that it transcends us, that it comes from beyond us, that it escapes our control and that we ultimately rely upon it.

In his now classic study of spirituality, *New Seeds of Contemplation*, Thomas Merton writes:

> Contemplation is the highest expression of man's intellectual and spiritual life. It is that life itself, fully awake, fully active, fully aware that it is alive. It is spiritual wonder. It is spontaneous awe at the sacredness of life, of being. It is gratitude for life, for awareness and for being. It is a vivid realization of the fact that life and being in us proceed from an invisible, transcendent and infinitely abundant source. (Merton 1961: 1)

Worthy of note here is the absence of a direct reference to a personal God. Contemplation is not the direct experience of God, not a mystical encounter with the Creator nor a personal experience of salvation (although such peak experiences may indeed occur in contemplative life). Contemplation is an experience of the *facticity* of being and of the contingency of earthly existence (what I will call existence's gift-quality), all of which astonishes the contemplative and leads to the terrifying but liberating realisation that we depend on that which transcends us. Many contemplatives are understandably monotheistic, but there is no reason why contemplation should not be identified with the atheistic Zen realisation of the 'suchness' (*Tathata*) of things.[8] Contemplation is an experience of the *goodness* of existence – an experience of goodness that is not at once a disavowal of pain and horror. Contemplation looks at the world not through rose-coloured glasses: the pain of existence and the suffering of all that lives remain visible to it. It is, rather, that 'being as such' stands revealed to the contemplative as *sacred*. So far away have we strayed from our religious origins that the word *sacred* is no longer understood. It means holy, set apart, that which we ought not to abuse or take for granted.

Merton was a pre-Vatican-II Catholic living in a monastery in what was then the most austere religious order in the Church, the Order of the Cistercians of the Strict Observance, also known as the Trappists. Can the contemplation of which he speaks be considered in any sense modern? Merton certainly thought so and understood his vocation to be one of sharing the gift of the monastery – contemplation – with the modern world. But can the virtue of contemplation, of perceiving being as a gift, be aligned with the practices of critique, control and calculation? Or are these seemingly incongruous approaches essentially opposed – premodern contemplation on one side, modern critique, control and calculation on the other? Does the person who contemplates 'being' forswear control and the person who controls fail to contemplate? I reject this dichotomy and find evidence for its fallaciousness in various places in European history: in Renaissance philosophy, which combined humanism and naturalism by uniting zeal for the development and expansion of the human project with contemplative reverence for the beauty and mystery of nature (Cassirer 1963); in the practice of modern science (as distinct from the philosophy of science), which is shot through with wonder; and, more prosaically, in the industrial activity of contemplative monastics throughout history. Concerning the last, it is worth noting that a monk is neither an idler nor a dreamer; all that he does, he does (or ought to do) in a spirit of contemplation or mindfulness. His meditation makes him more effective, not less. When European civilisation unravelled with the collapse of Rome, the monasteries became havens of learning, economic stability and technological innovation. Indeed, without the monks of Europe, there would be no modernity. Contemplation should not be confused with passivity.

We find, in fact – more centrally to the argument of this essay – a direct coincidence of the contemplative attitude to nature with the critical, controlling and calculating spirit of modernity in the widely misunderstood field of Renaissance Hermeticism, what I call neo-Hermeticism.[9] At the very threshold of the modern, as Europe emancipated itself from medieval traditions, secularised and began colonising the world, a contemplative attitude to nature was retrieved from second-century Hellenistic philosophy (specifically in the writings, rediscovered by Ficino in the fifteenth century, that have come down to us as the *Corpus Hermeticum*) and fused with Renaissance humanism. Nature and culture were not set against each other in the Renaissance; rather they were synchronised, in urban planning, in the role of art in public life, and in the ideal of the artist who is also a scientist. It has been argued that the Renaissance syncretism of Hermetic ideas and attitudes was the proximate cause of the scientific revolution (Yates 1964). In the neo-Hermetic view, nature was not mechanical nor reducible to matter; it was living, animated by a finite and volatile spirit or world-soul that the alchemists symbolised with the name Mercurius (related to but not to be confused with the modern element), quicksilver, *argentum vivum*. As an early-modern symbol, Mercurius stands not as a god to be worshipped but as the power that quickens and pervades everything that exists, rendering the multiplicity of beings, from molecules to ideas, one.[10] Mercurius unites opposites, makes nature alive; s/he is both an agent of transformation and a mediator between mind and matter. By isolating quicksilver in the laboratory, the alchemist (so it was believed) worked with the very principle of growth and change at the heart of creation. But to be commanded, Mercurius needed to be obeyed: only through careful and reverent observance of natural transformations, and through cultivation of an inner life bringing the soul of the scientist into alignment with the changes occurring in the alembic, could those natural processes be directed. To enter this sanctum of creation, this abyss of potency, was to descend into chaos, and it was at some risk to one's sanity that one did so. Such chaos was recognised not as disorder, but as proto-order, the ground of being and form; and it was to be accessed through the whole human being, through intellect, feeling, above all, imagination, all of which faculties vitally assisted the scientist in penetrating the mind–matter continuum.[11] This was a decidedly non-mechanistic approach to nature, one in which *Gelassenheit* (letting-be) had its place, as the scientist waited patiently for the manifestation of natural form to emerge from the abyss, without the interference of his will or agency, so that he might learn its secrets. Technology and experimentation were not disavowed in such an undertaking; rather, it was understood that the mechanistic thinking that usually attends certain processes involves abstraction from the real, a necessary detour from the infinity of incalculable relations in which we exist.

> Nature [for the Renaissance Hermeticist] is not a thing for the mind to meditate on in order to extract its laws and so increase mastery over the created world. It is the divine mirror thanks to which the reflective possibility of catching a glimpse of itself is offered to each mind that sincerely renounces the inevitably violent appropriation of such an 'object'. (Bonardel 1992: 79–80)

In our era of relativity, quantum physics and the advent of the technosphere (the end of mechanism in science), the Hermetic belief in nature as living and endlessly productive gains renewed relevance.[12] But lest I be misunderstood, my point is not that we need to or even could return to the natural science of the Renaissance alchemists; rather, we need to, and indeed can, retrieve something of the non-reductive and contemplative metaphysics of the Renaissance for the task of thinking nature in the Anthropocene. Such a metaphysics reveals the contemplative and calculative mindsets held in dynamic tension with one another, each offering a check and balance on the excesses and limits of the other. And to the objection that such an attitude is impossible for us because it is bound up with the ancient cosmology retrieved by the Renaissance, I answer with a question: was the *natura* of the Renaissance really simply the re-actualised *kosmos* of the ancients? On this position (mistaken in my view), Renaissance Hermeticism was nothing more than a last desperate bid to re-enchant nature before European civilisation's engulfment by mechanistic reductionism. While the Renaissance certainly did openly appropriate ancient cosmological science, especially astrology and alchemy, Hermetic *natura* is not the *kosmos* of the ancients; it is a finite *emergent* order, not a normative totality. It is creature, not Creator, and not to be mistaken for the divine.[13] Far from being a complete whole, an encompassing backdrop against which moral decisions are to be guided, nature was conceived to be as imperfect as we are. Nature was even thought to be in part fallen, infected by moral evil and thereby perfectible in our hands through our work. This attitude was quite foreign to the ancients, as unheard-of among the authors of the *Corpus Hermeticum* (whoever they were) as it was among the neo-Platonists and Stoics. For the neo-Hermetic, *natura* was to be worked, and that work was to be at once material and immaterial – or, if you like, physical and psychological. It was not, then, an object to be aesthetically and scientifically contemplated from a distance. The work called for brooked no separation between knowing and valuing: the alchemy succeeded to the degree that the alchemist achieved a *moral* transformation that was possible only in conjunction with science. The neo-Hermetic attitude to natural things was neither reductively utilitarian nor pantheistic; it was precisely what I have described as reverential. In this *alter-modernity*, if you will, we might come to envision approaches to developing science and technology that simultaneously revere the gift-quality of things while setting themselves upon the work of perfecting the world.

Contemplation is proposed here not as a separate fourth principle of modernity, but as a modification of the other three. And this contemplative modification changes everything. *Contemplative critique* is critique that emancipates human beings from ideology without taking the fatal misstep of arrogating to humanity power over truth. When the objectivity of truth is denied, truth is rendered a subjective imposition on a meaningless disordered 'real' (in Lacan's sense of the word). It is one thing to suspect oneself of being deceived; it is another to presume oneself the only meaningful source of order and the measure of truth. *Contemplative control* is the rightful assumption of responsibility for the development of the earth. But the earth is not ours alone; it belongs also to future humans and non-humans alike. It may be our vocation to develop and perfect it, but we will never possess it, and one of the lessons of the Anthropocene is that we cannot possess it, for it possesses us. Herein lies the meaning of stewardship in the Catholic interpretation of that much-maligned passage of Genesis (Gen. 1: 26): when God gives Adam 'dominion', God makes him a *steward*, not the possessor, of the earth. A steward, we recall, is responsible for lands and properties that are not his own possession (Francis 2015: 67). *Contemplative calculation*, non-totalising calculation, is means–end thinking that is not an end in itself – that is, not predicated on a reductionist ontology in which all qualities are reduced to quantities. Contemplative calculation is means–end thinking for the sake of the emancipation of the human and the just development of the earth, yes, but also for the sake of a deeper immersion in the beauty and mystery of all that is. That reason can be used instrumentally does not mean that it is nothing other than an instrument. Conversely, that reason has a *telos*, that it may in essence help us contemplate the whole, does not mean it cannot sometimes also be a tool.

With such promising possibilities firmly in view, I propose a retrieval of the religious origins of modernity in light of the unprecedented challenges facing us today, among others: climate change; the prospect of bio-engineered progeny, a geo-engineered planet and the end of wildlife; and the advent of the technosphere (technology that has become a self-organised system, that is, in some bizarre way, animate). Where others have approached such a retrieval in a systematic and scholarly fashion (and to different ends), in this essay I can only gesture to it – and recommend, as I do, a careful study of their work.[14]

In broader outline, one of the first results of a retrieval of the religious origins of the modern is the recognition that modern science and technology have presupposed a different sense of time – a decidedly theological sense of time – than that which pervaded the ancient world. No longer committed to Plato's concept of time as a moving picture of eternity (Timaeus 37c–e), the modern mind conceived time as *eschaton*, a progressive if undetermined unfolding of the new. In place of paganism's understanding of nature as the fixed and eternal backdrop of human life, modernity envisioned an emerging natural order, an evolutionary and open-ended production of being that includes human activity. As such, modern symbols of nature presuppose progressive time, that is, time as history, which is the legacy of the Biblical tradition: time progresses because it has a beginning and will have an end; nature emerges because it, too, is finite and historical. Within this properly historical sense of time, social mobility and individual freedom become possible for the first time – for only one who stands before the possibility of the radically new can be free of the past. At the foundation of this sense of time was a distinctive way of thinking of transcendence, not as the heavenly beyond of the ancients, but as *the future*. The transcendent future was the modern's hope in the possibility of change and the modern's trust in the open-endedness of time – a hope and trust that inspired both the modern's revolutionary spirit and her boundless energy for work with which we remain familiar today.

Time as history is the time of events, of the new, of the singular that disrupts the established pattern by bringing the transcendent future into the present. Notwithstanding the close intertwinement of the concepts of eschatological time and progress, however, it cannot be denied that the technocrat who succeeds the theologian begins from an assumption entirely opposed to the trust in the transcendent that grounds eschatology: where eschatology is poor in means and looks to the future precisely because it knows that it lacks the power to bring the Kingdom of God to the earth, the technocrat assumes the opposite, that technology is the means, and the technocrat alone the source, of order in the world; if technology does not put something in order, that thing will inevitably be disordered. It is thus that, in the historically continuous movement from eschatology to progress, a transformation occurs in the human sense of mastery, responsibility and vocation. The twelfth-century abbot Joachim of Fiore is often recognised as the first thinker of progress in Europe; his understanding of the future was Biblical and eschatological through and through. For Fiore, the Spirit would inaugurate the new age, the age of justice, just as it was the Son who had inaugurated the age of his own time.[15] Just a few hundred years later, however, early-modern thinkers would begin to describe progress such that the transcendent was no longer part of the picture.

Where early Christianity had embraced radicalism, medieval theology struggled with the disruptive and anarchic potency of eschatological time. Joachim was widely regarded as, if not heretical, certainly heterodox. The thinking of time as history had, for the most part, been buried in the Christian Middle Ages under the Augustinian bifurcation of two trajectories of time: the rise and fall of the City of Man, and the coming of the City of God. In Augustinian thought, the two trajectories of time are parallel lines and so never meet. The achievement of the City of God would signify the dissolution of the City of Man. Because Augustine anticipates the eclipse of one trajectory of time by the other at the end of history, he is not a thinker of ordinary time as progressive in any meaningful way (Augustine 426: XV, 1, p. 595). Until the Reformation made it possible for secular modernity to fully appropriate it, time as history only erupted on·occasion in revolutionary upsurges such as the radical Franciscan movement or the Peasants' Revolt, always to be suppressed again. It was not before New Testament theology was more fully retrieved in the Renaissance and Reformation that Fiore's eschatological time would become the reigning paradigm, albeit with a decisive twist: for modernity, history moves ineluctably toward the coming, no longer of God, but of man (Löwith 1949: 61f.).

The historical result of the transformation of eschatology into the cult of progress is modern disenchantment and nihilism. Löwith argues that modern nihilism appears when progressive history no longer has meaning, when time moves ineluctably into the new, but without order or *telos*. His argument highlights three steps in this process. First, Löwith explains, there emerged a conception of time as progressive rather than circular and repetitive: this was derived from Jewish and Christian eschatology. Next came the secularisation of the Jewish–Christian notion of eschatological time: here, the trajectory of history had to be recognised as directed not providentially but by the human will to justice. Following this shift, we needed to be disabused of our early-modern naïveté that progress always moves toward a utopian end: it goes without saying that with the horrors of twentieth-century warfare the bottom falls out of the cult of progress. But this collapse of faith in the future, according to Fiore, does not allow us to return to the pagan cosmos, either, with its consoling cycle of eternal forms anchoring human life in the divine. No one really believes in progress anymore, in the thick sense of the term, but neither do we believe in the Kingdom of God, and no matter how hard we try, we cannot find our way back to the circular *kosmos* of the pre-Christian world. Nihilism presents itself on the assumption that we are shipwrecked in an emerging but dys-teleological universe that will ultimately unravel. Regardless of how meaningful we believe our personal lives to be, the observations of science confound our search for deeper meaning. Our world, so the story goes, is the consequence of an unimaginable accident, the outcome of which was our planet's momentary favourability to the evolution of intelligent life. Even if we succeed in holding the chaos at bay for a few millennia more, our fate remains tied to the fate of all being: heat death, in which entropy, the natural tendency for structure to fall apart, destroys all possibility not only of life but of existence itself. The human being in the science narrative is nothing more than doomed matter that has become tragically aware of its fate. On such a view, reality is nothing more than particles in space combining unaccountably to form various compounds and substances before disappearing again, all without ultimate aim.

No people have ever lived under such a hopeless metanarrative as late moderns. No wonder we revolt against disenchantment. We feel abandoned by science to meaninglessness. The re-enchantment industry is a response to this exceptional situation in history. The programmatic re-enchantment of the world – based on nostalgia for the habits and attitudes of premodern cultures – fuels this esoteric movement. Millions are made on eco-retreats, consciousness-raising therapies, yoga and the paraphernalia associated with it, and on literature about angels and shamans sold in esoteric bookshops in every major city of the Western world. Re-enchantment is big business. Post-Christians are not irreligious. They are rather *desperately* religious, restlessly seeking new forms of divinity in various strategies of re-enchantment: travelling to South America to ingest psychedelics to feel, however briefly, reconnected with the world-soul; becoming yoga adepts; mapping the archetypes of the unconscious with the help of Jungian psychology; dedicating themselves with religious zeal to green tourism and cultural voyeurism in a frantic search for 'authentic' forms of human life (and at the same time, driving forward the eco-catastrophe that is the multibillion-dollar tourist industry). The statement attributed to Chesterton comes to mind: 'He who does not believe in God will believe in anything' (Cammaerts 1937: 211).

When Max Weber first speaks of 'disenchantment' in his famous Munich lecture of 1917, he coins the term that best describes modern malaise (Weber 1922: 8). Disenchantment is the fall from a state of comforting belief; it is the experience of a spell being broken. Cinderella arrives home from the ball barefoot, missing her fine gown and sparkling shoes. The palace, the horse-drawn carriage, the prince – all were a dream. But in the fairytale, of course, Cinderella's dream comes true in the end. Real-life disenchantment is far less fortunate. And it is irreversible. Children discover what they do not want to know and cannot unlearn, that Santa Claus is really a show put on by their parents, the TV studios and the shopping malls to make the world seem more magical than it is – and Christmas is never the same again. But presumably the one who is disenchanted is not to be burdened by the new knowledge but, rather, enlightened. Disenchantment is a positive thing, is it not, an ascent into truth from a state of ignorance? But if it is a kind of ascent, why do we regard it otherwise? Why do we flee it by pursuing programmes of 're-enchantment'? Weber presents his Munich address as bad news. His point is that, in the light of modern science – of evolutionary theory, contemporary physics and technological mastery – Europeans can no longer inhabit the universe of meaning that their forefathers did. For better or worse, traditional values and the consolations of Western religion are no longer rationally tenable. We must steel ourselves, Weber cautions, for a bleaker existence than our parents and grandparents had – for there is no natural moral law in the universe, no standard against which to measure our conduct, no ultimate sense of right and wrong, no divine justice balancing the scales. There is only us and what we do: politics, utilitarian ethics, critique, control and calculation. Moderns, Weber says, do not belong to a cosmos that cares about them. In a chaotic world void of purpose, he cautions, we must do the best we can, simply to keep going.

Enter the Anthropocene, that buzzword of contemporary eco-criticism. Notwithstanding the status of the term's scientificity (or lack thereof), I find in its account of the historical present the surgical precision of poetry. The Anthropocene can be interpreted either as the exaltation of the human become so awesome that it now constitutes a planetary force – or as humanity's humiliation. As the exaltation of the human, the Anthropocene signifies the ascension of civilisation to a position of power beyond that of any previous form of life on earth. *Homo sapiens* has become a geological force in the solar system; it is now capable of deliberately altering the course of natural history. No longer merely one form of life among others, the human species has finally overtaken the planet. It rules the world now, and its decisions will continue to influence the fate of other earthlings. As technology advances, we will remake the earth till it reaches full carrying capacity and then bid it farewell, to colonise other planets.

Considered from the other side, however – as the humiliation of the human – the Anthropocene confronts us with our vulnerability to hyperobjects such as the climate (or indeed the earth itself).[16] We find ourselves destined to suffer the unforeseen effects of evolution, ground down by blind, planetary forces, no more privileged than any other species, which had its day in the sun.

The contradiction that emerges in comparing these opposite perspectives is at the centre of contemporary ecological debate. Following Latour and Žižek, we ought to read the Anthropocene as an example not of the triumph of human reason but of its deflation. If we once thought ourselves godlike in our capacity to transcend the material conditions of our lives, we can do so no longer. Even the fantasy of a post-human uploading of the contents of the human mind is dispelled by the simple observation that someone is going to need to materially monitor the physical databank, which is anything but impervious to climate (try leaving your laptop out in the rain). But humiliation is not necessarily a terrible thing. To be brought down to earth (*humble*, Middle English, from the Latin *humus, ground*) may be the best chance we have of surviving our own success. Neither is the smashing of idols necessarily the death of nature; it might be its very unveiling. With the demolition of the romanticised sense of nature we find in so much environmental writing, of the 'balanced whole' that humans have upset by their rapacious technological will to mastery, nothing is lost but an ideological fiction.

Just as the god who expired in the nineteenth century could not possibly have been the Creator of heaven and earth, having become a mere prop designed by early-modern thinkers to bolster the teetering tower of human knowledge, so too was the nature that Dark Ecology has declared dead never alive. The question of nature is not only a question about the 'environment' but also and above all the question concerning the human being – and this question is far from closed. On the contrary, ecological iconoclasm reopens the question in a much more vital way than we have seen in years. 'Accept the risk of metaphysics', Latour writes, and I am inclined to take him at his word (Latour 2004: 232).

Two stories about the future of humanity are repeated wherever the facts of climate change are taken seriously. The first story is pessimistic. It foresees human civilisation regressing inevitably – as the irreversible impacts of climate change (desertification, food shortages, swamped coastal cities, armies of refugees) take hold – to a preindustrial economy, and at the expense of countless millions of lives. The other story is optimistic, and sees humans averting ecological collapse in their transit, in the next decade, from a fossil-fuel-based economy to one run on renewables. It is hard to know whom to believe. Perhaps Al Gore is right, and we can easily re-establish our Western liberal democracies on more sustainable terrain. Or it might be that the current dream of green consumerism is the noble lie we need to tell ourselves to prepare for what the embattled Pope Francis calls the 'ecological conversion' needed to save the planet and ourselves. What the pessimists and optimists in this debate have in common is their insistence that climate change is not a political fable concocted by the left; it is the most serious threat to human civilisation that we have ever faced. Wind farms are a good start, but there is so much more to talk about: renewing rural communities, jump-starting local agriculture, diversifying our economies and, above all, transcending consumerism. We will not wean ourselves from religious junk food until we can find ourselves a more compelling form of worship. Consumerism, I have argued elsewhere, is an *ersatz* experience of transcendence (McGrath 2014). My argument is not with capitalism as such, but with the form it has taken in late modernity. Capitalism has created the wealth which has undeniably improved the lot of countless human beings. But is it necessarily bound up with the degenerate form of secular Christianity which I identify with consumerism? Just as socialism drove nineteenth-century capitalism into self-regulation through the creation of the welfare state, so might environmentalism drive twenty-first-century capitalism into ecological self-regulation. This would require a recovery of the sense of the value of the non-human – not just utilitarian justification but, to use a tired phrase, a sense for the intrinsic value of nature or, better, the sacredness of nature. I am not advocating a new religion of nature, but I am staking my hopes on the possibility that the religious renewal of humankind will be occasioned by a new appreciation for the fragility and beauty – the sacredness – of what we have all been given in common: the earth. Francis is right: nothing short of ecological conversion can save humankind. We have no choice but to work toward it.

Notes

1. This is Bernard Lonergan's phrase for reality from the perspective of naïve realism. I have borrowed it here for different, but not entirely opposed, purposes. See Lonergan (1990: 106–7).
2. See Schelling's analysis of predicate logic in his celebrated essay on freedom (Schelling 1809: 343–5). For comment, see McGrath (2012: 121–3).
3. Schelling insists on the Platonic distinction between *me on* (non-being) and *ouk on* (nothing) as articulating the crucial difference between possibility as pure capacity to be and nothingness. See Schelling (1842: 113). The distinction has had an important if quiet effect on a central stream of modern philosophy, namely among those thinkers who understand being in an evolutionary sense, which is neither teleologically determined nor anarchically random. In addition to Peirce (1955), see Tillich (1967: I, 186–92), Berdyaev (1965: 27) and the late James Bradley (Bradley 2012).
4. Many have commented on this theological assumption of early modernity, but none as succinctly and with as much scholarly command as church historian Ernst Benz. See Benz (1965: 121–42).
5. The citation above is from Grant's lecture 'Philosophy in the Mass Age', which was broadcast on CBC in 1958.
6. Jung describes his breakdown and the play therapy in his *Memories, Dreams, Reflections* (Jung 1961: 173): 'I consciously submitted myself to the impulses of the unconscious. The first thing that came to the surface was a childhood memory from perhaps my tenth or eleventh year. At that time I had had a spell of playing passionately with building blocks. I distinctly recalled how I had built little houses and castles, using bottles to form the sides of gates and vaults. Somewhat later I had

used ordinary stones with mud and mortar. These structures had fascinated me for a long time. To my astonishment, this memory was accompanied by a good deal of emotion. "Aha," I said to myself, "there is still life in these things. The small boy is still around, and possesses a creative life which I lack. But how can I make my way to it?" For as a grown man it seemed impossible to me that I should be able to bridge the distance from the present back to my eleventh year. Yet if I wanted to re-establish contact with that person, I had no choice but to return to it and take up once more that child's life with his childish games. This moment was a turning point in my fate, but I gave in only after endless resistances and with a sense of resignation. For it was a painfully humiliating experience to realise there was nothing to be done except play childish games. Nevertheless, I began accumulating suitable stones, gathering them partly from the lake shore and partly from the water. And I started building: cottages, a castle, a whole village . . . I went on with my building game after the noon meal every day, whenever the weather permitted. As soon as I was through eating, I began playing, and continued to do so until the patients arrived; and if I was finished with my work early enough in the evening, I went back to building.'

7. See McGrath (2006: 120–50) and McGrath (2008b).

8. 'We know we are experiencing the "thatness" (*Tathata*) of reality when we experience something and say to ourselves, "Yes, that's it; that is the way things are." In the moment, we recognize that reality is wondrously beautiful but also that its patterns are fragile and passing' (Molloy 2006: 156).

9. Two dead ends for interpreting Renaissance alchemy must be carefully avoided: the first, stemming from Jung, sees in Renaissance alchemy nothing but the psychology of individuation; the second, prevalent in the history of medicine, finds in it a first and failed effort at modern chemistry – pseudo-science, born of the same genius that would give us the scientific breakthroughs of the seventeenth century, that is nonetheless properly relegated to the dustbin of history as a false start. From a wildly uneven literature, see Bonardel (1992), Faivre (1992), Yates (1964), Couliano (1987) and Foucault (1966).

10. See Jung's superb study of the figure of Mercurius in the Western alchemical tradition (Jung 1948).

11. By understanding the ground of being as potency rather than act (as in traditional Aristotelian-Scholastic theology), Renaissance alchemy was in the tradition of a certain reading of Plato (the Plato of the *Timaeus*). For this tradition, potency is not simply the absence of form or act, but the power to produce form, an excess that is never fully actualised in any particular form. The primacy given to the imagination over the discursive intellect in the Hermetic tradition is a consequence of the elevation of potency over act. The language I deploy in this sentence admittedly follows F. W. J. Schelling, who was deeply influenced by the alchemical tradition, especially the speculative Pietism of Friedrich Christoph Oetinger and the theosophy of Jakob Boehme. See Schelling (1809) and McGrath (2006, 2012). On the role of the imagination in Hermeticism, see Faivre (1992).

12. 'Far from sounding the death knell of hermetic-alchemical thought, symbolism, and practice, modern times have perhaps signaled their resurrection' (Bonardel 1992: 72).

13. On this point, see Cassirer (1963: 30–33).

14. See, above all, Gillespie (2009) and Dupré (1993). See also Karl Löwith's breakthrough study *Meaning in History* (Löwith 1949). Hans Blumenberg (1966) argues (against Löwith) that modernity has successfully extricated itself from the religion of its childhood (Christianity) and can therefore progress in a 'legitimately' secular (that is, atheist) key, but he does not deny the religious origins of secular freedom. Marcel Gauchet (1985) has revived Weber's thesis of the dependence of capitalism on Protestant Christianity, expanding it to argue for the dependence of political liberalism on the history of Christianity. Cf. Berman (2008).

15. On Fiore see Benz (1965: 35–48), Löwith (1949: 145–59) and Reeves (1976).
16. The term 'hyperobject' is Timothy Morton's and refers to beings that are so temporally and spatially massive that they defeat traditional ideas about what a thing is. See Morton (2013).

Chapter 2

Nature is a Symbol, but of What?

A certain sense of nature has died, no doubt. But nature, I will repeat throughout this essay, is a symbol, not merely a sign, and, as a symbol, it is not restricted to any univocal or discursive role it might have once played in metaphysical or scientific discourse; rather, it has become for us once again, over the course of the death of its premodern sense as the cosmos of meaning, and of the more recent death of its modern sense as the other of the human (either as mechanism or as normative real), a non-discursive symbol, a symbol in the hermeneutical sense of an overdetermined sign with one foot lodged firmly in the known and the other stepping tentatively into the unknown.[1] The death of nature is in one way the definitive disenchantment of the world, a hyperbolic disenchantment – disenchantment 2.0, if you will – which renders Weber's analysis quaintly outdated; but it is, in another way, a return to the mythical origins of the symbol of nature itself, a descent back into the dark womb of meaning that first gave birth to the variety of conceptions of nature that have held sway over the ages (*physis, kosmos, creatio, res extensa*, wilderness, et cetera). Nature in the Anthropocene sinks back into the *meon*, the place of possibility, not because it is meaningless and we must now get on with other concepts, but because, as an excessively meaningful or fundamental symbol, it is now giving birth to a new sense, an *Anthropocenic* sense, in which 'nature' means neither the cosmos that nests us in interconnected spheres of meaning (and by nesting us, denies the *anthropos* its specific difference), nor the mechanism that excludes the *anthropos* as its Big Other. As neither sign nor (scientific) term but rather non-discursive symbol, nature is now able to survive the extinction of one or another of its senses. The question remains: what can nature mean today? What new meanings does the symbol of nature give rise to in the Anthropocene?

We will not answer this question by arbitrarily *creating* a meaning for nature (apologies to Deleuze and Guattari) that promises to work in an age of 7 billion humans – of global consumerism and irreversible anthropogenic climate change. Creating a meaning for nature in the Anthropocene would implicate us in pure idealism, rendering us dangerously out of touch with the level at which ideas are shaping history. We must, rather, 'look and see' (Wittgenstein) what sense of nature is alive for us and might guide us toward the social and political transformations that must occur if humanity is to have a future on earth.

Two traditions in modern thought have advanced a sharp distinction between signs and symbols, but in somewhat different ways, and both will be useful to us in developing an Anthropocenic analytic of the symbolism of nature: first, the neo-Kantian tradition, beginning with Cassirer; and second, the psychoanalytical – or, better, hermeneutical – tradition beginning with Freud and Jung and developed by twentieth-century theologians and philosophers such as Tillich, Lonergan and Ricoeur. The neo-Kantian tradition builds upon the pragmatic and objective difference between symbols and signs: all symbols are signs (something that stands for or represents something else), but not all signs are symbols. What distinguishes 'signs that merely signal' from 'signs that symbolise' is use. Signalling signs *indicate*, either naturally (gathering storm clouds) or artificially (the ring tone on a phone), the presence or absence of something in a pragmatic context. The appropriate response to a sign is a specific action: take shelter; answer the phone. Symbols *express* sense; they are non-pragmatic, evocative of conception rather than action. The word that calls us to conceive (that is, the symbol in the neo-Kantian idiom) requires no particular action on our part, but rather a pause from action, and engages in us a contemplative attitude, inviting us to consider sense as it becomes manifest. In the Cassirerian tradition, any sign can be taken symbolically and any symbol can be reduced to a signal:

> Symbols are not proxy for their objects, but are *vehicles for the conception of objects.* To conceive a thing or a situation is not the same thing as to 'react toward it' overtly, or to be aware of its presence. In talking *about* things we have conceptions of them, not the things themselves; and *it is the conceptions, not the things, that symbols directly 'mean'.* (Langer 1957: 60–1)

Whereas sign usage is typical of all the higher animals, the symbolising function is unique to the human animal, constituting the specific way in which the human being inhabits its environment. It is not that humans have a world whereas non-humans do not, as Heidegger might want us to believe, but that each species of living being inhabits fundamentally different worlds, as Jakob von Uexküll was first to point out; each species has an environment organised proportionately to its own form of living. The specific difference that marks the human environment as other than, say, the environment of an octopus is the symbolic function.[2] To this important point, the point concerning the human difference, I shall return.

In the hermeneutical tradition beginning with Freud (but with roots in German Idealism), the distinction between sign and symbol rests on the difference between univocal and plurivocal bearers of sense. Signs are univocal whereas symbols are polyvocal and, as such, relate consciousness to unknown or unconscious possibilities of meaning.[3] In the neo-Kantian tradition, it is the *function* of the sign-that-stands-for-a-concept that renders it a symbol; in the hermeneutical tradition, it is the *ambiguity of sense* – double intentionality, as Ricoeur puts it (Ricoeur 1970: 16) – that renders some signs symbols. Since 'nature' is symbolic for us in both the neo-Kantian and the hermeneutical senses of the term *symbol*, I will hazard to fuse both traditions. The neo-Kantian tradition offers us a crucial means of underscoring the continuity and difference between human and animal thought; the hermeneutical tradition reminds us of 'the transcendent function' of the symbol (Jung 1971: 480), the unique way in which vague or overdetermined signs in human discourse open us up to emergent forms of meaning.

The symbol in the hermeneutical tradition has a magical aura because it maintains the connection between consciousness, on the one hand, and 'the unconscious' – conceived either reductively as the repressed (Freud) or productively as the possibility that has not yet emerged into actuality (Jung) – on the other. The symbol is the bridge between the two sides of the personality, preventing the complete dissociation of id / ego, unconscious / conscious, or collective / individual while compensating for their functional dissociation. As a symbol in the hermeneutical sense, 'nature' is still alive for us because, although the term is still evocative of sense and feeling, we are far from being clear about what the symbol of nature means in the Anthropocene – or about who we are with respect to it. Hyperbolic disenchantment has deprived us of some senses of the term (for example, nature as the other of the human; the normative real or mechanical order; 'the facts', over and against the values we impose on them), but older associations – some long displaced by the modern sense of nature as the human other, and others long relegated to the unconscious – are reawakening. In particular, the *finitude* of nature has returned to the sober light of day on account of climate change. Latour has addressed this finitude by retrieving James Lovelock's symbol, Gaia, and coining the more playful symbol OOWWAAB, that 'out-of-which-we-are-all-born' (Latour 2017: 159). I will argue that this contraction of nature, this finitisation of its mode of being – this rendering radically contingent that upon which we all depend – is not a new thought (notwithstanding Latour's theatrics), but a new way of reviving an old thought long forgotten: climate change reawakens a dormant *theological* sense of nature that was momentarily eclipsed in the mechanistic phase of early modernity and equally obscured by modernity's compensatory reversal, the infinitisation of nature in early Romanticism.[4] Nature is neither a machine nor a moral order, but of the same being as we are: dependent, contingent, non-subsistent: or, *creatio*.

'A symbol is a double-meaning linguistic expression' (Ricoeur 1970: 9). What does this mean? It means that a symbol in Ricoeur's restrictive sense does not name just any form of conception (as it does for Cassirer), but refers specifically to signs that are meaningful in two or more distinct ways: the symbol means one thing directly (the eagle refers to the predatory bird that inhabits North American coastlines) and other things indirectly (the American empire, sovereignty, power, et cetera). Dream symbols, Freud points out, have a manifest meaning drawn from everyday or literal associations, and a latent meaning expressive of vague or unconscious associations. Ricoeur is concerned to distinguish the double intentionality found in religious symbols, dream images and poetry from the univocal concepts of science – and finds Cassirer's functionalist approach too broad for his purposes. It is as a doubly meaningful signifier that the symbol calls for interpretation in the strict sense of negotiating polyvocal sense. 'Symbols occur when language produces signs of composite degree in which the meaning, not satisfied with designating some one thing, designates another meaning attainable only in and through the first intentionality' (Ricoeur 1970: 16). While Ricoeur's narrowing of the meaning of symbol in no way contradicts Cassirer (indeed, Cassirer's approach accommodates doubly intentional symbols), the hermeneutics of symbols does emphasise the role some symbols play in allowing us to transcend a certain limited form of rationality or discursive thought. Symbolic ambiguity does not simply frustrate literal thinking, but activates metaphorical thinking and evokes feeling. Lonergan agrees:

> For univocity, it [the symbol] substitutes a wealth of multiple meanings. It does not prove but it overwhelms with a manifold of images that converge in meaning. It does not bow to the principle of excluded middle but admits the *coincidentia oppositorum*, of love and hate, of courage and fear, and so on. (Lonergan 1971: 66)

The hermeneutics of suspicion (Marx, Nietzsche, Freud) unmasks illusions or dissimulations created by symbolic ambiguity; the hermeneutics of sympathy inaugurates a 'second naïveté' and frees up new possibilities of meaning production precisely through symbolic ambiguity. The archaeology of symbols (Freudian iconoclasm) must be followed, Ricoeur argues, by a teleology of symbols, a future-oriented production of new sense born of the death of older, outmoded meanings (Ricoeur 1970: 494 f.).

Tillich complicates matters further by adding to the hermeneutical line of distinguishing signs from symbols some considerations drawn from sacramental theology. Since what he has to say further underscores what it means for a symbol to die and, by implication, what it means for a symbol to continue to live – to survive one or other of its transformations – we cannot ignore him here. Symbols, according to Tillich, 'participate in the reality of that to which they point' (Tillich 1967: II, 239) in a way that signs do not. The sign is arbitrary and replaceable, has no intrinsic relation to what it represents, 'but the symbol grows and dies according to the correlation between that which is symbolised and the persons who receive it as a symbol' (Tillich 1967: II, 239). Symbols (the sacraments of the church are a preeminent though not exclusive example) engage not only the mind but also the body, that is, they evoke not only thought but, above all, feeling. They 'open up levels of reality, which are otherwise closed for us . . . otherwise hidden and cannot be grasped in any other way' (Tillich 1999: 42, 47). The precision of the sign represents a constriction on the symbol, which must be free to evoke, without restriction, feeling and anticipatory meaning. But this unrestricted evocation of sense, drawing as it does upon collective memory and unconscious feeling, is not something that is achieved deliberately or by definition: it is not the sign user who decides whether a symbol lives or dies. Symbols 'grow out of the individual or collective unconscious and cannot function without being accepted by the unconscious dimensions of our being' (Tillich 1999: 42). Tillich offers concrete examples of the life and death of symbols: the Star of David is a living symbol and, as such, it is irreplaceable and has not exhausted its power over the community that constellates around it; the Virgin Mary, on the other hand, is, for specific historical and theological reasons, no longer a living symbol for millions of Christians.

The hermeneutical symbol opens, not only onto history but into the individual, 'the hidden depths of our own being' (Tillich 1999: 42), 'levels of the soul, levels of our own interior reality' (Tillich 1999: 48). It follows that the life or death of the symbol is not up to us. 'If the dimension of depth is lost, the symbols in which life in this dimension has expressed itself must also disappear' (Tillich 1999: 3). 'Symbols do not grow because the people are longing for them, and they do not die because of scientific or practical criticism. They die because they can no longer produce response in the group where they originally found expression' (Tillich 1999, 43). This, then, is the crux of my dispute with the 'ecology without nature' or Dark Ecology movement: it is not for professors of philosophy to tell the human community that its symbols are no longer alive for them; it is for the human community to tell the professors about this, and such a telling consists in showing, in discourse, the continued evocation of sense effected by the use of the disputed term.

In my view, a hermeneutics of the symbol is exactly what is needed in ecological thought – not a re-enchantment of nature but a passage through its death into the new form it is taking for us today. 'The idols must die so that symbols may live' (Ricoeur 1970: 531). As a symbol in a hermeneutical register, 'nature' is irreplaceable and 'participates' in the reality of that for which it stands. But what is this reality? The question remains open, is indeed reopened today in an unprecedented way. The opening onto an indeterminate range of senses – as opposed to the closures that determine discursively defined literal sense – is the original event of symbolisation, an event, repeated with every transformation of meaning that renders human thinking originally contemplative. This question, then, is not to be decided by science. Ascertaining when symbols are being used scientifically or discursively versus polyvocally is crucial to understanding a statement or text, and this is especially so in environmental discourse concerning nature. The term 'nature', to repeat, is used, for the most part, vaguely, evocatively and not usually scientifically or discursively. It may indeed be the case that, as a scientific term, 'nature' has lost its meaning in the Anthropocene. And it is no defence to move from a positivist to a metaphysical use of the term, where nature means and still can mean 'being', *physis*, or, more restrictively, reality in space-time. Being in space-time is not the nature we worry about in the Anthropocene, not the nature we are striving to protect and conserve. No one is worried about the surface of the planet Mercury or about what is happening in the Alpha Centauri solar system. But we, some of us at least, are deeply worried about what is happening in our oceans.

As I have hinted in the opening lines of this essay, the crucial question to address is not *What is nature?* but rather *Who is the being who asks this question?* The being who asks this question is not part of nature conceived as a balanced whole or macro-organism, for it is a being who is manifestly free. Nor is this questioner nature's other, a transcendent spirit unrelated to the spiritless thing over and against it. For the being who asks this question is manifestly animal, that is, material, and dependent upon the same life-giving processes that make possible every other form of life. Nature can be neither an organism – for the human being is no part of a whole – nor a mechanism – for it includes us, and we are not machines. The future of nature and the future of the *anthropos*, then, cannot be thought apart from one another. 'Man [sic] stands opposed not to the part (to a particular celestial body [i.e., the earth]) but to the whole, to which he relates as its *logos*, as that which is authentically existent [*eigentlich seyende*]. He is the *universal* being' (Schelling 1854: 491). The future of nature is *Anthropocenic* nature, nature profiled against the *anthropos*, both in a practical sense – that is, what we do will affect everything – as well as in a semantic sense – how we conceive ourselves at this stage in history will determine how we continue to conceive nature. Nature is neither (contra the ancients) an organism nor (contra the early moderns) a mechanism, because in neither of these paradigms are we able to think the nature that thinks nature, *thinking nature*. Organic wholeness defines the ancient (Greek, Roman, Hindu, Taoist, et cetera) conception of nature. This conception unravelled in medieval Christendom under the pressure of Biblical revelation to reconcile two central mysteries of faith: creation (divine causality) and the fall (human causality). Some vague sense of the uncontainable quality of the *anthropos*, its non-mereological relation to the whole, compelled early modernity to conceive nature as separate from us and the *anthropos* as transcendent – effectively replacing the Creator–creature binary with the culture–nature binary – and it was in this transition, rather than in the Bible, that nature first became humanity's other. At the same time, in the same movement, nature was conceived as mechanistic, lacking *telos* or integrity and ready to be disassembled and reassembled at will. But conceiving nature as a mechanism is no longer tenable today, in the Anthropocene, because even if we are free, we can no longer pretend to be free of nature, nor can we presume mastery over that which is, at least from a quantum perspective, incalculable.[5] In ancient prejudice, the reciprocally causal relation of the organic part to the whole of which it is a part renders properly human causality (morally imputable causality) impossible. As part of a whole, the human is at best capable of secondary causality, which is not genuinely moral at all (at least from Kant's perspective on what constitutes a moral act, which is much stricter than Aristotle's or Aquinas's). But in modern prejudice, *anthropos* vanishes into thin air – for as neither part nor machine, it becomes *noumenal*, both ineffable and inexplicable.

Among other things that have died in the Anthropocene is a certain kind of naïve naturalism. The challenge today is to think nature in a way that neither reduces human causality to secondary causality nor denaturalises the human. A naturalism is needed that is not at the expense of the human, and a humanism that is not at the expense of the natural.

But what precisely 'nature' means for us at this late hour, with only twenty-five per cent of the planet's surface still wild (and rapidly disappearing) and no corner of it untouched by humankind, is an open question.[6] The ancient sense of nature as eternal and reliable moral order is no longer compelling for an age on the cusp of designing life in a laboratory. The cosmos understood as an infinitely coded container resonant with archetypes and quivering with sympathies and antipathies – the magical *kosmos* of Plato and Hermes Trismegistus – is spent. That this magical sense of nature persists as a cultural commodity, fuelling, as I have already considered, the re-enchantment industry, is only further indication, if more is needed, that we no longer genuinely inhabit an infinitely meaningful cosmos. And the

Romantic sense of the infiniteness of nature, of the boundlessness of life, is also gone – along with the vanished (indeed vanquished) wilderness and our Romantic naïveté.

So, what is left for us to think when we think nature? This is not an easy question to answer. And yet a certain undefined religious aura still surrounds the term, even though nature can no longer be for us what it was for the ancients, medievals or Romantics. This religious residue will be my clue to explicating a contemporary, twenty-first-century Anthropocenic sense of nature. Let us not expect quick results: I may be unable to say what nature means, in the end, or to prove to a critic of my argument that we should care about it. My results will be largely negative. In a move analogous to the *via negativa* of medieval theology, by stripping away most of nature's familiar predicates, I hope to make even more manifest the symbolic power of nature in the Anthropocene.[7]

Certain important eco-theorists, notably Žižek, Morton and Latour, have reinvigorated environmental philosophy by urging us to dispose of the term 'nature' altogether because, it is claimed, it no longer serves the environmental cause. Even though there are important differences – to be discussed in what follows – between Žižek's Lacanian critique, Morton's Buddhistic object-oriented immanentism and Latour's Actor Network Theory, I will refer to this movement provisionally (for now) using Morton's term 'Dark Ecology'. According to Latour, 'nature' died in the science wars (Latour 2004). Close consideration of his use of the term 'nature' reveals that he takes issue with its deployment as a scientific or discursive symbol, not as a symbol in the hermeneutical sense. His claim that political ecology needs to let go of nature is thus less extensive than it first appears. For Latour, considering nature as an order of value-free facts to which natural scientists have unsullied access on account of the strictness of their methodology, and of which natural science alone is the trusted gatekeeper, is no longer tenable. We know too much about the constructed, evaluative and political quality of scientific discourse to continue to believe in such a sense of nature. Most importantly, Latour claims that the persistence of this sense of nature in popular scientism is an obstacle to political ecology insofar as it allows much of the non-human world to be ruthlessly exploited by humans who continue to regard such exploitation as a non-political act. Again, this sense of 'nature' is univocal. It is the sense of nature at work in science's claim to be directly reporting the 'facts of nature' rather than interpretations or social constructions: nature as pre-established order, value-free and indifferent to our judgements and methods of observation.

If we follow Timothy Morton, however, we extend the critique to other symbolic uses of nature. For Morton, the Romantic sense of nature – infinite wilderness, the inexhaustible freshness of 'the wild' celebrated by nineteenth-century poets and fetishised by early environmentalists – dogs environmentalism today with a consumer fantasy. The continued romance with so-called wild nature, Morton contends, perpetuates a concealed anthropocentrism that is lethal in our present context. In the face of systemic corporate green-washing, self-indulgent eco-tourism and the false advertisement of rural cultures and pristine natural landscapes – landscapes that not only no longer exist but that have been destroyed by the very global capitalism for which the ads were engineered – it is hard to deny his point (Morton 2007). However, to repeat (and it bears repeating, for it is the core of our argument), a genuine symbol is never restricted to a single sense. Symbolic uses of the term 'nature', then, cannot be declared dead simply because the early scientific meaning of 'nature' is now recognised as inaccurate or because the Romantic sense of nature has proven itself to be untenable. There may be, and no doubt are, other senses of nature that live and perhaps thrive with the demise of both scientific realism and Romanticism.

What Latour and Morton rail against is using the term 'nature' to buttress the eco-ideology that derails the environmental cause. And it cannot be denied that we are awash today in eco-ideology, from the eco-tourism that is apparently the last hope for the 'pristine' places of the earth (a so-called green economy that turns agrarian labourers into service providers, effectively re-indenturing rural communities), to the recycled cups from which we sip our four-dollar Starbucks lattes. The consumer machine knows we are concerned and has found a financially profitable place for that concern. When I can add charges to an airline ticket to offset my 'carbon footprint', ultimately enriching a corporation that is busily flying as many planes as it profitably can, I know that I am duped. There is no shortage of examples of eco-ideology at play in contemporary politics, but a particularly exquisite case is Donald Trump's overhaul of the Environmental Protection Agency – the EPA, the leading American scientific research institute addressing global warming – to purge it of climatologists. Trump appointed Scott Pruitt, a spokesperson for the oil and gas industry and known climate-change sceptic, as director of the EPA, and Pruitt proceeded to gut the EPA of its climatologists. Defending this bizarre appointment in a press conference, Trump boasted that now, the US will protect air and water through the stimulation of American manufacturing. Trump has long exempted himself from the duty to speak truthfully; now he no longer even needs to speak coherently. Trump standing before the world to defend his protection of the environment – having undertaken actions that are plainly destructive to it – is the essence of eco-ideology. The ideologue lies with so much conviction that we can scarcely believe how he can fail to see the contradiction. In the same week that Pruitt was appointed, Ivanka Trump was cued to make climate change her signature issue (when not busy marketing her clothing line). The very week of Trump's overhaul of the EPA, more than 250 people were killed in a flash flood in a village in Colombia, swept away, while they slept, by spring rains twice as heavy as expected. The story barely made the US news. Signs of disaster are all around us but we pretend not to see them, while political leaders like Trump help us to feel that disavowal is the new normal. In a recent interview, Latour offered a disturbing answer to the question, *How is it possible for elites to persist in denying anthropogenic climate change, when the consensus of international science refutes them?* The elites are indeed aware of the ecological disaster befalling us, Latour replied, but they keep silent because they are investing in a future outside the world held in common – in other words, in their own private future. They know, in other words, that they and their descendants, the one per cent, will inherit what is left of the earth; who cares about the rest?[8]

The Romantic era did not die with Nietzsche or even Heidegger. Instead, it entered a new and more aggressively disavowed key, in which the Romantic longing for wholeness and a return to a cosmocentric worldview – a longing no longer sustained by natural vistas and hiking tours of the Alps (there are too many highways and cafés and fellow tourists to keep that nineteenth-century fantasy alive) – is now managed by CGI-manipulated advertisement (Morton 2007: 94–9). Romantic nature is now primarily a virtual phenomenon. It is maintained by large-budget HD documentaries, carefully designed 'safaris' and Disney-themed parks. It is not uncommon for children to complain that genuine wildlife-spotting is far less interesting than watching staged drama on the nature channel. But does the critique of Romantic nature not miss the point that 'nature' is, and for the most part always has been, primarily a symbol? To disabuse us of one symbolic association of nature is not to deny the possible legitimacy of others. Nature was a symbol for the Romantics and remains a symbol for us today, which is not to say that its meaning has not changed.

Latour's sense of nature as the order of facts is what Cassirer calls a 'discursive symbol': it is univocal, abstract and determinate; Morton's sense of nature as the Romantic wild is 'presentational'. Both concepts are symbols, according to Cassirer's theory, but the Romantic presentational symbol of nature as 'the wild' is polyvocal, vague and for that reason evocative of feeling. When the scientist speaks of 'a fact of nature', she does not equivocate but defines; when Goethe waxes poetic about 'nature', he does not define anything but, rather, evokes feeling.[9] The two critiques represented by Latour and Morton find an important point of convergence in contemporary eco-ideology. Both the scientific and the Romantic symbols of nature are deployed in service of the ecological idol of *holism*. The eco-ideologue will use both symbolic senses for the nature that needs protecting, alternating between them as necessary. So we are told in one breath that we are living out of harmony with nature and that nature will restore balance at our expense (Romantic and vague symbol of the whole to which we belong), and in the next that we need to preserve nature for the enjoyment of our children's children (scientific and determinate symbol, which stands for the order of things without us). That these symbols contradict each other (for the scientific conception excludes us while the Romantic concept includes us) does not disturb the eco-ideologue, for his purpose is not to speak coherently but to use rhetoric to achieve an end. It does not matter to the ideologue that a nature that is eternally balanced cannot need or even receive our protection. As order of facts or natural system of being, nature is the solid, structured reality – sutured together by law – to which scientific language ostensibly corresponds. As infinite wilderness, the scenic verdant backdrop of human life, nature is approached principally through art and imagination. Both scientism and Romanticism assume a separation of the human from the natural: the human is, on the one hand, the scientific observer, and, on the other, the artistic genius – and in both instances separate from what is observed or meditated upon. That science understands the whole to be calculable while Romanticism regards it as infinitely surpassing understanding does not disturb the structural similarity between the two attitudes. Nature is conceived as a whole objectified by the scientist as much as by the Romantic, even if the two use different means to produce discrepant accounts of this wholeness.

The myth of a stably structured reality over and against the neutral scientific eye does not work at the quantum level, nor does it make sense of what scientists do when they debate what is and is not deserving of a name.[10] Neither does the infinitely meaningful cosmos survive the debasement of Romanticism by consumerism. When the Romantic is exposed to be at heart a consumer who experiments with identity through shopping, the 'intuition' that ostensibly connected him with everything is seen in a less kindly light. In a reversal of the history of the concept of intellectual intuition, Romantic intuition has come to appear far closer to Fichte's notion of it than to Schelling's: it is not the intuition of the universe but the intuition – or should we say *projection*? – of an idea of the self that unites early Romanticism and its late-modern variant, consumerism. What the Romantic enjoys in 'nature' is his own self enjoying nature.[11] This, then, is the sense of nature that has died for us: nature as the balanced order of being to which we and all other living things belong. When nature as cosmological whole becomes a finite object for calculative science and Romantic aesthetics, it is no longer a whole, for it leaves something out: the calculator and aesthete, who are able to objectify and aestheticise the whole by virtue of their transcendence of it.

The purely ideological use of the dead sense of nature as cosmological whole is most visibly at work in environmentalism. At the core of every ideology is a disavowal: we refuse to acknowledge and live out of what we know. But ideology goes further, for the disavowal at its root is constitutive of a form of life. The ideologue does not *want* the truth, for it interferes with a form of life she keeps perpetuating because her identity is bound up with it. In the ideology of scientism, the supremacy of science over every other discourse consists in its having recourse to 'reality' as the bedrock of truth that confirms or disconfirms the scientist's propositions and theories. The image of infinite wilderness likewise consolidates, however inversely, the supremacy of the Romantic aesthete. Environmentalism dips freely into scientistic or Romantic ideology as needed, in order to confirm the environmentalist's need to be one who belongs to the universe. We have upset 'the natural harmony of things' with our technology, our hubris, our calculative reductionism, we are told, and climate change is the consequence. The impacts wrought by the warming atmosphere are evidence of nature's equilibrium reasserting itself at our expense. If we could only embrace moderation (a life of meditation, vegetarianism, voluntary simplicity, et cetera) 'in harmony' with nature, we might be able to begin ceasing to destroy it.

The ideals of early environmentalists live on in the often repeated claim that consumerism and consumer-driven technology are 'out of balance' with the natural order to which we belong. Insofar as this trope persists, climate change, disappearing wildlife and mass extinction are regarded as symptoms of an imbalanced relationship to the whole of which we are only a part. The ideological core of environmentalism is particularly unmistakable in the environmentalist who fetishises Native American or other traditional non-Western attitudes to living: the Western environmentalist knows, even if he denies it, that holism is not characteristic of his culturally native understanding of nature. It is not unusual, then, to find committed environmentalists who are also interested in non-Western religious rituals that have as their aim the awakening of a sense of belonging to the whole, a sense that Western thinking's mind–body and subject–object dualism ostensibly represses. From yoga retreats in tropical resorts to neo-shamanism, from Ayurveda to Peruvian psychotropic healing rituals, environmentalism is not only a spirituality but also a politics of denial, and a lucrative one at that.

This is not to say that environmentalism is simply New Age. A great deal of science has been marshalled in support of the effort to retrieve a sense of belonging to the whole. Here the environmentalist shifts ably from Romantic ideology to scientism and back again. To cite a rather heavyweight example, the physicist David Bohm is referenced frequently in environmental discussions. Bohm sees the ambiguous results of quantum physics as evidence of both the illusoriness of the subject–object distinction and the abstractness of surface conceptions of space, time and causality. These structures of thought create the illusion of a mechanistic 'outsidedness' of thing to thing, of merely efficient causal relations among events, concealing a deeper order of unimaginable interconnectedness, one that in curious ways resembles the ancient *kosmos* with its signature microcosm–macrocosm homology (Bohm 1980). In Bohm's understanding of the significance of quantum physics, all that is exists interdependently in the undivided whole of being. On the explicate level, we see linear causality, discrete particles and multiple levels of duality, but on the implicate level revealed by quantum physics, nothing is fundamentally separate or independent. Environmentalism tends to align such observations with a futuristic optimism that is deeply modernist: the future can be better than the past if only we can render science and technology holistic before our delusions of 'duality' kill us.

The holistic ideal is in fact as old as the environmental movement itself. Arne Naess's 'Deep Ecology' got underway in the early seventies with a highly influential essay on Spinoza (Naess 1977). Naess's Spinoza is a thinker of the cosmos as a balanced whole, of nature as God, *Deus sive natura* – if not an organism in the typical sense because of the absence of a notion of final causality in Spinoza, nevertheless an undivided unity in which everything that exists shares in the one infinite essence of substance. Spinozistic immanence allows Naess to deny any hierarchical relations among beings that could justify elevating the interests of human beings or human communities above those of their non-human counterparts.

Deep Ecology rejects most environmental ethics for its anthropocentricism – for example, the application of utilitarian or deontological ethics to environmental problems. Such ethical models, presuming that the human is the measure of the good, merely extend traditional ethical paradigms to include the non-human. Naess calls for a new ontology in which the human being is understood to be only one being in a system of interconnected beings, one with neither special privilege nor responsibility. *Pace* Kant, it is not the human being who uniquely deserves our respect; the living environment as a whole has 'intrinsic value' – value that is not a function of the value judgements of human beings. As such, 'inalienable' legal rights ought to be transferred to all living things and the non-living matter that supports them, without regard for their specifically human utility.

Apart from Spinoza, Naess could find little support in the Western tradition for his biocentric ethics. But in the East, he found plenty. A scholar of Gandhi, Naess draws on the latter's beloved *Bhagavad Gita* to expand Deep Ecology into metaphysics and spirituality. *Gita* 6:29 speaks of the realised human being who sees himself in all being and all beings in himself. 'With self by Yoga integrated, [now] he sees / The self in all

beings standing,/All beings in the self:/The same in everything he sees'
(cited in Zaehner 1938: 348). In Naess's reading, the *Gita* expresses the
maxim of self-realisation that he also finds in Spinoza. Since everything
is interconnected, the self-realisation of any living being is part of the
self-realisation of every other living being. Spinoza speaks of the *conatus*
in all modes of substance, which is the desire of every individual thing to
persist in its being and, in the case of living things, to realise its potential
and maximise its power or essence. 'Everything, in so far as it is in itself,
endeavours to persist in its own being' (*Unaquaeque res, quantum in se est,
in suo esse perseverare conatur*) (Spinoza 1883: Part III, Prop. VI, p. 136).
Spinoza comments:

> Individual things are modes whereby the attributes of God are expressed in a given
> determinate manner; that is, they are things which express in a given determinate
> manner the power of God, whereby God is and acts; now no thing contains in
> itself anything whereby it can be destroyed, or which can take away its existence;
> but contrariwise it is opposed to all that could take away its existence. Therefore,
> in so far as it can, and in so far as it is in itself, it endeavours to persist in its own
> being. (Spinoza 1883: 136)

Unlike those readers of Spinoza who see in the doctrine of *conatus* nothing
more than an ethics of self-maximisation (not at all at odds with either
liberalism or corporate capitalism), Naess reads Spinoza as an ecological
thinker who places the interests of the whole above the interests of the part.
The enemy of environmental holism is the liberal consumer who presumes
that the human being is separate from the whole, an individual negatively
free to carve her own path of destruction through the material world. Deep
Ecology shares (for example, with the extreme right) deeply conservative
assumptions about the relation of the individual to the community. The
good of the individual is to be subordinated to the good of the biotic
community, the social expanded to include all living things on the planet
and the non-living materials upon which they depend. Is it a surprise, then,
that in its most extreme forms, Deep Ecology becomes fascistic, advocating
the demolition of the doctrine of human rights in the interest of an ethics
of the whole? Naess himself believed in radical population control aimed at
reducing the human population to about 100 million people. He failed to
specify what was to be done with the other 7.3 billion.

Environmental holism can also take an apocalyptic turn. Consider the
conventional reading of Lovelock's 'Gaia hypothesis' (Lovelock 1979):
the planet is an organism, the hypothesis goes, and, like any organism, it
regulates itself. Every part is ordained to the whole of which it is a part.
When the organism is healthy, there is a balanced subordination of part to
whole, and the whole thrives. Sickness, then, is an imbalance in homeostasis: one of the parts steps out of the whole, becomes autonomous and

inflamed, operating as though it were itself the whole – like a cancer cell reproducing maniacally without consideration for the life of the organism on which it depends. The human community, Lovelock contends, is the infection, and climate change is the planet's attempt to restore homeostasis (Lovelock 2006):

> We have grown in number to the point where our presence is perceptibly disabling the planet like a disease. As in human diseases, there are four possible outcomes: destruction of the invading disease organisms; chronic infection; destruction of the host; or symbiosis – a lasting relationship of mutual benefit to the host and the invader. (Lovelock 2006: xvii)

Like a fever, the planet seems to be cooking the human infection. That this likely means the end of human life on earth is really bad news only for humans.

Lovelock's recent books are so bleak in outlook that they should be regarded as belonging to the genre of dystopian apocalyptic literature. In terms of the science, he does little more than repeat the now well known theory of anthropogenic climate change: 'Nothing so severe has happened since the long hot period of the Eocene, fifty-five million years ago, when the change was larger than that between the ice age and the Nineteenth Century and lasted for 200,000 years' (Lovelock 2006: 7). In terms of politics, Lovelock's work is a desperate plea for a transformation in attitudes. Since global warming is a consequence of the last century of industrial activity, it might already be too late for humanity, Lovelock muses gloomily. His 2006 book *The Revenge of Gaia* ends with a passage that could have been pulled out of Walter Miller's *A Canticle for Liebowitz*:

> Meanwhile in the hot arid world survivors gather for the journey to the new Arctic centers of civilization; I see them in the desert as the dawn breaks and the sun throws its piercing gaze across the horizon at the camp. The cool fresh night air lingers for a while and then, like smoke, dissipates as the heat takes charge. Their camel wakes, blinks and slowly rises on her haunches. The few remaining members of the tribe mount. She belches, and sets off on the long unbearably hot journey to the next oasis. (Lovelock 2006: 159)

To be sure, Lovelock is not entirely certain that this decline of civilisation into climate-precipitated tribalism is the only option for us, even though he regards the effects of the climate change already caused by the past century of industrial activity to be irreversible. If there is a chance for us, he contends, it resides in a remembering of nature: 'We need most of all to renew that love and empathy for nature that we lost when we began our love affair with city life' (Lovelock 2006: 8). But what does 'nature' mean in this context? What should we love if Lovelock's advice is to be heeded?

Notes

1. On the distinction between sign and symbol, and between discursive and non-discursive symbol, we will follow the Cassirerian tradition and its classic statement, Susanne K. Langer's all but forgotten *Philosophy in a New Key* (Langer 1957: 53–102). On the psychoanalytical sense of symbol, see Ricoeur (1970: 9–19). These two traditions are not as conflictual as Ricoeur suggests they are.

2. See Cassirer (1944: 23): 'It would be a very naïve sort of dogmatism to assume that there exists an absolute reality of things which is the same for all living beings. Reality is not a unique and homogeneous thing; it is immensely diversified, having as many different schemes and patterns as there are different organisms. Every organism is, so to speak, a monadic being. It has a world of its own because it has an experience of its own. The phenomena that we find in the life of a certain biological species are not transferable to any other species. The experiences – and therefore the realities – of two different organisms are incommensurable with one another. In the world of a fly, says Uexküll, we find only "fly things"; in the world of a sea urchin we find only "sea urchin things".' Cassirer's philosophy of symbolic forms extends Uexküll's biological approach to the diversity of environments to the question of human difference. 'In the human world we find a new characteristic which appears to be the distinctive mark of human life. The functional circle of man is not only quantitatively enlarged; it has also undergone a qualitative change. Man has, as it were, discovered a new method of adapting himself to his environment. Between the receptor system and the effector system which are to be found in all animal species, we find in man a new third link which we may describe as the *symbolic system*. This new acquisition transforms the whole of human life. As compared with other animals man lives not merely in a broader reality; he lives so to speak, in a new *dimension* of reality' (Cassirer 1944: 24).

3. On the hermeneutical distinction between sign and symbol, see, in addition to Ricoeur, Tillich (1967: II, 238–9), Lonergan (1971: 64–9), Jung (1971: 473–81). The early Schelling is an unacknowledged source for this tradition. See the differentiation among schema, allegory and symbol in his *The Philosophy of Art* (Schelling 1802–3: 46): 'That representation in which the universal means the particular or in which the particular is intuited through the universal is schematism. That representation, however, in which the particular means the universal or in which the universal is intuited through the particular is allegory. The synthesis of these two, where neither the universal means the particular nor the particular the universal, but rather where both are absolutely one, is the symbolic.'

4. By 'theological', I do not mean confessional or tied to an particular religious dogma; I mean, rather, horizoned by transcendence. A theological sense of nature profiles nature against its genuine other: the transcendent. We need not know anything about the transcendent save that it transcends the finite (the natural), and is therefore infinite. Hegel would not like this argument, but Schelling would, because it is in fact his. See my forthcoming book *The Late Schelling and the End of Christianity* (Edinburgh University Press, 2019).

5. The destruction of the notion of nature as mechanism is a central theme of the new materialism. See Bennett (2010).

6. On these statistics, see Williams et al. (2015).

7. My project is allied with Anthony Paul Smith's to some degree. See Smith (2013).

8. Eric Aeschimann and Xavier de La Porte, 'Bruno Latour: "Les super-riches ont renoncé à l'idée d'un monde commun"', 19 March 2017, on the Bibliobs website, <http://bibliobs.nouvelobs.com/idees/20170316.OBS6702/bruno-latour-les-super-riches-ont-renonce-a-l-idee-d-un-monde-commun.html> (accessed 20 September 2018).

9. Cassirer's taxonomy of signs and symbols is no longer well known. Below is a summary of the principal distinctions. See Langer (1957: ch. 4).

Signs	Discursive symbols	Presentational symbols
indicative	expressive	expressive
non-conceptual	univocally conceptual	polyvocally conceptual
contextual	abstract	trans-contextual
determinate (conventional)	determinate (defined)	overdetermined (vague)
practical	indifferent	evocative of feeling

10. This is now a commonplace in science and technology studies, but it was not when Latour and Woolgar wrote *Laboratory Life* (1979).
11. This is perfectly clear to see in a close reading of Schleiermacher's second speech on religion (Schleiermacher 1799). It is not 'the infinite without' that one feels in Schleiermacher's religious experience, but rather 'the infinity within' as imaged by nature without. On the difference between Fichte's and Schelling's notions of intellectual intuition, see Vater (1978).

Chapter 3

The Theology of Disenchantment

The first to speak of the death of nature was Carolyn Merchant in her book of the same title (Merchant 1980), a seminal text in eco-feminism that describes patriarchy, technological domination and mechanistic science as related features of an axial seventeenth-century shift in thinking about the human being's place in the world. Merchant locates the most recent appearance of the notion of *kosmos* in the Renaissance, when followers of Ficino, who rediscovered and translated the lost *Corpus Hermeticum* – and of Paracelsus, the peregrinating medical doctor and alchemist of Switzerland – inundated the bourgeoning book industry with lavishly illustrated texts elaborating the possibilities of a science that works within *kosmos*, and promising the empowerment of the human community. Merchant contrasts androcentric Enlightenment atomisation, objectification and dissection with this Renaissance version of holism, which, she argues, preserved the premodern idea of cosmos and – most importantly for eco-feminism – promoted a fundamentally gendered approach to reality:

> The female earth was central to the organic cosmology that was undermined by the scientific revolution and the rise of a market-oriented culture. . . . For sixteenth-century Europeans the root metaphor binding together the self, society and the cosmos was that of an organism. (Merchant 1980: 278)

She contends that nature conceived as an organic whole simultaneously knitted individuals together in concentric circles of belonging: family, community, state, creation. The good of the individual was, in the order of things, subordinated to the common good. The 'dominion' model of techno-science, in contrast, sundered humanity into atomistically self-interested individuals and reduced the earth to an exploitable resource.

I have two objections to Merchant's thesis, objections that are central to the argument I wish to formulate concerning the form of modernity I believe to be the most promising way forward. My first concerns the gendering of the technology/nature distinction. Without for a moment underplaying the crucial contribution of eco-feminism to the literature of environmentalism, we need to ask ourselves if the correlation of the early-modern utilitarian attitude to nature and violence against women still adequately characterises the ecological situation that is the Anthropocene. Male technology raping female earth is too simple a figure to describe, for example, the techno-sphere, which no one seems to control, which is self-reproducing, and which could hardly be described as male and patriarchal.[1] The technosphere is rhizomatic rather than arborescent, uterine rather than phallic, and relational rather than hierarchical. The digitally sutured 'second nature' in which most of us now live, move and have our being (we humans as well as the domestic plants and animals dependent on us) is no longer the product of linear thinking, phallocentric domination of the wild, et cetera; it has itself become a new form of wilderness, proliferating without plan wherever there is a cellphone to connect to the web – that is, everywhere. In fact, the struggle of traditional models of male-dominated economic power to maintain control of the technosphere – from corporations suing individuals for file sharing, to wildly speculative geo-engineering projects aimed at fighting climate change – indicates that the perceived binary op-position between phallocentric technology and feminine nature is no longer tenable. Technology itself has now assumed characteristics associated with the 'female earth': the technological is not a tool but a 'space', a receptacle, for the growth and development of organic life; it is deeply relational, creative of a proliferation of communities both human and non-human, as well as of new forms of social and political life.

For a number of reasons, including the global reach of its networks, its mode of evolution . . . its correspondingly great separation in scale and complexity from the gene – the unit of biological selection – and its dependence on non-biological pro-cesses (radio waves, for example) and materials (such as aluminum and steel), the technosphere can be treated as a novel Earth phenomenon in its own right, i.e. with its own emergent dynamics that is coupled to, but distinct from, the biosphere. In this view, humans and domesticated animals and plants, while biological, are intim-ately linked into as well as producing the technosphere, within which they can exist in large numbers and outside of which they cannot. Alternatively, noting the critical role of humans and other organisms in the function of technological systems, the technosphere might be taken as an extension of the modern biosphere or perhaps as a parasite on it, given that it consumes quantities of biological products to help sus-tain its own metabolism. Conversely though, it provides the means to sustain larger numbers of organisms (up to some point) and rapidly transform ecological structure (species richness, evenness, biomass, etc.). In developing the present perspective we treat the technosphere as inextricably linked into the biosphere – in effect parasitis-ing it, but with the potential to become commensal. (Williams 2015: 13)

Symbiosis can be parasitical, as when one organism depends on another, to that other's detriment. It can be mutual, as when both organisms benefit from the relation (as in a good marriage). And it can be commensal, as when one organism benefits from the other, but that other is unaffected. The hope is that the technosphere, which is at the moment parasitical in relation to the biosphere, might yet evolve such that it becomes commensal with it. In any case, the technosphere has several things in common with the biosphere, a fact that disrupts the technology–nature binary assumed by Merchant: both spheres consume biological materials to sustain themselves; both are non-anthropocentric, that is, both develop and reproduce independently of human agency; both are platforms the conditions of which render new forms of life possible or impossible; both are webs of interdependence and information exchange. The technosphere has taken on many of the grounding and life-enabling functions previously held to be signature qualities of the biosphere: many life forms, not only human, now depend on the technosphere and cannot exist apart from it. Without the technosphere, millions of domesticated animals, from the animals we raise for consumption to the pets we choose to live with, would perish. We are indeed dealing with something new in our midst, something unprecedented in other eras: the creation of a new material support system for both human and non-human life. It cannot be dismantled without causing global catastrophe. It is not in the command of any one central authority. For every population privileged by it, another segment of the population (certain species of canine, for example) is enabled. For every non-human species sacrificed by it (reptiles, for example), other non-human species benefit. The technosphere is too all-inclusive, too decentralised and too unpredictable to be vilified as a new expression of the patriarchal domination of nature. But neither is it to be regarded as benign (any more than the earth may be regarded). It is the new home of life in the Anthropocene, the new form that nature has taken in our age, and if we have no choice but to live in it, we must learn to live in it justly.

Second, and more apposite to the thesis of this essay, Merchant's case for the continuity between ancient holism and Renaissance alchemy underplays the theological orientation of the latter, as though Ficino, Agrippa von Nettesheim, Paracelsus, et al., were just Greeks and Romans disguised as Christians. The Renaissance alchemists were by and large either Kabbalists or Christian Hermeticists: that is, they were not neo-pagans but Jewish–Christian thinkers. The theological context of early-modern alchemy was not mere window dressing or political diversion. Although a doctrine of *creatio ex Deo* is developed in the *Corpus Hermeticum* – one that affirms the material world as the body of God in a way that corrects and exceeds the spiritualism of other Hellenistic philosophies (Platonism,

Stoicism, Gnosticism), and that resonates with Jewish–Christian attitudes – early-modern alchemy is possessed of a will to perfect the universe, a will to continue the work of the Creator, which is deeply bound with ontological assumptions derived from Genesis and political assumptions derived from the New Testament. I will discuss these in some detail in the pages to come. For now, I note that Renaissance Hermeticism is arguably not holism at all. The Renaissance magus has a different relation to the universe from the ancient magician; he is not the microcosm of the ancient world, but rather the *imago Dei* who most images the transcendent Creator in his capacity to raise himself above material processes and actively intervene in natural history. As has been argued by many, the transposition of Hermeticism into a Jewish–Christian key in the Renaissance was not incidental to the rise of science. Renaissance Hermeticism was, on the contrary, the womb of the scientific revolution.[2]

Nevertheless, Merchant should be credited for having reminded the environmental movement that cosmological holism is a central if forgotten theme of the Western tradition. Various Hellenistic schools, from neo-Platonism to Stoicism, from Hermeticism to Epicureanism, could be marshalled in support of the construction of a holistic cosmology that understands the universe to be a balanced whole, and the human being a part of that whole, subordinate but also belonging to it. Heraclitus speaks of the *logos* at the heart of the world: 'All entities come to be in accordance with this Logos' (Heraclitus, Diels-Kranz 22B1). *Logos* in this passage can be translated as *reason* or *order*. The flux and flow of time follows the *logos*; the planets obey it, as does the human body. *Logos* reveals itself in the blossoming of a flower. The task for the sage is to hearken to the *logos*, to listen to it sounding in everything inside and outside of himself so as to live in harmony with all things. Similar statements can be found in Stoicism, in the *Corpus Hermeticum* and in Plato's *Timaeus*. Without exaggeration, we could argue that holism is the predominant cosmology of the ancient world. The ancient *kosmos* was not a collection of extended objects or an aesthetic consumable. It was an unobjectifiable, self-normed and self-regulating totality that included everything within it – gods, mortals, nature and culture. The human soul or intellect had no transcendent vantage point from which it could make sense of things. It was merely one part of a greater whole that necessarily exceeded its comprehension, hence the relatively seamless blend of science and aesthetics in ancient philosophy. Ancient imagination and analysis worked hand in hand, for the task of knowing was an infinite one.

Modernity began with the consciousness that we no longer belong to the cosmos, when the symbol of nature as cosmic totality no longer worked. But when exactly did this change occur? When did we kill the cosmos? The easy answer, the one Merchant offers – the seventeenth century – is almost certainly wrong: suddenly, inexplicably (the story goes), seventeenth-century Europeans became Cartesian subjects, capitalistic reductionists and exploiters dedicated, with Bacon, to torturing nature to wrest her secrets from her in the service of humanity. It is certainly true that nothing like a transcendent Cartesian subject appears before the seventeenth century. And it is clear that the seventeenth-century instrumentalist folding of science into technology made possible the great advances we now associate with modernity – not only with Newtonian mechanics and the discovery of thermodynamics, magnetism, gravity and electricity, but also the political liberalism that would sound the death knell for traditional models of community. It would be naïve not to see a connection between Cartesian transcendence, instrumental reason and political atomisation. These are distinct aspects of a single, complex phenomenon. The problem with locating the demise of holism in the seventeenth century, however, is that it explains nothing. Vilifying the seventeenth century as the sudden interruption of human history by technocracy only begs a further question: whence the technocratic subject? What historical causes are responsible for these seismic shifts in epistemology, economy and politics? Did the technocrat really set upon the seventeenth century fully formed, like Athena sprung from the head of Zeus directly, armed and fully grown?

Clearly not. Even Athena has deeper origins.[3] The better answer to this question, I submit, repeats Lynn White Jr's famous argument concerning the theological roots of the environmental crisis (White 1967) – but with a different, more deeply Weberian spin. The technocratic subject is the product of the dominant religion of Europe: Christianity. Socratic thinking did not bring it into being (as Heidegger believed), nor did modern unbelief. Technocracy, liberalism and secularism are three different sides of a single historical phenomenon born of Europe's most deeply held religious beliefs. That church Christianity (especially Roman Catholicism) objected to reductionist science, revolutionary politics and privatised religion is not proof that these movements were not Christian in origin.[4]

I can only sketch in outline here arguments that have been developed by others at great length.[5] Reductionist science presumes that chaotic singularities can be intelligible in a way that would make no sense for Plato or Aristotle or the science of the ancient world that in one way or another proceeded under their influence. Since the free will of God is the origin of beings, every singular thing has its own unique mode of intelligibility and exhibits lawfulness that cannot be traced back to the recurrence of universal forms. This trust in the deep intelligibility of matter inspires the early-modern scientific method and has everything to do with Jewish–Christian monotheism and, more specifically, with Jewish–Christian voluntarism (the thesis that creation is the effect of the absolutely free will of God and is preceded by nothing – such that moral law, the forms of things and the good itself are all contingent on God's will) and its offshoot, medieval nominalism. Nominalism replaces the Aristotelian–Thomist cosmos with a theatre of singular chaotic events, putting in the place of a system of cyclically recurring forms in a closed universe an emerging and contingent order that can at any moment reverse itself or produce aberrations. One can spin this point from the other side and show the voluntarist underpinnings of modern scepticism. If everything that exists is contingent on the will of God rather than recurring patterns, there is no way to know anything apart from empirical investigation:

> Since each individual being for Ockham is contingent on God's free will, there can be no knowledge of created beings prior to investigation. As a result, humans cannot understand nature without an investigation of the phenomena themselves. Syllogism is thus replaced by hypothesis as the foundation of science. (Gillespie 2009: 23)

Late-medieval trust in providence, on the one hand, and early-modern scepticism about human cognitive abilities, on the other, are in fact two sides of the same coin: the more we trust in God, the less we trust in reason and the more weight we give to the empirical experience of singularities in the formation of knowledge. Theological voluntarism, nominalism and epistemic scepticism give birth to the new confidence in empirical methodology that characterises early-modern science.

Medieval nominalists were hardly unbelievers. On the contrary, the reality of universals was rejected because those universals impinged upon the freedom and sovereignty of God (Gillespie 2009: 19–43). Seen from its historical origins, there was nothing atheistic or irreligious about the empirical turn of the seventeenth century. In his 'Preparative Toward a Natural and Experimental History' (1620), Bacon writes:

> I want this [natural] history to be compiled with a most religious care, as if every particular were stated upon oath; seeing that it is the book of God's works, and (so far as the majesty of heavenly may be compared with the humbleness of earthly things) a kind of second Scripture.[6]

As if every particular were stated upon oath – that is, the singularities of sensible experience are not ontologically impoverished or incapable of explaining themselves, as in Platonism: they are legitimated and warranted by the will of God, to which they owe their essence and existence. Because the empirical singularity we encounter in sensation is the direct effect of the will of God, the nominalist can trust that it has its own substantial truth, that it is more than an appearance or instance that merely refracts the universal form into singularity. The method of understanding this singularity, as Bacon puts it, is not anticipation (deduction via abstraction) but interpretation (induction via experimentation) (Bacon 1620: aphorism 26). The ancient preference for deduction and abstraction is rooted in the assumption of the transitory and ultimately illusory nature of sensory experience: what is most real are the eternal forms cycling through the cosmos, rendering time the moving image of eternity (*Timaeus* 37d). The modern privileging of the singular instance over the universal form, in contrast, presupposes the separation of eternity and time, and the independence of nature from God; it is a-cosmic in orientation and typical of the voluntarist attitude of Jewish–Christian monotheism.[7]

The transcendence of the Jewish–Christian God not only anchors the singular to the will of God, granting it the ontological weight it lacks in the idealism of Plato and the ancient world; it also renders nature an autonomous object, a free-floating thing that can be broken down and rebuilt in various ways. Curiously, the more real the singular becomes, the more precarious nature appears, and we suddenly see the point of a robust doctrine of universals: to mitigate the significance of the singular and thus underwrite the contingency of merely apparent nature with the necessity of an invisible eternal nature. The technological deconstruction and reconstruction of nature are in this light understood to be the human vocation. The thing is not to know the world (in the contemplative sense) but to change it.

> In Bacon's naturalistic scheme there is no place for a knowledge which has for its purpose mere contemplation – the activity assigned by Aristotle to his meta-physician. The aim of all knowledge is action in the production of works for the promotion of human happiness and the relief of man's estate. Through inductive science man is to recapture his dominion over nature long forfeited and long prevented through the efforts of erring philosophers and men of learning. (Anderson 1960: xxvii)

Many others, from Weber to Grant and his mentor Leo Strauss, have made the point that modernity hinges precisely on this severance of nature from the eternal law that regulates the archetypal cosmos of the ancients. What is original in Gauchet's *The Disenchantment of the World* is the way Gauchet links the disenchantment of nature to the Jewish–Christian theology of creation. The Jewish doctrine of *creatio ex nihilo* simultaneously elevates the divine to unreachable transcendence and untethers the world from eternity.[8] Yahweh does not *horizon* this world, nor is the latter an emanation of Yahweh's mind or being. Rather, the Creator wholly transcends this world, belongs to another order entirely – such that this world is to be explicated and experienced on its own terms. In Gauchet's phrase, Jewish transcendence 'autonomises' the world (Gauchet 1985: 141). The transcendent God of the Jews is present only in absence – as an artist is said to be present in his art but in fact appears nowhere in it. The Creator is *revealed* in nature and history, which means God is initially hidden and concealed in what God reveals. The singularities of nature are related to God as artworks are related to the artist: they show forth divine providence and give glory to God, but they do not image God (with the important exception of the human being). They are other than God, and therefore understandable on their own terms.

With the autonomisation of the world comes the liberation of the human from the determinism sotypical of premodern life. 'The greater the gods, the freer humans are' (Gauchet 1985: 51). The premodern sense of the sacred subordinated humanity to gods who were assumed to be continuous with the world: when not sharing the same form as humans and other animals themselves, these gods at least participated in the same natural order (albeit at a higher level). The hierarchical continuity assumed in paganism between the natural and the divine was the presupposition grounding the theological and social determinism that so immobilised ancient human beings. Everything that occurred in the premodern world was associated with and dependent on the divine. In such a world, the thought of freedom cannot really occur, for in it goodness is the same as alignment with the will of divinity (or the moral law of nature), and evil is nothing more than failed alignment. A discussion of praiseworthy and blameworthy action might occur in this context, but it would not presume the radical freedom, the absolute autonomy, of the individual that is so central to modern thought.

But Judaism on its own does not emancipate the human for the transformation of the world; it could easily lead to a renunciation of the world, as it did in the prophets and in various ascetic movements (the Essenes, for example). Needed for the world to be fully autonomised was the Christian doctrine of incarnation. Only when the transcendent God of Judaism becomes human in a very specific and concrete sense – only then is the world 'ontologically complete' (Gauchet 1985: 77). As Hegel reminds us, a general incarnation of the transcendent in a variety of human beings, or in nature in general, cannot grant the universal salvation possible only through the *unique* hypostatic union of the divine and human natures in one historical man. Christ – the 'concrete universal', the singularisation of the *Logos* – alone can equally distribute divinity among all. A conception of the recurrence of incarnations in a variety of forms maintains the hierarchy of the divine and the human, as well as an aristocracy of spiritual beings above and beyond the reach of the average human; a singular and unique incarnation demolishes such hierarchies.

Hegel notes divine 'incarnation' is common in many religions. But the Lamas of Asian religion, for example, actually function to exclude the everyday person, for the incarnation is reserved to a particular elect and thus excludes the vast majority of everyday people. To be truly universal, therefore, the representation must be singular, must be in one person, 'This individual is unique; [there are] not several [like the Lamas]. In one [all are encompassed]. (Gilbert 2017: 21)[9]

Paradoxically, the hypostatic union of human and divine natures in Christ is the moment at which the two orders (the eternal and the temporal) become most clearly distinguished from one another; it is the moment of the abolition of the hierarchical principle that governed paganism from Greece to India. This is also Schelling's reading of the Chalcedonian formula defining the hypostatic union: it is not that Christ combines in himself two pre-existing natures, but that the two natures become distinguishable precisely in their union. Prior to the incarnation, there is neither a distinctly human nor a distinctly divine nature: the two are only differentiable in the event of their conjunction.[10] The split between nature and divinity is not mitigated by the Christian doctrine of incarnation, for it is a false Christology that sees the point of the hypostatic union to be the deification of nature. The hypostatic union is the *humanisation* of the divine, not the deification of nature; it humanises God in a way that is far more extreme than any anthropocentric mythology. The incarnation of Jesus, far from resuscitating pantheism, spells the definitive death of *kosmos* and the absolute removal of the transcendent divine from the orbit of human experience. It spells, in other words, the negation of false transcendence. Thereafter, the infinite God is present only in absence, as Luther reminds us. Thereafter, there are no more natural signs of God to be deciphered: God fully inhabits the form of the Son, and the Son is the crucified one whose material body is so essential to him that it is resurrected. God is no longer 'present' in nature, not even in 'humanity'; God is incarnated in a single, ordinary individual. The divine Father is simultaneously manifest and veiled by the fully human nature of Christ.

It also follows from the doctrine of the incarnation that investment in this world is a Christian duty. If the transcendent God deemed the earthly order sufficient for incarnation – if God elevated ordinary human things (birth, infancy, motherhood, fatherhood, community, family, work, friendship, love and death) to the divine – then it is apostasy to turn away from the world in ascetic neo-Platonic detachment. The ascetic's scorn for this world is not an originally Christian posture, but far more typical of Hellenistic philosophies such as neo-Platonism and Stoicism. Christian monasticism owes more to the Hellenistic worldview than it does to the Jewish–Christian Bible.[11] The Christian's duty is fulfilled, not in an ascetical renunciation of earthly life, but in the work of improving human society through the construction and maintenance of schools and hospitals, economic productivity and the pursuit of scientific enterprise. Christianity *invests* in the world in the name of salvation. The specifically Christian call is neither to renounce the world as does Gnosticism or Stoicism, nor to simply accept it as is (a position Gauchet holds to be typical of Islam); rather, the Christian is called to work on the world, to work with the Creator in bringing creation to perfection. God leaves nature incomplete so that we might become more like God through our work of transforming matter. The Stoic tries to change not the world, but the self. The Christian, by contrast, tries to remake the world in accordance with divine will.

> In this way, the world gets an unprecedented 'ontological completeness' and an unheard-of validity, leading eventually to its full autonomy. While the search for salvation from of old meant a turning away from the world, the doctrine of the Incarnation leads to an appropriation of the world and to its transformation, precisely in the name of salvation. (Cloots 2008: 17–18)

On a related point, the revolutionary politics of the modern age are dependent on eschatological hope, as Ernst Bloch has argued at length.[12] And private religion, which is the basis of civic tolerance, would not have existed without the robust theological notion of human dignity that underwrites political liberalism (see Gauchet 1985; Berman 2008). Far from abolishing religion, secularism develops upon and consolidates the basic beliefs of one particular form of religion, Christianity, and Pauline Christianity in particular. In Gauchet's broadened theory of secularisation, it is not this or that Christian doctrine that secularises – not, for example, as in Weber, the Calvinist work ethic that secularises (Weber 1905) – but Christianity as such. The 'religious logic' of Christianity itself is secularising. Nor is it specific aspects of modernity (capitalism, for example) that are made possible by Christianity, but modernity as such. Gauchet understands secularism in the conventional sense as post-religious, and thus can write that Christianity is 'the religion of the departure from religion' (Gauchet 1985: 4). If we follow Charles Taylor and Frédéric Lenoir and argue that secularism is not post-religious but pluralist and therefore hyper-religious, we can see Christianity as emancipating humanity not from religiosity as such but from religious nationalism, religious dogmatism and religious intolerance (Taylor 2007; Lenoir 2003). Even with this modification, Gauchet's general point remains valid: a traditional hierarchy of divine and natural related as higher and lower – the ontological continuum that consolidates the cosmological dependency of human civilisation on a doctrine of eternal law meditated by cult and priesthood (religion) – comes to an end with the preaching of the Gospel by Paul.

The universalism of Paul has been commented upon often enough before. The point to be made in the context of the present essay is that Paul's emancipatory politics breaks with the hierarchical organisation of society associated with a deterministic doctrine of nature as *kosmos*, wherein everything and everyone has a pre-assigned place and a predetermined set of possibilities and duties in the system of being.[13] 'There is no such thing as Jew and Greek, slave and freeman, male and female; for you are all one person in Christ Jesus' (Gal. 3: 28). Notice how Paul relates the bondage of humanity prior to Christ to a specific understanding of the elemental world (that is, the *kosmos*):

> We were slaves to the elemental spirits of the universe, but when the term was completed, God sent his own Son, born of a woman, born under the law, in order to purchase freedom for the subjects of the law, in order that we might attain the status of sons. (Gal. 4: 3–5)

In sharp contrast to the pagan wisdom of hierarchical mediation and cosmological subordination of the singular to the universal, Paul asserts the immediate access of each individual to the emancipatory Spirit, and thereby elevates difference above unity, and individuality above cosmic belonging. Such a gospel of freedom is repeated wherever revolutionary politics raises its voice in protest against any form of naturalised tyranny or enforcement of social immobility on the basis of a cosmological principle of pre-established hierarchical order.

The break with the holism of premodern philosophies of nature can also be underscored with reference to the new thinking of freedom and morality associated with modernity. In ancient holism, morality is not something unique to human beings; it is inscribed into the material order itself. The good is the way of nature; it is the functional relation among all parts of the whole, the result achieved when these parts effectively – and, at the human level, deliberately – are ordered like the organs of a properly functioning body toward an end common to the whole. What makes an action right or wrong is the degree to which it obeys the natural law governing the whole. If we follow nature, we do right and thrive; otherwise we do wrong and die. Moderns, by contrast, are authors of themselves; they are uniquely capable of good to the degree that they are uniquely capable of evil (understood as unnatural or perverse behaviour). Human beings, Schelling argues, are never just animals; they are destined to be either above or below the animal, depending on how they dispose of their freedom.[14] Environmental holism, whether it knows it or not, hearkens back to a pre-Christian vision of the hierarchically ordered cosmos in which humans are not free to decide for good or evil. Just as the ancient Platonist must in the end deny radical freedom both at the level of the One and at the level of the finite human being – who does not freely *decide* for good and evil but obeys the eternal moral law to the degree that intelligence and virtue enable such obedience – the environmental holist must deny any real distinction between good and evil. Moral wrongdoing is a mistake in judgement: having misconceived the inferior path as better and more desirable than the superior, the errant soul disturbs the natural order. The solution is to train the soul in virtue so that it more effectively wills what is in its own interest, the genuinely good.[15]

Such a return to pagan naturalism serves the agenda of the environmental holist, for whom distinguishing between the human and the non-human on the basis of the presence or absence of the capacity to choose freely between good and evil is 'speciesism', that is, anathema. On this view, which is now commonplace, humans are not special or distinctive: every being is destined to fit into the balance of the whole in its own way. To live well is to do good and to do good is to follow the order of things. Such talk, however inspiring to early environmentalists, is falling on hard times these days. For some theorists, the point of quantum physics is not that there is a hidden 'implicate' order wondrously balancing the most distant points of the universe. On the contrary, the fact that only statistical probabilities obtain at this level indicates that there is no predetermined natural order. Breakthroughs in genetics demonstrate that no 'nature in itself' prevents us from altering the course of our evolution or from creating artificial life.

> Because so called natural objects are all amenable to manipulation 'nature' melts into thin air . . . nature is no longer 'natural,' the reliable 'dense' background of our lives, it now appears as a fragile mechanism, which at any point, can explode in a catastrophic direction. (Žižek 2008)

Without subscribing to Žižekian cynicism, we can still identify several internal problems, even logical inconsistencies, in environmental holism. For example, there is the question of locality. Deep Ecology, Earth Firsters and James Lovelock speak of the earth as an organism that balances itself homeostatically. But if this blue-green garden is in fact a singularity in the universe, an accident in an unfathomable expanse of space populated by uninhabitable chunks of rock and balls of gas – the entirety of it the product of accident, of collision and explosion – then our earth-centred holism is most certainly an illusion. Holism must go all the way or else it is not holistic. It cannot be the earth alone that is a balanced whole; it must be the solar system, the galaxy, the Milky Way – the universe. David Bohm is able to consider this latter possibility, but the thought otherwise exceeds the speculative capacities of your average environmentalist. And it appears to be disproven by scientific observations of randomness at the quantum level – and on the astral level, of a tendency toward entropy.

A further problem is the environmentalist's refusal to discriminate between the human and the non-human, or recognise any species' unique role in the natural balance, is increasingly untenable in the era of anthropogenic climate change. The Anthropocene has brought renewed urgency to the question of humanity's responsibility for the current crisis. Given our evolutionary and technological achievements, we are not merely the chief perpetrators of climate change; what we do now, today, will certainly have an impact on the future of all life on earth. It is not the planet itself that is going to solve this one, but human morality and politics. We must, then, change our ways, first by taking responsibility for what we have done, and then by making amends for our wrongs. There is no use in lecturing other species on their respective contributions to the problem or its solution. Not only are they incapable of understanding us, they are not free to do other than they do. Human exceptionalism returns in the Anthropocene with a vengeance.

What is the appeal of eco-holism, and why does it persist despite so many arguments against it? Eco-holism attracts us because, in the first place, it promises to restore our lost sense of belonging to the universe. Contra predominant scientific narratives, it offers us the consoling belief that we are not an accident, not an absurd awakening of self-consciousness destined ultimately to witness the forces of entropy consume the ground of its possibility. Holism assures us, rather, that we belong here. We are made for this universe. We fit into it, or at least can fit into it, as organically as a beaver in a pond or a tiger in a jungle. If in modern angst we note the all-too-human longing for a proper home, in holism we find the answer to that longing. Holism re-enchants the world. Nature is not mindless or spiritless, and not, as early modern Deists would have it, a carefully designed mechanism set in motion by a now-absent Creator. Rather, nature is *divine* once again, as it was for Lao Tzu or for Heraclitus or for the Vedas. If we want to understand divinity, we have only to understand nature, which offers us concrete and sensuous things to feed our recalcitrant Romantic impulses: craggy peaks, stormy seas, the starry heavens above, or, if you like, labyrinthine subatomic universes beneath the surfaces of bodies, not to mention distant nebulae on the edge of visibility.

I would not for a moment consider mocking these sentiments. I wish rather to understand them. It bears keeping in mind that they emerge from a sense of threat. The modernity that won the day is now constitutively homeless. Humanity has been evicted from the cosmos. But other forms of modernity are possible. In order to access these possibilities, free them up from underneath the sedimentation of traditional presuppositions, we need to re-examine the religious roots of disenchantment. It was not an increase in knowledge that disenchanted the world, but a change in religious orientation. Long before the seventeenth century set upon nature and tortured her for her secrets, the Jewish–Christian religion had disenchanted nature, evacuated it of divinity by introducing an ontological difference between created and uncreated being. Jewish–Christian theology locates God *elsewhere*. The revelation of God is not natural; it is, rather, an intrusion of transcendence into nature, the breaking into history of God's words and deeds.

It took many centuries for the significance of this religious revolution to be realised. The Catholic Middle Ages obstructed its movement by retaining Hellenistic cosmology as the underside of Jewish–Christian transcendence, the *natura* that *gratia* perfects rather than destroys (Aquinas, *Summa theologiae* 1a, q.1, a.1). As anyone familiar with the theological debates of the high Middle Ages would appreciate, this grafting of the Hebraic onto the Hellenic was hardly seamless. It was fraught with tensions that eventually fractured it into two in the Reformation. Consider the implications for nature of Luther's *theologia crucis*. Luther contrasts the quasi-pagan natural theology of the Scholastics with what he regards as the genuinely Christian theology of the New Testament. The Scholastics, under the influence of Hellenistic thought, privileged a theology of glory – *theologia gloriae* – an aesthetic theology of the divine presence in nature, over the theology of the cross, the *theologia crucis*, that is, the theology of God's absence and, for Luther, the core of New Testament revelation. 'The condition of this life is not that of having God but of seeking God', Luther argues contra Aquinas, Scotus and all those who would underwrite revelation with a theology of nature (Luther 1516: 225). In the Heidelberg Disputation, we find the following declaration:

> That person is not rightly called a theologian who looks upon the invisible things of God as though they were clearly perceptible through things that have actually happened. He deserves to be called a theologian, however, who understands the visible and manifest things of God seen through suffering and the Cross. (Luther 1518: theses 19–20)

God as revealed in the New Testament appears not as a lord of nature but as the crucified and failed Messiah. Luther's point is that no amount of reflection on the being of nature can bring one to the Christ. From Jewish voluntarism to the Lutheran theology of revelation, to the nominalism, reductionism and mechanism of early-modern science and capitalism, a direct line of historical influence becomes clear. Modernity inherits from the Reformation a theology in which God is understood to be discontinuous with nature. Based on this inheritance, we launched the political, scientific and economic overhaul of civilisation that continues to condition us today. The Creator in Reformed theology is so transcendent that his interventions are all miraculous. His first and final appearance in space and time is a singular incarnation culminating in his crucifixion and resurrection.[16]

In the form of the modernity that vanquished Renaissance humanism, the binary of a transcendent unfathomable first cause and its contingent and autonomous effect was transposed into an atheistic key: it became the culture–nature distinction, which simultaneously elevated the human and rendered it incomprehensible. *Natura's* original pairing with transcendence made possible the atheist transference of transcendence to humanity. Transcendent spirit became identified with the human, no longer the divine. Early German Idealism might have celebrated this move as the apotheosis of the human: released from the shackles of theology, we became free to capitalise on our own exceptionality. But by the beginning of the twentieth century, things looked less promising. Rather than delivering the world into our hands, the scientific revolution seemed to have cut it adrift into meaninglessness. Today, in the Anthropocene – the ultimate humiliation of our species – we face the hard facts. How bad indeed we are at playing lord of nature.

With the idea of transcendental freedom, a fundamentally new conception of human being entered philosophy. Where Scholastics described the soul as an immaterial *substance*, subsuming humanity under the same genus as animals and plants (which were also thought of as substances), the moderns drew a line between the human and the non-human that not only distinguished between but separated them. Transcendental subjects, reflective and free, belong to a genus of their own. What distinguishes European philosophy from all others before it (and contemporaneous with it) is precisely this assumption that the human being is not a part of nature but supervenes over it. Notice the change that has occurred in the transposition of transcendence: in the Christian paradigm, human being emerges out of nature and is called to elevate itself above it, thereby raising material nature, in which it participates, into union with the divine; in the modern paradigm, human being stands over and against nature, as that which is alien to it, and has nothing above it. The apogee of this position is Fichte's, in which nature is no longer simply other than human; it is an other posited so that transcendental subjectivity *might realise its freedom* in conquering it. Nature is a means to human freedom, stuff to be used as we will, without any intrinsic intelligibility (for it is thinking that renders it intelligible) or value (for it is only of use value to us).

We should not simply vilify this attitude, as we may be inclined to, even if we recognise the need to move beyond it. Behind the seventeenth-century sea change was also the awakening of the will to develop and improve the human condition – a value largely absent in premodern societies. For moderns, technology is not only about mastery, but also about justice. Ancient empires could do without technology as we know it because they understood slavery to be a natural condition.[17] It is not out of ignorance that the ancient Greeks or Egyptians or Hindus did not develop modern technology. It is because they were not particularly interested in human equality. Buddhism breaks with the assumption of natural slavery as well, but in an other-worldly direction. Beyond *samsara*, we are all equal, equally nothing, *sunyata*. With the Jewish–Christian doctrine of the dignity of the human being, the universality of access to the divine principle – which is the historical presupposition of the doctrine of human rights (Berman 2008) – slavery is condemned. While slavery persists in Christendom – even to this day, in the form of the sweatshops that make consumerism possible, or the garbage services that the developing world still provides for so-called first-world waste – it does so as a guilty stain on the consumer conscience, something that needs to be hidden from view or repressed to be continued. Early-modern technology and political liberalism were both motivated by a commitment to the universality of human equality; the ancient solution to the diversification of labour and the production of the leisure and special-isation essential to civilisation – slavery – could no longer be tolerated, or at least, could no longer be openly and guiltlessly endorsed. Contra Aristotle, no human beings were born to be enslaved; rather, all were in principle entitled to the maximum flourishing and happiness possible in this life.

The movement from *creatio* to the death of *kosmos* to the secular is neither an *a priori* necessity nor a random historical fact; these three concepts are organically if not logically related. It is only in light of divine transcendence that the divinity of nature is denied. And it is only in the wake of nature's desecration that society is secularised and the individual set negatively free. Politics and science are secularised in the name of precisely this freedom. The erosion of the concept of natural community, which, it should be noted, is the shared presupposition of both Marxism and liberalism, is part and parcel of desecration. When nature is set up over and against spirit, understood as transcendent God or transcendent human reason, the eternal essences theorised by the ancients either disappear entirely, as in nominal-ism, or lose all power over the human being. They become mere categories, media of cognition rather than manifestations of the deep structure of being that also determines humanity.

We must be soberly realistic about what is possible for us now and what is not. The nostalgia of moderns who pine for a return to the lost *kosmos* of the ancients is somewhat contradictory, for those who truly participate in nature have no sense of themselves as participating in it. Rather, they are wholly immersed in it, lacking the critical distance presumed in the act of valuation in which the re-enchanter distinguishes the premodern from the modern. What the re-enchanter wants is not the unconsciousness of the premodern but the sense of belonging attributed to him. But herein lies the contradiction: the re-enchanter does not want to belong at the expense of consciousness and differentiation. And yet it is precisely consciousness and differentiation that exile us from belonging to the *kosmos*. The re-enchanter wants belonging without relinquishing the sense of separateness that could appreciate it. Such a fantasy is like wanting to be present at your funeral to see your friends and family grieving for you. We want to be present at least enough to appreciate our own absence.

Alongside the disenchantment of the world there emerged a demand for universal equality rooted in a doctrine of intrinsic human dignity, which has been witnessed for the most part only in its being breached, no doubt, but which has nonetheless steadily transformed ethical discourses around the world. The freedom of the Christian proclaimed first by Paul gave rise to experiments in egalitarian communal life – for example, the house church (*domus ecclesiae*) of Rome and some Middle Eastern cities. At the same time, the theology of the New Testament precipitated a transformation in basic anthropological concepts and the definitions of personhood, rendered urgent at the Church councils of Nicea and Chalcedon that convened under Constantine in the fourth century. In the Middle Ages, the ethics of personhood was held in check by a momentary return of ancient, hierarchical, political models, but it continued to define Church teaching until it emerged full-blown in the Renaissance. When Christianity was rejected or at least suspended in the public sphere on rationalist grounds in the seventeenth, eighteenth and nineteenth centuries, the concept of the dignity of the person still played a determinative role in politics, even if in degenerate forms, for example in the liberalism of John Stuart Mill.

In the present day, the Christian ethics of the free individual has been in one way or another exported to every culture on the planet and now functions, in abstraction from its theological context, as the inner engine of the global consumer–capitalist system, the system which has abolished every other major system of social organisation and exchange. When non-Westerns 'modernise', they become secular individualists and, in that moment, disenchanted, no longer inhabitants of a hierarchical, eternal order.[18] One can visit Gurgaon in India (near Delhi) and witness this happening in real time. A couple of decades ago, Gurgaon was the agricultural belt of the ancient city of Delhi, a rural village where traditions addressing social stratification, family, gender relations and religious duties – all stretching back to the Vedas – determined all aspects of life. It has since become the leading financial and industrial hub of India, boasting the third highest per capita income in the country. Once a rice paddy inhabited by simple farmers, Gurgaon is now coveted real estate for Delhi's upper classes and the tech corporations for which they work. Farmers who once lived on a hundred rupees a week are now selling their farms for millions. Malls have opened with glistening surfaces and shelves full of Western commodities, and freeways have been built through rice paddies to connect them to Delhi. A gap has opened between the older generation, who still inhabit the ancient Hindu universe of meaning, and the new generation, who dress in Western style and sip lattes that cost more than their fathers once earned in a day – a gap that makes the intergenerational struggle between the baby boomers and their straight-laced parents trivial by comparison. These parents go to temple and offer sacrifice to Shiva or Vishnu, no doubt seeking forgiveness for their children – whom they scarcely recognise – clad in designer jeans, partnering casually, and generally following suit with the Western fantasy of self-fulfilment.

We seem to be caught on one or the other side of two horns of a dilemma, faced with a stark choice between belonging to the whole and forswearing technological progress, or pursuing progress and forswearing wholeness. A culture founded upon *creatio* will have the conceptual presuppositions necessary for technological development, but by virtue of those very presuppositions will deprive its citizens of the sense of belonging that gives meaning to life. A culture founded upon *kosmos* will have the presuppositions necessary for a rich sense of community and for holistic ethics and politics (along with the sense of belonging that accompanies them), but will, in light of these presuppositions, lack the linear concept of time and anthropology of the human as self-maker without which progress would be unthinkable. No wonder we are immobilised with anxiety and cannot imagine a way forward. The only possibility for the flourishing of the earth community appears to be the extinction of the modern human being.

Notes

1. On the technosphere, see Williams et al. (2015) and Haff (2014). See also Jeni Fulton, 'What Is the Technosphere?', 5 October 2015, at the Spike website, <http://www.spikeartmagazine.com/en/articles/what-technosphere> (accessed 20 September 2018).
2. This argument is well known in the small circle of scholars working in the area of Western Esotericism. See the classic studies relating Renaissance Hermeticism to modern science by Francis Yates (1964) and Ioan Culianu (1987). Worthy of mention is the work of those scholars who have identified the close relationship between Renaissance Hermeticism and German Idealism. See, for example, Magee (2001) and O'Regan (1994). See also McGrath (2012: 44–81). A crucial move in the transition from medieval to modern thought, religious in origin, was the move from the hierarchically ordered cosmos of Aristotle, Plato, Plotinus and their first Christian followers (Augustine, Boethius, Pseudo-Dionysus) to the homogenous universe of the Renaissance. Cassirer has demonstrated the role of Nicholas of Cusa's radical revision of neo-Platonism in this movement. See Cassirer (1963). God is so other than creation in Cusa's view that there is no ladder of perfection that can be scaled to reach the divine. The gap (*chorismos*) between the infinite and the finite is unbridgeable – there is no hierarchy of being. It is not only that the earth is no longer the centre of the universe as a consequence of this thought; there cannot be a finite centre of the universe: every thing is equally distant from and equally near to God conceived as an infinite sphere, whose centre is everywhere and whose circumference nowhere (Cusa 1440: 108). Cassirer points out that Cusa's maximisation of the distance that separates the creature from the Creator does not devalue the world; rather, it renders everything in the world, which exists only by virtue of participation (*methexis*) in

the infinite, equally symbolic of the divine. The transcendent One manifests itself in infinite multiplicity and diversity – a standard neo-Platonic thought. But the diversity is not ordered in terms of degrees of values and perfection, as it was for the first Christian Platonists: every individual is of immeasurable significance and value because each is a unique and irreplaceable manifestation of the One. Cassirer's book uncovers the genetic relation between Cusa's remodelled Christian neo-Platonic mysticism and Renaissance humanism, on the one hand, and early modern empiricism, on the other: just as the human individual is elevated above the universal by virtue of his or her immediate relation to the divine, so too are the singular irregularities of the material world rendered intelligible and worthy of thought on their own material terms, and not merely by means of the universal which they instantiate. Cusa's neo-Platonism is thus foundational for both modern politics and science. See Cassirer (1963: 31–32): 'From the religious point of view, the individual is not the opposite of the universal, but rather its true fulfillment. . . . Each particular and individual being has an immediate relation to God; it stands as it were, face to face with him.'

3. Zeus, having slept with Metis, the goddess of craft, feared that she might conceive a rival to him. So he swallowed her up. He had a terrible headache as a result. When his head was split in two with an axe to relieve him, Athena leaped out with a shout, 'and pealed to the broad sky her clarion cry of war' (Pindar, *Seventh Olympian Ode*).

4. Neither are we justified in singling out Protestantism for the crime, as some Catholic thinkers (e.g. von Balthasar) are inclined to do. The presuppositions of disenchantment, namely divine transcendence, human autonomy and the finitude of creation, are not uniquely Protestant beliefs; they are uniquely Christian beliefs.

5. See in particular Michael Allen Gillespie's *The Theological Origins of Modernity* (2009) and Charles Taylor's *A Secular Age* (2007).

6. Bacon, cited in Gascoigne (2010: 216).

7. See Gilson (1955: 498): 'Considered under its purely theological aspect, this doctrine [nominalism] is dominated by the first words of the Christian creed: "I believe in one God, the Father almighty". . . . The God in whom Ockham believes is Yahweh, who obeys nothing, not even Ideas. Duns Scotus had submitted to the free will of God the choice of the essences to be created; instead of letting God be free to choose between essences, Ockham suppresses them. Abelard had made Ideas the privilege of the divine mind; Ockham suppresses universals, even in God. It is because there are no universal Ideas in God that there is no universality in things. The so-called Ideas are nothing but the very things producible by God. God needs no Ideas in order to know; by the very fact that God is God, he knows all.'

8. While the Scholastics sought to heal the rift between Biblical voluntarism and Greek metaphysics, they were too good to miss the different ontology that the Biblical doctrine of creation demands of Christian theology and science. Without delving into the Scholastic disputes about *essentia* and *existentia* (or *essentia* and *esse*), it is worth highlighting the agreement between Scotus and Aquinas on what distinguishes the being of the Creator from the being of creation. The former is independent, *esse subsistens*, first being and being in its proper sense (*ipsum esse*); the latter is dependent, *esse non subsistens*, consequent being and being in its derivative sense. Characteristic of *creatio* are contingency, change, potency, growth and decay. We should read Aquinas's 'Five Ways' (or five proofs) as a meditation on the nature of contingency. What is at issue in each of these proofs is not the necessary nature of God (which on the terms of each of the proofs is inconceivable), but the non-necessary nature of nature. Aquinas describes nature variously as potency, which depends on an act that it does not itself possess; as the effect of another rather than the cause of itself; as possibility mysteriously awakened into actuality without its own help; as graded approximation to perfection rather than perfection itself; and as being directed toward ends that it has not set for itself. See Aquinas, *Summa Theologica*, 1a, q.2, a.3. What

is most characteristic of nature in both the medieval and modern senses, we might say, is that it need not be. *Creatio* is disenchanted matter, a thing bereft of divinity. To be sure, it is designed, ordered and preserved by God, but that is precisely the point: it does not possess its own self-ordering principle or *telos*, as in Aristotle. The principle that orders it lies outside of it.

9. Gilbert cites the third volume of Hegel's *Lectures on the Philosophy of Religion* (Hegel 1832: 114).

10. See Schelling (1831: 526–43) and Tritten (2014). Gauchet's argument is strikingly similar to Schelling's, describing Jesus' 'inverted messiahship'. See Gauchet (1985: 119): 'The incarnation of the invisible used to be the archetypal means for showing the continuity between the earthly hierarchy and the celestial order; here it became the very signifier of their mutual exteriority. . . . Instead of attesting to the other's substantial proximity, it began to refer to its infinite distance; instead of identifying the collective body with its external foundation, it highlighted the enormous gap separating them. For God's truth to reach us, he had to adopt a shape analogous to ours, a spectacular way of announcing his unimaginably foreign nature. His proximity through Christ is an inexhaustible sign of his unrepresentable remoteness.' The Arian option attempted to reinstitute the traditional pagan hierarchy of being, preserving cosmic continuity by subordinating the human to the divine. By rendering the divine and the human equal in Christ, the hierarchy of being is abolished. 'The Incarnation was no longer to be understood in terms of the old political logic of higher and lower, but in terms of a purely metaphysical logic of otherness; and in this framework the absolute difference of the human and the divine allowed us to think their complete union. . . . Here, the complete union of both natures in Christ – "the same perfect in Godhead, and the same perfect in manhood, truly God and truly man" – draws our attention to the complete disjunction of the human and the divine' (Gauchet 1985: 126).

11. This was, of course, a central argument of the early Reformation against Roman Catholicism. See Chadwick (1964: 104–13). For a history of the fusion of Christianity and Hellenistic thought in early ascetic and monastic movements, see Bigg (1886).

12. See Bloch's three-volume *Principle of Hope* (Bloch 1954). See also Benz (1965: 49–63) and Taubes (1947).

13. See Badiou (2003), Taubes (2004) and Žižek (2000), the last especially at pp. 119–21: 'Christ's death is *not* the same as the seasonal death of the pagan god; rather, it designates a *rupture* with the circular movement of death and rebirth, the passage to a wholly different dimension of the Holy Spirit . . . Christianity (and, in its own way, Buddhism) introduced into this global balanced cosmic Order a principle that is totally foreign to it, a principle which, measured by the standards of pagan cosmology, cannot but appear as a monstrous distortion: the principle according to which each individual has *immediate* access to universality (of nirvana, of the Holy Spirit, or, today, of human rights and freedoms); I can participate in this universal dimension *directly*, irrespective of my special place within the global social order. . . . Christianity asserts as the highest act precisely what pagan wisdom condemns as the source of Evil: the gesture of *separation*, of drawing the line, of clinging to an element that disturbs the balance of All . . . Christianity *is* the miraculous Event that disturbs the balance of the One-All; it *is* the violent intrusion of Difference that precisely *throws the balanced circuit of the universe off the rails.*'

14. Schelling's discovery of this point marks his departure from the pantheistic, immanentist nature philosophy of his youth and the beginning of the philosophy of religion which will occupy him unto his death. See Schelling (1809: 23).

15. See Plato, *Apology*, 37a: 'I am convinced that I never wrong anyone intentionally'.

16. See Gogarten (1953), who, according to Blanco (2013: 305), sees 'secularization as the effect of the Christian faith itself, because the Biblical conception of God deprives the world of its sacredness'.

17. On this point, see the forgotten classic by Hilaire Belloc, *The Servile State* (Belloc 1912). Belloc exaggerates his points, and skewers history to suit them, but on the fundamental assumption of his critique of capitalism, Belloc is spot on: slavery is understood to be the normal economic condition of human civilisation prior to Christendom. Often overlooked, especially in Heideggerian circles, is the relation between the rise of modern technology and the late medieval desire for universal social justice. One of the reasons why technology develops in Europe is because of the medieval Jewish–Christian heritage. Technology was not only desired because it allowed us to lord it over nature; it was also desired because it allowed us to emancipate human beings from servile labour. The Christian has a will to technology because she believes (uniquely in the history of humanity) that slavery is immoral. On this point see Grant (1987).

18. Individualism is a residue of authentic Christian personalism. As a politics it would not have been possible without the Christian elevation of the person, the one who stands in an absolute relation to the absolute, as Kierkegaard put it, above the universal (Kierkegaard 1843: 56). But Christian personalism is not individualism; the latter is a reduction and a distortion of the former. See Maritain (1940: 74–82).

Chapter 4

Eco-anxiety

If the first death of nature was the Jewish–Christian eclipse of *kosmos* as a normative whole in favour of the assertion of a transcendent God (God over nature), the second death of nature was the denial of both nature and God: no *kosmos* – but no spirit, either. Such is the desperate bleakness of late modernity: neither natural law nor transcendent spirit can save us anymore. 'Today, since the apocalypse is technically possible and even likely, it stands alone before us: no one believes anymore that a "kingdom of God" will follow it' (Anthers 2007: 115). The fundamental psychological state of the modern is consequently not only disenchantment but also metaphysical *disorientation*. 'Who gave us the sponge to wipe away the entire horizon? What did we do when we unchained the earth from its sun? Whither is it moving now? Whither are we moving now?' (Nietzsche 1882a: 181–2). The late nineteenth century reels in the vertigo of this metaphysical disorientation, deprived both of the normative order of nature and the moral order of freedom. Characters in Dostoevsky are rendered literally sick by the thought of the meaninglessness of human existence. Raskolnikov must test himself against the truth of nothingness to see if he can endure the thought that nothing matters, that there is neither good nor evil but only the praise or blame of society. One who can live with this thought, Raskolnikov concludes, is a master with the right both to transgress law and to determine history. Wondering if he himself is up to the task, Raskolnikov murders his landlady to see if his conscience is free of self-deceit and able to live with the deed. Unlike Dostoevsky's protagonist, contemporary culture no longer tests itself against despair, and has instead settled itself into the abyss – making a home in it – by adopting an attitude of cynical indifference.

Compared with the planetary catastrophes on offer today, from nuclear holocaust to the collapse of the material support of human civilisation (that is, a stable climate), nineteenth-century nihilism appears quaint. The meta-physically tormented anti-heroes of Dostoevsky's novels are self-absorbed, spoiled young men, concerned only with the salvation of their own souls. We, on the other hand, have the extinction of humanity to worry about. Perhaps one of the reasons so few people genuinely worry about climate change is that the stakes are so unbearably, unimaginably high: if there is anything to it, we have everything to lose. Meanwhile, the facts mount up, and the most disturbing predictions of climatologists increasingly look to be accurate.

There is no other place for such disavowed horror but the unconscious. We repress the disturbing recognition made at the 2015 United Nations Climate Change Conference that we are far away from the global policies needed to reduce emissions sufficiently to keep global warming from exceeding the two degrees beyond which eco-collapse is inevitable. The problem is that no one knows how to get there from here. Astrophysicist Neil deGrasse Tyson in 2014 shouted on television about the imminent doom of the fossil-fuel age but no one appeared to be listening:

> We're dumping carbon dioxide into the atmosphere at a rate the Earth hasn't seen since the great climate catastrophes of the past, the ones that led to mass extinc-tions. We just can't seem to break our addiction to the kinds of fuel that will bring back a climate last seen with the dinosaurs, a climate that will drown our coastal cities and wreak havoc on the environment and our ability to feed ourselves. . . . The dinosaurs never saw the asteroid coming. What's our excuse? (deGrasse Tyson, cited in Toadvine 2017: 223)

'Government alone is helpless', Latour wrote shortly before the Paris Climate Change Conference, 'it needs all its citizens in this effort' (Latour 2015). The challenge facing policy-makers and activists alike in the decade to come is Herculean: how do we mobilise the entire human community to change our ways of living? Paul Gilding is right: an adequate global response to climate change will require collective action on the scale of the mobilisation of Western democracies to fight fascism in the Second World War (Gilding 2011). Gilding means this to be a hopeful point: we did it before; we can do it again. But it is one thing to expect people to actively respond to an immediate threat to their existence – we might even succeed in eliciting compassion for the people in the developing world who are already disproportionately suffering the effects of climate change – but how to drum up support for the not-yet existing, the future generations who are destined, it seems, to bear the brunt of our indifference? At stake is nothing less than the hyperbolic amplification of the already widely ignored notion of 'the common good'. We are accustomed to extending our ethical concerns to our fellow human beings (and maybe some of the animals with whom we share the planet). We include our children and perhaps our grandchildren in the orbit of our ethical considerations. But what climate-change activists are hesitant to tell you is that the reductions they are calling for, the limitation of emissions to 350 p.p.m. or the confinement of global warming to two degrees above pre-industrial times – which will require immense economic sacrifice and a degree of collective self-limitation that we have perhaps never before seen – is not primarily for the sake of our children, or even our children's children, but for future humans who will likely not even remember our names. If we cannot treat our contemporaries justly, those whose suffering is tangibly manifest daily on countless screens, how are we to tackle intergenerational justice (Fritsch 2017)? James Lovelock has been arguing for a decade that our children are *destined* to suffer the effects of the greenhouse gas emissions of the last century, regardless of what we do now. It is the children of the *next* century whose very lives are at stake in our response to climate change.

It will be possible to limit global warming to two degrees above pre-industrialisation levels, the Intergovernmental Panel on Climate Change (IPCC) concludes, only if global carbon emissions are reduced to zero by the middle of this century. While this is the strongest language to date from policy-makers, critics note that the Paris Agreement is not legally binding and presumes the continued goodwill of governments, a presumption which, in the Trump era, is increasingly dubious. Even more disturbingly, no one knows how to move a global economy totally dependent on fossil fuels to zero emissions within three decades. The consensus of climate science is that the 'current trajectory of global annual and cumulative emissions . . . is inconsistent with widely discussed goals of limiting global warming at 1.5 to 2°C above pre-industrial levels' (Edenhofer et al. 2014: 113). In a disturbing understatement, former chairman of the IPCC Rajendra Kumar Pachauri argues that 'stabilizing temperature increase to below 2°C relative to pre-industrial levels will require an urgent and fundamental departure from business as usual' (Pachauri et al. 2015: v). Meanwhile, the earth races closer to the two-degree increase, with NASA declaring that 2016 was the hottest year on record (2015 and 2014 being the runners-up). The planet is warming faster now than it has at any time in the previous 1,000 years. The Arctic will soon be free of summer ice for the first time in 100,000 years. Global warming limited to one and half degrees above pre-industrial averages (the Paris target) is still certain to bring about a destruction of much of the flora and fauna of the planet. The last time the planet was that warm was the Pliocene. It will almost certainly mean that in the next century sea levels will be ten to forty metres higher than they are today (Kahn 2015), submerging New York, London and Rome, and displacing millions. The IPCC is, in effect, already planning for this.

The most radical solution to climate change on offer is the total abolition of the modern system of exchange and the inauguration of the zero-growth economy (Rubin 2012). This option attacks the problem at its root, the classical economic calculus that fails to reckon with the finite material basis of all economic growth. Economics, the law of the household (the *nomos* of the *ecos*), is conventional and constructed and can be altered to suit various ends; ecology, the order of the household (the *logos* of the *ecos*) is not up to us and must be heeded in any economic plan. If we have only five acres of land to share among a community of farmers, then any system of exchange the community decides upon will be limited by that fixed material base. We have only one earth, and one delicately balanced climate that makes life and economy possible; any system of exchange that imperils that material presupposition is unsound, not only unsustainable but self-destructive. If nothing less than the end of the classical theory of endless economic growth is required for the planet to be habitable for future generations of humans – not to mention countless imperilled species of animals and plants – then we must be prepared to imagine a post-consumer civilisation. But here our powers of imagination fail us. What does a modern civilisation look like when standards of living no longer change as a result of increased productivity, when people live for something other than shopping? Regardless of our lack of imagination, Gilding argues that we have already come to the end of economic growth; it is simply that economists and policy-makers have for the most part failed to realise it. Faced with disappearing natural resources, rising seas and a ballooning human population, we can no longer *afford* to live beyond the means of our planet's ecosystems and resources. Economists and governments still talk of stimulating the sluggish global economy – choosing not to notice that while we remain dependent on fossil fuels, this stimulation comes at the expense of the earth that makes human life possible.

We know that fear-mongering, which the media are only too willing to facilitate, will not bring about the required ecological conversion. Psychological studies have noted that the typical response to the 'disaster data' pouring out of the media on the topic of climate change is a moment of horror followed by indifference (American Psychological Association 2011). If all the known deposits of oil are developed and burned, 10 trillion tons of carbon will be released into the atmosphere, causing average global temperatures to soar – and yet we continue furiously to develop the fossil-fuel industry. We blame the oil industry, but as long as demand exists, it will keep extracting. Fossil-fuel companies, for example, are projected to triple deep-water exploration investments by 2022, spending upward of $100 billion. Elizabeth Kolbert in *The New Yorker* speculates on what the earth will look like if all known deposits of oil are consumed:

> After ten thousand years, the planet would still be something like 14 degrees hotter than today. As a society, we seem to have trouble planning more than a year or two in advance. It's true that right now our fossil fuel resources remain vast; but it's also true that, if we keep burning through them at current rates, they'll be gone in less time than it took for the Roman Empire to rise and fall. If earlier societies had done what we're doing, the world as we know it wouldn't exist. If we keep doing it, in spite of all we know, future societies will still be contending with the consequences thousands of years from now. As they explore the flooded ruins of our cities, they will wonder how we imagined this would end. (Kolbert 2015)

It would be a mistake to describe our contemporary attitude to climate change as apathetic; it is, rather, desperate. Both the magnitude of the problem and the doom it foretells for future humans rob us of our capacity for action (Lertzman 2013). The deferral of the worst effects of climate change is in fact a defensive mechanism that has as its side-effect an intensification of politically immobilising horror: 'Fear of loss leads to it being split off and projected into the future. The present continues to feel safe but at the expense of the future becoming terrifying' (Randall and Brown 2015: 119). Empirical evidence suggests such strategies of disavowal are less successful for northern indigenous communities, where the adverse effects of climate change on mental health are measurable (Cunsolo 2012). And it is not as though the mental health effects of climate change denial are not also visible in Western democracies: millennials live with the pervasive sense that there is no future for them. When talking to this generation, I have noticed that the rhetorical strategies that I habitually use to convince academic audiences to pay attention to this issue are not required: the conviction that anthropogenic climate change is happening now and that indeed it 'changes everything' (Klein 2014) is universally present as an atmosphere of anxiety in which young people live.

It is no surprise that eco-criticism is equally divided between those who have given up on humanity and those who have given up on nature. 'The death of nature', the rallying cry of Dark Ecology, is a deeply ambiguous phrase, the vagueness of which contributes to its affective power. Since it is not clear what the term 'nature' means in the expression, the phrase has a nightmare effect on us, just as the terror-instilling power of the monster in the horror film increases to the degree to which its figure cannot be clearly discerned. Without losing the urgency of the moment, I believe we need to decouple these concepts, Anthropocene and 'death of nature', so that we can move into a new and more productive era of ecological discourse. We need to begin to think in terms of an era of *Anthropocenic nature*. Eschewing the false forced choice between a self-deluded return to enchantment and a dystopian shipwreck of technological disenchantment, an ecology of Anthropocenic nature is a resolutely political one. For nature can no longer be left to flourish or languish in a depoliticised no-man's land of so-called facts; the future of Anthropocenic nature plainly depends on politics. But it is still *nature* that is at issue.

I will eschew a definition of nature in this essay, for we must pass through the negation of what we mistook for nature. As a heuristic notion, I think of nature as the one that is not all: the one that is the origin of all that exists, but which is itself not infinite, and therefore incomplete, that outside of which there is always something.

In his recent Gifford lectures, Latour makes the claim that if the Gaia hypothesis is to be re-actualised, it will not be in the interest of a return to the myth of the earth as a balanced whole (Latour 2017). Political ecology, it seems, 'must still let go of nature' (Latour 2004), even when resurrecting Gaia – a rule that Latour promptly violates on practically every page of his lectures, in which he speaks of nature in too many senses to be easily numbered. Latour reaffirms Chakrabarty's point that natural and human history are now connected, like the two ends of a twisted length of paper that are attached to form a Möbius strip (Latour 2011: 9). What we do with our economy and politics has a direct impact on the earth; what happens on the earth has unforeseeable and unstoppable implications for economy and politics. Like all other organisms, humans do not merely adapt to an environment; they change their environment to suit their needs, much as life on planet earth has produced, and continues to reproduce, the climate that makes it possible. One can spin this collapse of natural history into human history in one of two ways: either everything is now technology (or subject to it) and modernity is deprived of its Big Other (Žižek 2008); or everything is now part of one non-hierarchical material continuum that includes human technology and deprives us of moral agency and responsibility in the strong (that is, Kantian) sense of the term (Morton 2010b). I reject both of these options, much as I do their premise, that natural history and human history are now indistinguishable. It is indeed the case that they are inseparable, as they always have been, even if Cartesianism and the linguistic idealism of the twentieth century made it seem otherwise. What has changed is our perception of the intertwinement of the natural and the human, which are no less distinct for being intertwined. Nature in the Anthropocene depends on us as much as we depend on it.

The current talk about the death of nature should be distinguished from one of the first iterations of the same trope. Bill McKibben used the phrase 'the end of nature' in a book of that title to decry the loss of wilderness and the extinction of species resulting from unbridled human and technological development (McKibben 1989). The 'end' or death at issue in McKibben's book has little to do with changing conceptions of the human being and its relationship to matter; it is, rather, concerned with the far more concrete problem of ecological destruction. As such, McKibben's book is an expression of a first wave of eco-anxiety, a wave that foresaw, with Heidegger, the advent of total technological domination of the globe at the expense of other species, of wilderness and of the sense of meaning that we have derived from them. At the keynote address of the 2007 conference of the International Association for Environmental Philosophy, Stephanie Mills crystallised the nostalgia, melancholy and sense of tragedy characteristic of first-wave eco-anxiety. A well known eco-activist and environmental states-woman, Mills has edited and authored books such as *In Praise of Nature* (1990), *In Service of the Wild* (1996) and *Turning Away From Technology* (2007). Under the title 'Going Back to Nature When Nature's All But Gone', Mills struck exactly the balance of sorrow (for all that is irretrievably lost), enthusiasm (for a natural order more beautiful and meaningful than most will ever know) and defiance (in the face of imminent eco-collapse) that is so typical of early environmentalism. The environmental movement has failed, Mills reminded us. After over three decades of activism, the wilderness is 'all but gone' (Mills 2008). Resources are disappearing in direct proportion to the ballooning human population. When ecology got underway in the early 1970s, there was so much more at stake. Now, after decades of globalised consumerism, there is far less left to protect and preserve. When Mills turned activist, publicly renouncing her right to motherhood because she did not want to bring a child into an already overtaxed planet, not only were the stakes different, but the conception of nature was different too. Nature was a pre-established harmony with which we had lost touch at the expense of our own demise. Nature was Mother Earth, all that was wholesome, fresh and invigorating. Technology was unwholesomely artificial.

Marshall McLuhan points out that every advance in technology comes at the expense of the atrophy of a natural human capacity (McLuhan 1962). The invention of writing led to the atrophy of human memory, the invention of the printing press to the atrophy of visual culture, and so on. McLuhan's view on technology is nuanced, cautious and ambiguous; Heidegger's is not. Not only is the external environment at risk in the technological order, according to Heidegger; even more disturbing is what we are doing to ourselves. A human being out of touch with nature (*physis*) is also a human being exiled from the depths of its being. While nature is commodified and reduced to what Heidegger calls a 'standing reserve', the human essence is eclipsed (Heidegger 1954: 19). I tentatively follow Heidegger on this point, for it touches my own thesis, that what is at stake in thinking nature in the Anthropocene is rethinking the nature that thinks nature. As the planet teems with consumers, human culture approaches a nadir of devolution. *Homo erectus*, a brave hunter-gather in a jungle of predators, has become *Homo consumptus*, a bored and distracted shopper in a sea of products. Heidegger's words in the 1950s prophesied such disaster:

As soon as what is unconcealed no longer concerns man even as object, but exclusively as standing reserve, and man in the midst of objectlessness is nothing but the orderer of the standing reserve, then he comes to the very brink of a precipitous fall; that is, he comes to the point where he himself will have to be taken as standing reserve. (Heidegger 1954: 27)

When I call this kind of thinking first-wave eco-anxiety, I am not saying that it is behind us. The notion of nature as precarious cosmic balance, a moral order eclipsed by technology, remains pervasive, especially in certain pop-culture movements: alternative medicine, New Age spirituality and so on. The point is that the notion of nature born of first-wave eco-anxiety is no longer our principal source of eco-anxiety. Our deepest fear today is no longer that we have disturbed the balance of things. It is rather that technology is powerless to tame or counterbalance what we increasingly regard as an inherently chaotic material universe.

Heidegger draws upon Kierkegaard to make an important distinction between anxiety and fear (Heidegger 1927: para. 40; Kierkegaard 1844). In the experience of fear, he explains, I direct my fear toward a specifically fearsome object or event. For example, I fear that the plane I am in might crash, or that I might have cancer. Fear is intentional and as such always pertains to a determinate object. In the experience of anxiety, on the other hand, I tremble before the unknown. Anxiety cannot name that about which it is anxious because it does not fear any one thing. It is anxious in the face of reality itself. It is crucial to note that one can feel both fear and anxiety at the same time. Fear is often a disguise for anxiety. I am anxious about death, and I fear the plane crash. The plane safely landing does not assuage my anxiety but merely suspends it until the next occasion. For Freud, neurotic anxiety is something one cannot get away from, something free-floating and paralysing precisely because it is the psyche's anxiety over itself (Hall 1999: 64–8). Eco-anxiety is not fear of catastrophe: fear is conscious and may lead to productive action. Rather, eco-anxiety is an unconscious and paralysing anticipation of the end of everything.

The films that gave expression to first-wave eco-anxiety are not films about nature as such. They are films about technology – *2001: A Space Odyssey, THX 1138, Logan's Run, Blade Runner, The Terminator, The Matrix* – the same story, over and over again, of technology run amok – and it goes something like this. Our evolutionary success overtakes us and we ourselves become an exploitable resource, managed, quantified, liquidated and ground down into fuel. Our technology blocks out the sun and chokes the air, either in a pedestrian way, through an irreversible population bubble brought about by advances in biology, or, more speculatively, by becoming intelligent, usurping us and becoming our overlords. Machines awaken and take the initiative (inaugurating 'the singularity'); they reproduce themselves without our permission and begin programming themselves to pursue their own aims. In all such scenarios, we humans find ourselves entirely alienated from nature. The dark satanic mills that so disturbed the Romantics become the murderous HAL in *2001*, or the faceless bureaucracy that forbids human love in *THX 1138*, or the Tyrell Corporation, the corporate giant in *Blade Runner* that satisfies our demand for slave labour by mass-reproducing human beings.

The irony in *Blade Runner*, as has been noticed often enough, is that the clones – the replicants – with their four-year lifespan are more human than human, as Tyrell puts it. It is the people in the film – the police, the bureaucrats, the dejected and defeated crawling about in the endless rain of a pollution-cloaked LA – who seem to have lost their humanity. What they have lost, of course, is nature, as the popular cut of the film makes abundantly clear with its happy ending wherein Rick Deckard and his replicant girlfriend, Rachael, flee to the wide-open spaces of Canada in their hover car. The replicants are more natural, more intensely sexual and hungrier for life than the humans in the film.

The association test that ascertains humanness – the Voight-Kampff test – is an emotional reaction test loosely based on Jung's association experiment. An intelligent being with more than four years of life experience will have a physiologically manifest emotional reaction – a shortening of breath, a dilution of pupils – to certain verbal suggestions. It is not that the replicants show no emotion; it is, rather, that they show unusual emotional reactions to certain kinds of provocative language. In fact, they demonstrate more emotion, not less, under interrogation, reacting vigorously to certain emotionally suggestive images put forward by the one conducting the test. The implication is that twenty-first-century humans are deadened, put to sleep by technology, whereas the replicants remain alive.

> HOLDEN: You're in a desert, walking along in the sand when all of a sudden you look down . . . and see a tortoise. It's crawling towards you. . . . You reach down and flip the tortoise over on its back, Leon. . . . The tortoise lays on its back, its belly baking in the hot sun, beating its legs trying to turn itself over. But it can't. Not without your help. But you're not helping.
> LEON: Whatcha mean, I'm not helping?
> HOLDEN: I mean you're not helping! Why is that, Leon? (Fancher and Peoples 1981)

The replicant is human being under siege by machine; his very essence has become technologised. The spontaneity of life itself has become replicable: second nature has colonised first nature so as to become indistinguishable from it. The replicants' subjective experiences, their joys and sufferings, hopes and desires, are as manufactured as their bodies. Their personalities are the products of memory implants engineered by the Tyrell Corporation so that the impression of their humanness is impeccable. The moral dilemma of the film arises from the identity of the indiscernibles. The replicants are not robots, they are our doubles: they feel pain and pleasure; they remember, reflect and desire; they search for happiness, struggling with their sense of identity and purpose in a universe that does not care about them. If they are in all essentials the same as us, save in origin, why should they be denied the respect due to persons? The Tyrell Corporation anticipates this dilemma and so designs the replicants with a four-year lifespan so that they do not get out of hand. They are made for specific work in deep-space exploration: manual labour in extreme conditions, or, in the case of Priss, a 'standard pleasure model', for the enjoyment of off-world colonists. If replicants step out of line, they are to be hunted down and 'retired'. The leader of the rebel replicants, Roy Batty, rails against this instrumentalisation, and in his death scene, he elevates himself above his origins. By saving his enemy rather than killing him, Batty asserts not his superiority over Deckard but his solidarity with him – and with all humanity, cloned or natural. He proves himself to be human – that is, capable of good, not only in appearance but in essence. To deny the humanity of the replicants, to deny them respect, is to denigrate the human itself. In this regard, the true villain of *Blade Runner* is not Roy, the replicant, but Tyrell, the company that has commodified humanity.

The technology–nature binary at the root of eco-anxiety is resolved when one swallows the other. The opposition of technology to nature is of course a version of the modern binary that replaces the traditional duality between God and nature. In modernity we became nature's other and, in that moment, unnatural. Our technology becomes a blight on the planet, an iron cage, a system of circuits and wires that displaces rather than perfects natural processes. We make the world ugly and denigrate ourselves in the act of so doing. We are bound to a chain, every link of which we have forged ourselves, and are no longer free to undo it.

If first-wave eco-anxiety is motivated by the fear that 'the moral order of nature' will become totally technologised, second-wave eco-anxiety is tormented by the opposite fear. What if our technology breaks down, no longer works to keep nature in control? A different concept of nature lies at the root of this latter fear, one decidedly less cosy. The greenhouse effect, extreme weather and super-viruses hold before us the prospect of a nature that breaks with and out of the grid. No longer a safely managed consumable, nature becomes, once again, something that consumes us. First-wave eco-anxiety is obsessed with such technology-precipitated problems as overpopulation, pollution and engineered dystopias. Second-wave eco-anxiety focuses on the failure of technology in the face of unmasterable, inhuman, horrific nature. On this view, unchecked oil extraction, global warming and lethal weather will see the civilisation experiment meet an inglorious end.

Humanity will be reduced to prehistoric life conditions, for which we will be, after 10,000 years of civilisation, no longer prepared.

What is worth noting here is the transformation that has transpired in the popular conception of nature. First-wave eco-anxiety assumes a premodern cosmos of balanced forces, a home for humanity full of beauty and significance, one we have ignored or interfered with at our peril. Second-wave eco-anxiety works with a much starker model of nature – culled from popular accounts of planetary science and quantum theory – one that depicts the universe as an inhuman horror of meaningless material events capable of, in a single moment, sweeping aside all that we consider good, true and beautiful.

We might celebrate eco-anxiety as liberating us from the fundamental fantasy that the human being – with its values, decisions and cultures – has a home in the universe. Like the Lacanian analysand who is 'cured' by the realisation that everything he most values is a fantasy constructed by his unconscious to shield his delicate ego from the horror of the real, humanity is being divested of the illusion of the possibility of a return to Mother Earth, which never existed in the first place. The Romantic nostalgia for a home in the cosmos has become, in present circumstances, life-threatening. That is why we must not renounce instrumental reason, Žižek argues, but *use* it to better organise and distribute our finite resources – and to postpone for as long as possible the inevitable failure of civilisation (Žižek 2008: 62).

First-wave eco-anxiety is anxious about technology and despairs that we are destroying nature; second-wave eco-anxiety is anxious about nature and despairs that we are mismanaging technology. Rising seas, desertification, water scarcity – and the disappearance of fuels for our fertilisers and factories – do not bring about the collapse of *nature* but the collapse of technology. Heidegger's intimations of a future of endless energy – the *Blade Runner* fantasy of unlimited artificiality – seem naïve in 2018. It seems far more likely, in the framework of second-wave eco-anxiety, that the unmanageability of matter will trump technology. Since the stabilisation of the earth's climate made possible the invention, some 10,000 years ago, of agriculture and its side-effects (writing, science and history), human culture has been predicated on controlling the natural environment and emancipating itself from that environment's contingencies. The 'unthinkable' facing us now is not the advent of some situation that has never before existed, but the return to a scenario that our prehistoric forbearers knew all too well: life in a flux of chaos in which the forces of nature overwhelm, such that there is little space for cultural activity beyond a rudimentary level. Nature is coming back, we anticipate. Unfortunately, it is not a panoramic scene bathed in golden sunlight and surveyed from a BBC helicopter – not Sierra Club's nature, something that can be enjoyed aesthetically from a distance. This is a nature that bites.

Second-wave eco-anxiety has, at least, shaken us from the delusion of nature as something that needs our protection. It is rather culture, civilisation and technology, and the non-human earthlings and their eco-systems, everywhere imperilled by technology, that are fragile and in need of care. This form of eco-anxiety, then, could be an occasion – indeed, our opportunity – for recognising that the human is not the other of nature. On the contrary, pitted *against* nature, the human does not stand a chance.

The 2009 John Hillcoat film *The Road*, based on the Pulitzer Prize-winning novel of the same name by Cormac McCarthy (2006), follows the hopeless journey of a father and his son through post-apocalyptic America. The sky has grown permanently grey, lit up intermittently with flashes of sporadic lightning. The cold rain nourishes nothing: all plants and most animals have died. The detritus of our civilisation – wrecked cars, abandoned high-rises, rusting ships – is covered in a layer of grey dust. That the film withholds details of the cause of the catastrophe only adds to the brute facticity of it. All we are told is that something very bad has happened. As in the aftermath of the K–T extinction event – the asteroid, ten kilometres in diameter, that struck earth 65.5 million years ago, wiping out the dinosaurs – the conditions supportive of life have collapsed. The impact of the K–T asteroid, a billion times more potent than the bomb that destroyed Hiroshima, included large-scale fires, earthquakes measuring more than ten on the Richter scale and continental landslides creating tsunamis. Blasted material flung into the atmosphere shrouded the planet in darkness, causing a global winter and killing off half of all species on earth. The human survivors in *The Road* wander a similarly devastated landscape in a daze of hunger and fear, cannibalising each other's emaciated flesh. The nameless boy and his father make their way on foot toward the sea, for no apparent reason other than a vague hope that they will find 'good people' there. They live in perpetual fear of the marauding bands of cannibals who hunt down the weaker to store them in cellars, where they are eaten alive, limb by limb. The nature successfully technologised by the Tyrell Corporation in *Blade Runner* here returns like the repressed in a Freudian trauma. This nature is not just outside us; it is inside as well. In the extreme situation of total ecological collapse, what would prevent us from becoming monsters? If we got really hungry, the boy asks his father, would we eat people? No, the father answers, and the answer fails to convince either the boy or the audience. Insofar as they compete for disappearing food supplies in a zero-sum game, they *are* eating people. When the father leaves a thief standing naked in the wind after taking everything from him, the boy berates him for failing in his commitment to 'carry the light'.

Can the savage instinct inside us be maintained within moral limits even in the most extreme situation imaginable? *The Road* is, on the surface, a film about a man desperately trying to maintain moral standards in a post-apocalyptic return to a Hobbesian state of nature. At its heart, however, it is a film asking us to redefine nature. Cormac McCarthy denies us the idealised postcard fantasy of the natural order wherein the power of nature is displayed selectively in planets of moderate temperatures, in sunlight balanced by rain and in verdant forests and fecund seas – conditions optimal for human life. If nature is to mean anything, it surely also includes the surface of the moon, or of Venus for that matter, where temperatures are routinely 460°C.

A younger Venus is believed to have possessed earth-like oceans, but these evaporated as the quantity of carbon dioxide increased in the atmosphere and a greenhouse effect far more extreme than anything predicted for earth's immediate future kicked in, leaving the planet a dimly lit inferno. Although winds on Venus are slow, moving at only a few kilometres per hour, the high density of the atmosphere renders them lethal dust tempests blowing rocks across a barren surface. Scientists speculate that the atmosphere of Venus was once like earth's, leaving us to draw the uncomfortable conclusion that our bright blue planet will in the distant future very likely look like the glowing ember that is Venus. It will not matter whether human-generated carbon dioxide has anything to do with it or not. The solar system is quite capable of producing such devastation itself.

In *The Ends of the World* Déborah Danowski and Eduardo Viveiros de Castro name the root cause of second-wave eco-anxiety as the horror of a 'worldless humanity': 'there will be nothing in the end, just human beings – and not for long' (Danowski and de Castro 2017: loc. 1339). In their analysis of *The Road*, they praise Cormac McCarthy for having hit the apogee of nihilism along this line:

> In McCarthy's novel, in fact, death threatens to capture the few living beings that remain by subtracting the world from them: denying them objects, eroding their human memory, and gradually corroding language itself; ravaging their bodies with disease and hunger; transforming them into the fodder of cannibal predators, ex-humans who have lost their souls, that is, their *humanity*, precisely. Aphasia preludes anthropophagy. It is hard to read this book without the distressing sensation that we already live in the world of the dead, and that the metaphorical 'fire' that some characters still carry is no more than a half-life. . . . The whole world is dead, and we are inside it. The boy's father dies; the boy travels on with people he met on the road, and who appear to be trustworthy. But they have nowhere to go. Those who journey down the road will come to no place, for the simple reason that there is no place left to come to. There is no way out. (Danowski and de Castro 2017: loc. 1361)

Is this effort to think what Derrida calls the 'phantasm of remainderless destruction' (Derrida 2007, cited in Toadvine 2017: 221) a genuine breakthrough to a new ontological situation? Or is it merely an expression of dystopian machismo, a bid to out-dark the darkest nihilism by displaying that you can think what most find unthinkable, the dys-teleological end of time? Ray Brassier's *Nihil Unbound* (Brassier 2007) positively celebrates the inevitable annihilation of not only the species, and not just the earth, but of the universe itself, because it allows for a speculative apotheosis of the limits of thinking, situating thought in a place that is void of sense. In a perverse reversal of the Pauline idea that we are already living the resurrection to come, Brassier enthuses that 'everything is dead already' (Brassier 2007: 119). The task for philosophy in the face of the absolute fact of the coming extinction of all life is to annihilate thought, devalue it entirely, not even holding out some significance for thinking the unthinkable end of thinking. Brassier attempts to radicalise disenchantment to the point where we 'clear the way for the intelligibility of extinction. Senselessness and purposelessness are not merely privative; they represent a gain in intelligibility' (Brassier 2007: 238).

First-wave eco-anxiety idealises the non-human as a pre-established harmony with which we have lost touch, to our peril. On this view, technology stands between us and the source of all that is true, good and beautiful. Second-wave eco-anxiety unmasks nature as a meaningless theatre of contingency. Here human technology, which might otherwise have brought about a sustainable way of life for the species, becomes prostituted to consumption and fails us. While the valences shift between these two models – in the first, nature is good and technology is bad, and in the second, nature is value-free and technology is the best means we have of keeping the monster from taking over – they have an assumption in common. Both presume that nature and technology are mutually antagonistic. Where technology reigns, nature does not, and vice versa. Reversing a binary does not displace it in any way; rather, it compounds it from a different angle.

A superficial reading of Heidegger enlists him in support of this dichotomising perspective, claiming him to have characterised technology as the enemy of *physis*, which technology reduces to a standing reserve. If one looks closer, however, the text of 'The Question Concerning Technology' claims something quite different. Far from being mutually opposed, technology and nature are united at the root: they are both causes, both ways of coming into presence.[1] As such, they both stand subordinate to truth conceived in its primordial sense as *aletheia*, the unveiling of being. 'The essence of technology is by no means anything technological' (Heidegger 1954: 4). This paradoxical claim means that technology is not a term for the things people make, but the name for a historical shift in attitudes, a transvaluation of values, if you will, for which no one is responsible but in which moderns find themselves uniquely caught. This modern attitude, which I have characterised in terms of critique, control and calculation, is a spontaneous irruption of being, as unexpected and unfathomable as a Newfoundland summer. Its source is every bit as mysterious and uncertain as its duration. Does this mean we should be indifferent to technology, or watch it passively from a safe aesthetic distance? On the contrary, says Heidegger, we are called to 'shepherd' technology as much as we are called to shepherd the earth, the air and the water. Dwelling poetically does not mean living without technology, but rather living with it in such a way as never to lose sight of its contingency. For technology is not absolute; it need not be, and, like all beings, tends to conceal the mystery of its origins. We can read Heidegger as an advocate of voluntary simplicity, no doubt, learning to live freely with technology means, on occasion, saying no to what it offers us. This reading is not inaccurate, but it has become stale. We could also read Heidegger in a more Anthropocenic key, that is, as challenging us to see the whole modern machine as a gift, no doubt ambiguous, but in its own way as sublime as Gros Morne National Park.

Note

1. Heidegger is retrieving the Aristotelian distinction between two types of causality: natural (by means of *physis*) and technical (by means of *techne*). See Aristoltle (*Metaphysics*, Bk V: ch. 4).

Chapter 5

Dark Ecology

Breaking with the folksy and somewhat frumpy environmental holism of the 1970s and 1980s, Timothy Morton's Dark Ecology is a new form of environmentalism, one that is wise to contemporary theory and the deep cynicism that inhabits it. Morton confirms the growing conviction in Continental-philosophy circles that we must move beyond phenomenological critiques of calculative science and into a new, hypermodern re-inscription of technological thinking (as in, for example, Badiou, Meillassoux, speculative realism and object-oriented ontology). Ultimately, what is discarded by Dark Ecology is not the quantifiable and manipulable material 'order' (however contingent) that has been the guiding construct of natural science since the seventeenth century, but any account of matter as cohering in an intelligible whole, organic totality, or *kosmos*.

The force of Dark Ecology's critique of environmental philosophy derives from its exposure of the political impotence of eco-phenomenology, Heideggerian ecology, Deep Ecology and eco-feminism. We have been reading Heidegger for the better part of a century, Morton reminds us. We have generated countless pages of phenomenological descriptions of embodiment, emplacement and so on. And we have had two centuries of Romantic gushing over ennobling experiences of wilderness. And yet we have no political will to change the course of our economic and technological development, which is almost certain to end in total ecological and economic collapse. Witness how quickly global warming fell from the agendas of the major players of world politics with the 2008 financial crisis. The message was clear: in a forced choice between clean industry and economic growth, the latter wins every time. Environmentalism has found a place in our political rhetoric, but our political unconscious remains driven by capital, or, more specifically, consumption. How are we to change this?

The failure of environmental concerns to transform the political cannot be denied. When water from a melted Greenland icecap submerges most of London, New York and Dubai, we may, finally, see the mobilisation of a planetary will to reform our unsustainable ways of living, but by then it will certainly be too late – if it is not already. Morton has written several books on the subject of Dark Ecology, but he has yet to achieve the rhetorical force of the public figure who is obviously his model in eco-criticism, Slavoj Žižek. The most direct statement of the attitude and desperate mood of Dark Ecology is Žižek's:

> Today, with the latest biogenetic developments, we are entering a new phase in which it is simply nature itself that melts into air: the main consequence of the scientific breakthroughs in biogenetics is the end of nature. Once we know the rules of their construction, natural organisms are transformed into objects amenable to manipulation. Nature – human and inhuman – is, thus, 'desubstantialized,' deprived of its impenetrable density, of what Heidegger called 'earth.' This development compels us to give a new twist to Freud's title *Unbehagen in der Kultur* – discontent, uneasiness in culture. With the latest developments, the discontent shifts from culture to nature itself: nature is no longer 'natural,' the reliable 'dense' background of our lives; it now appears as a fragile mechanism, which, at any point, can explode in a catastrophic direction. Biogenetics, with its reduction of the human psyche itself to an object of technological manipulation is, therefore, effectively, a kind of empirical instantiation of what Heidegger perceived as the 'danger' inherent to modern technology. What is crucial here is the interdependence of man [sic] and nature: by reducing man [sic] to just another natural object whose properties can be manipulated, what we lose is not (only) humanity but nature itself. In this sense, Francis Fukuyama is right: humanity itself relies on some notion of 'human nature' as what we simply inherited, namely, the impenetrable dimension in/of ourselves into which we are born/thrown. The paradox is, thus, that there is man [sic] only insofar as there is impenetrable inhuman nature. With the prospect, however, of biogenetic interventions opened up by the access to the genome, the species is able to freely change/redefine itself, its own coordinates; this prospect effectively emancipates humankind from the constraints of a finite species, from its enslavement to the 'selfish genes.' However, there is a price for this emancipation. . . . Should we not apply here the fundamental lesson of Kant's transcendental idealism: the world as a Whole is not a Thing-in-itself, it is merely a regulative Idea of our mind, something our mind imposes onto the raw multitude of sensations in order to be able to experience it as a well-ordered meaningful Whole? The paradox is that the very 'In-itself' of Nature, as a Whole independent of us, is the result of our (subjective) 'synthetic activity'. (Žižek 2008: 57)

Here is Dark Ecology in its starkest outlines: biogenetic developments divest us of our illusions of possessing a depth dimension, a human nature, and simultaneously demolish time-honoured distinctions between culture and nature, artificial and natural, organic and mechanical. From the perspective of what we actually believe when we do science (always, for Žižek, the final court of appeal), there is no natural order. Žižek adds that there never was: nature as the whole that contained humanity was a necessary illusion, a

Kantian regulative ideal, a Lacanian 'fundamental fantasy' to be traversed if never totally abolished. Breakthroughs in genetics demonstrate that no 'nature in itself' prevents us from altering the course of our evolution or artificially creating life. When these things happen, as they inevitably will (if they have not already), the comforting fiction of a natural order grounding the intelligibility of our language and the morality of our actions is shown for what it is: a projection, however inevitable or even necessary on a day-to-day level.

According to Morton, the nature that appears to have recently died is not to be mourned at all; it was, in fact, never alive, for 'nature' as such is nothing more than an environmentally dubious construct, a Romantic leftover (even if it does still inspire eco-phenomenologists, eco-feminists and Walt Disney alike), something over and against us, to be aesthetically enjoyed as the beautiful and sublime backdrop of our lives (Morton 2007: 10). The distance assumed between nature as aesthetic object and the natural aesthete is, according to Morton, the nub of the ecological problem itself. By holding ourselves apart from an idealised nature, we indulge a number of ecologically disastrous beliefs: that the structure of the visible is an accurate measure of the structure of the invisible; that things will go right if we simply let nature be; that we are at the centre of a universe of meaning that subsists apart from us; and that we have a 'natural right' to the ownership of matter. As an alternative, Morton offers us a neo-Darwinian 'mesh of interdependence', which, not accidentally, has a Buddhist ring to it (Morton is himself a Buddhist): a material ontology in which 'everything is related to everything else' to such an extent that any effort to distinguish things or species of things must be ultimately seen as empty abstraction. Morton combines claims from contemporary biology and physics with deconstruction (the somewhat tired critique of essentialism) to mount a multi-fronted attack on the self-identity of 'nature' and 'natural' beings: things do not stand apart from other things, but are assemblages of them. If we look beneath the skin of our most cherished natural being – say, the drowning polar bear desperately in search of an ice floe – we do not find a definable essence that justifies our distinguishing it from another, but rather an interweaving net of chemical and physical properties that are not themselves stable, but in a state of continual transformation.

This kind of hermeneutic-deconstructive conceptual genealogy advances, no doubt, the environmental philosophical discussion, which too often becomes nostalgic and philosophically stale, recycling hackneyed images of a wholesome, refreshing and invigoratingly 'warm green' nature (to borrow Latour's phrase). Dark Ecology has raised the question concerning nature and, although Morton and Žižek have no intention of leaving it open, once it has been raised, the question cannot easily be closed again. Morton in particular shows us, as much by his literary bombast as by his historical insight, that the concept arguably most central to the environmental philosophies of the last century, the concept of nature itself, remains obscure and uninvestigated.

Part of the reason for the success of Dark Ecology is that, contrary to its rhetoric of radicality and novelty, it does not, in fact, challenge the dominant twentieth-century epistemologico-ontological discourse, namely structuralism (the rightful heir of transcendental philosophy). Dark Ecology is preceded by structuralism's ontology without nature; the affinity between them is demonstrated by the facility with which Žižek, the grandmaster of neo-structuralism, has appropriated Morton's critique of environmentalism into his own tireless Lacanian analysis of Western decline. For Žižek, the significance of Dark Ecology is that it unmasks the Big Other as a Big Lie: nature as the aesthetic and moral background of our lives is the fiction constitutive of our vacuous subjectivity. Nature is the lie that does for us what God did for Christendom. The projection of a stable order of being as our Big Other is inevitable, Žižek adds, for our material situation is unthinkably bleak. Environmentalism is eco-ideology, a new opium for the people, replacing the moribund Western religions with an equally self-serving myth that functions as an external authority in human affairs. To traverse the fantasy and mobilise genuine political will for environmental policy (as distinct from the empty rhetoric of our elected representatives), we need to practise that curious Lacanian two-step of acknowledging the inevitability of the Big Lie that constitutes our subjectivity and becoming more at ease with the necessity of lying, that is, of 'enjoying our symptom'. 'Along these lines, 'terror' means accepting the fact of the utter groundlessness of our existence: there is no firm foundation, no place of retreat, nothing on which one can safely count. It means fully accepting that 'nature doesn't exist' (Žižek 2008; 56).

It is no doubt odd that environmentalism has found an ally in structuralism, for nothing seems to be less ecological than Saussure's semiotics. But Dark Ecology is primarily about eco-politics, not the 'intrinsic value' of clean air, verdant forests and teeming seas. The upshot of Dark Ecology is that there is nothing outside the political, and this is clearly familiar structuralist terrain. The structuralist revelation of the arbitrariness of signification is already, for the early Lacan, sufficient grounds for denying an extra-lingual order of intelligibility. If signification is mere convention, the signified, tethered as it is to the signifier, has no more ontological subsistence than the signifier. In short, we are securely on medieval nominalist terrain: talk is always only talk about talk. The key to coherent speech (spoken or written) is neither the authentic expression of transcendental concepts nor reference to an extra-lingual state of affairs, but the successful application of a sign within a system of differences. A natural referent (the 'transcendental signified') or a prelingual order of things has no role to play in language; on the contrary, language is possible only in the absence of the prelingual thing. Where we can speak, there nature is not, and where we cannot speak, there we are not.

In the proto-structuralism of medieval nominalism, the problem of universals was ostensibly solved by making thought a self-generative system, independent of an extra-symbolic order. Transcendental philosophy mediates medieval nominalism and late-modern structuralism. The effect of Kant's reduction of intelligible structure to modes of cognition was a severance of thought from thing. While Kant was still alive, there were protests against this de-naturing of thought: Schellingian nature-philosophy refused the dichotomy of thought and nature, mind and matter, subject and object: nature thinks itself in me, according to the young Schelling, which means equally that thought thinks nature outside of me: thought is not an intra-subjective affair (Schelling 1797).

But outside a relatively small circle of nineteenth-century speculative philosophers, the Schellingian objection was not heeded, and the human sciences developed in the direction of nominalism and structuralism. Early philosophical hermeneutics found fertile ground for its history–culture distinction in transcendental philosophy. For Wilhelm Dilthey, the hermeneutical sciences (the *Geisteswissenschaften*) concern the self-generative world of thought: the material thing, if it could still be affirmed to exist, was the subject of natural science (Dilthey 1883). The early Heidegger and his disciple Gadamer reject this ontological reduction of hermeneutics to the cultural, but the effect of their collaborative widening of the hermeneutical circle to include ontology is not a return to realism, but quite the opposite: in their view, reality becomes merely a manner of speaking about beings whose existence in every way depends on our speaking about them.

Freud's psychoanalysis initially appeared to be founded upon a naturalism foreign to transcendental-structuralist ontology. Trained as a biologist, Freud believed he was interpreting psyche as a natural phenomenon – if not a material thing, at least a thing obeying something analogous to the laws of matter, and explicable, like matter, in a purely non-teleological and mechanistic way. The mind–matter dichotomy of early modernity, like the related culture–nature dichotomy of transcendental philosophy, was to be overcome not by denying the mind-independent existence of nature, but by proving that mind and culture are not unnatural; the ego, along with other precious products of human civilisation, is to be understood as the defensive formation of a highly evolved material organism ultimately driven by the same dual drives of life and death that one can observe in an amoeba.

At the heart of Lacan's 'turning Freud inside out' like a glove, as Lacan puts it, is the French psychoanalyst's break with this psychoanalytical naturalism. In Lacan, Freud's lifelong effort to make a natural science of psychoanalysis is laid to rest; a natural history of the psyche is no longer possible, for in Lacan's hands, psyche becomes an order of linguistically structured experience to be explicated *sui generis*. In the mirror stage, which gives rise to the ego, the pre-subjective mind of the infant seeks release from the chaos of its uncoordinated body by dis-identifying with its lived experience and learning to identify with the unified and defined body revealed to it in the mirror. Mommy and Daddy help this along by pointing at the reflection and chirping brightly, 'It's you!' Such misidentification marks the child's entrance into consciousness – first into 'the imaginal', which is, for Lacan, not the immediately sensible but the base stratum of false consciousness upon which the full network of the symbolic order rests, and later into 'the symbolic', the world of meaning substituted for 'the real'. The child's identification with the coherent image of itself in the mirror is a repression of the lived experience of its body. Repression is thus the condition of the possibility of subjectivity – repression not only of basic sensations and drives, but of anything that challenges or threatens the ideality around which the psyche consolidates its virtual identity. The child, liberated by the mirror from the coil of appetites and drives that compose its awkward and disobedient body, is henceforth an 'I', an 'immaterial subject' able to author its actions and enjoy an interior life about which it can then speak with other subjects. But this liberation is bought at a price. 'The real' withdraws in the repression only to return in the inevitable slips and breaks, crises and pathologies, which characterise human existence (Fink 1995).

Lacan's structuralist theory of subjectivity simultaneously evacuates interiority of 'authentic' meaning and relegates exteriority to the absurd, the remainder that thought cannot think – not because it exceeds comprehension, but because it gives no intelligibility to be thought. Subjectivity is a virtuality publicly constituted 'in' the psyche of every speaker by the language she speaks. Language, without which subjectivity could not exist, forces the subject to expel itself from life and destines it to desire this expelled life as the only thing that can complete it. The life from which consciousness withdraws haunts it as the unimaginable 'real'. Because regaining 'what was lost' can only mean the extinction of the subject, the psyche is trapped in a no-win situation of fantasy, desire and denial, condemned to perpetually desire an integrity, wholeness and unity with matter that must always elude it (hence the inevitability of 'nature' as phantasmic aesthetic object: the subject must on some functional everyday level experience itself as in exile from a primordial state of belonging). Žižek again:

There is no subject without some external 'prosthetic' supplement that provides the minimum of his phantasmic identity – that is to say, the subject emerges via the 'externalization' of the most intimate kernel of his being (his 'fundamental fantasy'); the moment he gets too close to this traumatic content and 'internalizes' it, his very self-identity dissolves. (Žižek 1996: 36)

The 'prosthetic supplement' of eco-ideology is nothing other than *nature itself*, the fantasy of a cosmological whole, the universe of meaning from which modernity has putatively alienated us. The eco-ideologue simultaneously longs for union with the cosmological whole and holds herself at a distance from it by idealising it as the lost home of humanity. Were she to achieve the object of her desire, union with the cosmological whole, her identity would dissolve.

Suffering the insubstantiality of subjectivity is at the heart of Lacanian neurosis, but such suffering cannot be avoided; it can only be accepted as inevitable, and to some degree mitigated. Lacanian subjectivity is a nothing (here we note the place of its interface with Morton's Buddhism), an absence of reality, a zero constituted by the negation of immediacy. Language, a system of self-contained and self-generative significations that is always incomplete, exposes the nothingness of the subject by denying it the possibility of shaping a 'true' self: every time the subject utters a word, his utterance is sabotaged by unintended significations. The Lacanian unconscious – that which is expelled, denied, forever misplaced – is not a source of meaning, creativity or life. It is the wound left in us by language, by the excision of the infant from pre-symbolic life – not a reservoir of meanings and intuitions that have slipped beneath the threshold of consciousness, but an idiot that apes the *logos*, playing with language without understanding what it utters, mechanically proliferating – without intention or meaning – the differences and ambivalences that are as integral to language as is grammar.

The Lacanian 'subject' is the Cartesian subject living in a disenchanted world, the subject of modern science and, I might add, the Hegelian subject, a subject deprived of 'roots' in 'nature' by the structure of consciousness itself (Žižek 1996: 119). Subjectivisation is not a reversible procedure: there is no way back into pre-subjective 'nature'. This is the significance of Lacan's 'Vel', the mathematical sign for an either–or choice. The human being is faced with an impossible choice, one akin to the pseudo-choice offered by the mugger: 'Your money or your life'. The choice is between subjectivity (rationality, symbolic life, et cetera) and being (natural life, immediacy). Like the mugger's victim, who cannot choose to save his money without losing his life (and therefore losing his money as well), the modern subject cannot choose nature over subjectivity without losing nature (for there would be no one left to enjoy the choice) (Lacan 1973: 211). Subjectivity is possible only on the basis of a severance of consciousness from 'the real' (the cut effected by 'the symbolic'). The unconscious is the trace of this scission: it is not 'the remains of nature' (as though some dimension of humankind's natural origins exists on a subterranean level of the psyche), but rather the gap necessary to the maintenance of the bubble of the symbolic. The Lacanian unconscious is neither substance nor subject; it is the absence of both; pure lack.

Lacan coins the term 'extimacy' ('something strange to me, although it is at the heart of me'; an 'intimate exteriority' [Pound 2008: 87]) to articulate how subjectivity is constitutively exteriorised by the symbols without which it would not exist. The most interior is the most exterior, and vice versa: the unconscious is noisy with cultural chatter, and 'the great outdoors' is filled with subjective constructs. The community of speakers who give me my identity and position in the symbolic are not outside me; they occupy the innermost sanctum of my subjectivity. Conversely, 'outside me' is no natural order, but the social and political collective that grants me an identity, that is, a position within the symbolic order. At its core, my existence is not nature but the marketplace of collective meaning that has engendered my identity. Žižek likens 'extimacy' to the Kinder Surprise one can find in every German grocery store. The delicious chocolate egg promises a rich, gooey interior. When one breaks it open, however, one finds that it is hollow. Inside, wrapped in a plastic capsule, is a toy made in China, a piece of indigestible junk.

The Lacanian symbolic is a reaction to an unthinkable real far more disturbing than Kant's *Ding an sich*: the directionless material origin of our existence. Nonetheless, we must not miss the echo of the transcendental in Dark Ecology: for Žižek and Morton as much as for Kant and Lacan, any experience of nature as an organic whole or universe of meaning can only be the result of the substitution of a psychogenetically structured totality for the material chaos of the universe. However necessary our fantasy of interior depth and infinite meaning, Dark Ecology demolishes both senses of Aristotelian *physis*: there is no 'essence within' that could render the unconscious a richly mysterious source of meaning, and no 'cosmological whole without' that could ground culture in something other than convention.

Morton and Žižek are not claiming that *kosmos* has ever been an important scientific ideal for the West: rather, as a fantasy with little purchase on the real, it has allowed environmentalists to dream about a nature that truly exists only in Romantic poetry, while consumer-driven capitalism proceeds to ravage the planet. What remains for Dark Ecology is modern techno-science with its seemingly irresistible will to mastery, a machine that Dark Ecology hopes is separable from the capitalist ideology that currently holds it hostage. With the collapse of Romantic and post-Romantic vitalist models of nature, there is nothing left for us to do but recognise technology as the only reasonable response to the senseless contingency of matter: at least we might try to hold the monster at bay for a while. Disburdened of our Romantic ideal of a universe of meaning, we must, Morton and Žižek agree, begin to think much more realistically and sustainably about how we use the fraction of inhabitable matter the universe has arbitrarily entrusted to us. What is required in such a hopeless, indeed gnostic, *Geworfenheit* is not less instrumental reductionist thinking, but more. Let us stop waiting for God; if technology cannot save us, nothing will.

The gnostic overtones of Dark Ecology require no elaborate hermeneutical work to expose. Notice the not-so-subtle nihilism in the following quote from Morton: 'Dark Ecology is no solution to the problem of nature, which has more in common with the undead than with life. Nature is what keeps on coming back, an inert horrifying presence and a mechanical repetition' (Morton 2007: 201). One thinks of Lars von Trier's 2009 film *Antichrist*, in which the doomed couple simultaneously come to terms with the disavowed violence at the root of their sexual life, visualised in scenes of genital mutilation, and the repressed monstrosity of 'nature in itself', epitomised in a deformed fox that pauses from eating its own entrails to declare, 'chaos reigns'. Von Trier's ludicrous CGI sequence is a nihilistic version of Disney's talking animal, it seems: what beasts would really say if they could speak. As in ancient Gnosticism, there are those who can accept the bleak truth that 'mother nature' is a monster – and those who cannot. The former stand to the latter as the initiated and elite (those who have experienced gnosis) stand to the uninitiated and ignorant. The difference between ancient and modern Gnosticism is dramatic nonetheless: for modern Gnostics like Lacan, Žižek and Morton, there is no salvation in gnosis save the smug satisfaction of knowing better than others, and whatever joy the perfunctory disposal of the history of religion and metaphysics affords them.

It is important to note the difference between Morton's ecology and the political ecology of Isabelle Stengers, Bruno Latour and Michel Serres. Stengers, Latour and Serres use deconstructive anti-foundationalist claims to challenge the entrenched de-politicisation of techno-science. The questionability of modernity's cherished fact–value distinction – and the related distinction between primary and secondary qualities – destabilises techno-science by removing any last objections to including the fate of the non-human in political discussion. The demotion of natural science from its place of apolitical prestige to that of one politically driven discourse among many – as such, an epistemology founded in certain ethico-political decisions and meaning-generative practices – gives Latour licence to reconceive, without recourse to a stable and unified order of nature outside the collective, political relations between and among humans and non-humans. Dark Ecology, by contrast, at least in its Žižekian form, is not, in fact, anti-foundationalist at all. On the contrary, the undisputed authority on post-human material interdependence remains, for Dark Ecology, the natural scientist.

If Dark Ecology is on the extreme left, a kind of structuralist-Marxist collectivisation of what can no longer be distinguished – a politics of indiscernibility, if you will – Latour's political ecology sits squarely in the centre of the political spectrum. Latour, just as emphatically as Morton and Žižek, proclaims the death of nature as a good thing for environmentalism – although he means nature in a different sense. Latour's target is not Romanticism and its idealisation of nature as a balanced organic whole, but modernism and its objectification of nature as a static universe of entities assumed to be already real and awaiting our discovery. In the modernist paradigm, nature is excluded from 'the due process' that governs political life – the slow and collaborative construction of propositions or hypothetical entities and the ordering of their relations to each other. The exclusion of 'nature' from politics results in an intolerable shrinking of the political. Latour's is a liberal-democratic approach to collectivist ecology, one that maintains the basic presuppositions of classical liberalism: the individual as the basic political unit; the constructed nature of every political association of individuals; and the need to protect individuals from unjust exclusion from the political process through representation in a political assembly. Only now, for Latour, an individual is not exclusively a human person, but anything that acts and can be identified as such. Latour's target is not the Romantic *flâneur* enjoying the aesthetic show of 'pristine' wilderness, carefully staged in national parks and wilderness preserves. Latour has his guns aimed at something far more foundational for modernity, in fact: the other side of the Romantic aestheticisation of nature, what he calls Science (with a capital S), the supra-political authority on the facts of nature (assumed to be already real out there) that emasculates public life. 'If politics stops', Latour declares, 'even for a second, there is no longer anything but a point, a lie, a madman who says, "we all" in the place of others' (Latour 2004: 148).

Latour is a constructivist, but not in the traditional sense of one who denies there being any reality outside human discourse. On the contrary, the non-human, the matter observed by science, collaborates in the construction of propositions and deserves the title 'agent' or 'actant' just as much as human persons do. Science as it is in fact practised is nothing other than an association of human and non-human actants in a trial designed to guide the construction of what is real and what is not; or, as Latour would put it, science is the election of entities to be included in the common world, with the inevitable repercussion that is the exclusion of those the collective has decided not to take into account. Traditional ecology has made itself powerless to the degree that it has promoted what Latour calls the 'bad bicameralism' of nature and culture, or facts and values (Latour 2004: 115), a two-house system of representation that greatly limits the power of the political. The upper house in the bad bicameralism is 'the house of nature,' to which the scientist alone has privileged access, and which is by definition apolitical, objective and epistemologically and ontologically binding – the order of facts. The lower house is 'the house of society,' where associations of humans debate what is left for them to debate when the non-human is excluded from extra-scientific discussion – the order of values. As an alternative to this untenable limitation of the political, Latour proposes a new bicameralism that will finally 'bring the sciences into democracy', a good bicameralism that distinguishes two representative powers: 'the power to take into account', that is, the work, which has its democratic procedures and rules, of giving reality to new non-human agents by naming them; and 'the power to put into order', that is, the work, which follows equally democratic procedures, of debating how we, the association of humans and non-humans recognised by the first house, can live together in a common world (Latour 2004: 109). This new bicameralism replaces the obscure distinction, which Latour regards as the presupposition of modernity, between facts and values. The fact–value distinction justified a separation of nature from politics and of science from society; but the distinction itself is untenable and cannot withstand the constructivist critique of how science actually does its work. Science is not the detached description of an existing order, progressively unveiled through objective experimentation, but an entirely interested, socially constituted, ethico-politically motivated debate among trained researchers interacting with the unexpected behaviour of un-defined matter in order to construct language to give epistemico-ontological reality to the 'actants' at play.

Thus 'nature', for Latour, refers to the pseudo-order of objective facts rep-resented by Science (capital S). Since facts are constructed, not discovered, and the real work of scientists is as procedural and constructivist as the work of politicians, there is no hard distinction between nature and politics or between science and society. The debate concerning what is real and what is important no longer needs to await an authoritative word from the upper house. Political ecology is therefore not concerned with nature but with 'the common world' constituted by the unpredictable interactions of humans and non-humans. 'Political ecology has nothing to do, or rather, finally no longer has anything to do with nature, still less with its conservation, protection, or defense' (Latour 2004: 19). At the heart of political ecology is the debate, hitherto left to the scientists, concerning 'the multiplicity of nonhumans and the enigma of their association' (Latour 2004: 41). We can no longer pretend that this debate is the prerogative of a few specialists who stand outside society and its concerns.

> Once we have exited from the great political diorama of 'nature in general,' we are left with only the banality of multiple associations of humans and nonhumans waiting for their unity to be provided by work carried out by the collective, which has to be specified through the use of the resources, concepts, and institutions of all peoples who may be called upon to live in common on an earth that might become, through a long work of collection, the same earth for all. (Latour 2004: 46)

Here an obvious objection arises. The political is the domain of speaking beings, of those who can argue and make a case for certain interests prevailing over others. How is the non-human, which is defined by its lack of speech, to enter into this domain? The same way it has always entered into the domain of the human, Latour answers. If the non-human cannot speak, we must speak for it. The sciences do this all the time; this is in fact their chief activity: to represent the non-human to the human community. The structure of liberal government, with its assemblies of representatives pleading the causes of those they represent and ordering the priorities of the collective accordingly, ought to be the structure of political ecology. To see that there are no epistemic obstacles to including scientific debates in public life, or vice versa, it remains only to recognise that representation and ordering are the daily procedure of the sciences.

While the political solutions offered are slightly different, both Latour's political ecology and Dark Ecology address the same nature idolatry, albeit from different sides, for the nature fetishised by Romanticism is the other face of the nature objectified by modern science. In both instances, an unsound separation of the human from the material order sustains the construct. In the case of the Romantic, the reflective powers of the human being make possible the aesthetic pleasure that the show of nature affords, and arguably ground the consumerist approach to matter as an accessory for identity construction. In the case of the modern, reflection is held to demonstrate the spirituality of the human being, who has no home in matter and can therefore stand over and against it as pure observer. Dark Ecology and Latour's political ecology meet when they counter this human–nature dichotomy with the familiar eco-trope of 'interdependence'. That which distinguishes the human from the non-human is far less significant than that which they share, namely a material universe upon which both human and non-human depend for their existence.

In the Gifford lectures, Latour appears at first to be constructing a new quasi-religious object for us out of Gaia. But in this very gesture, in the precarity of the new divinity, which depends on us as much we depend on it, he destroys religion altogether – at least religion insofar as it contains an essential gesture toward transcendence. Gaia, the new god, is not and cannot be transcendent – so Latour tells us. Gaia is not outside and beyond but inside and within. Our intimacy with her is so profound that it was largely unthematised until space travel and climate change rendered her objective for us. But what we look at when we look at Gaia, the shimmering blue planet shining on the black horizon of space from the window of the International Space Station, is not the beyond, that which transcends humanity and delimits it; rather, it is the picture of us looking at ourselves for the first time. We must not miss the deeply irreligious trajectory of Latour's thinking (even more pronounced in his book *Jubiler*, which is ostensibly the book in which he comes clear on why he still goes to church, apparently for no particular theological reason whatsoever [Latour 2002]): every bit as much as do Nietzsche or Deleuze, Latour wishes to disabuse us of transcendence. With Gaia installed in the place of the old gods, or, for that matter, the Abrahamic God, we ostensibly foreclose political theology, theology that has always short-circuited the political with reference to a transcendent that norms the political without itself being open to politics. This transcendent God, with his Tables of Law– and, significantly, the nature he grounds – is irrefutable, unrevisable and unavailable for discussion. In the place of this God, Latour tells us, we are to put Gaia, and with her, deliberation, construction, deconstruction, assembling and disassembling.

At the centre of Anthropocenic politics, Gaia stands resurrected, like a Greek goddess appearing suddenly in the agora, beautiful but finite – and all the more beautiful for her finitude and fragility – demanding recognition. How is she to be represented? How are her legitimate needs and demands to be articulated in such a way that they give rise to a new constitution for the collective? It is no accident that Carl Schmitt is quoted on the opening page of the Gifford lectures (Latour 2017), for at the heart of Latour's lectures is a not-so-subtle polemic against classical political theology (which Schmitt invented), the politics that would justify sovereignty on the grounds that it images the transcendence of God. The *nomos* of the earth, the politics of Gaia, will not be grounded in transcendent law; it will be fully constructed on the basis of this-worldly materials and arguments, and will be, as such, not an absolute law but a relative law, not eternal but subject to deconstruction and critique. Lovelock's Gaia hypothesis goes astray in one respect: Gaia is presented as a system that regulates itself. But Latour would have us characterise Gaia otherwise: there is nothing pre-established about her; she is a historical being like ourselves, a contingent product of evolution, and so she has a history, and not just any history, but a history that includes all other histories.

While I disagree with Latour on the question of transcendence – without transcendence there is neither law nor order, for without it there can be no justice (as Plato so memorably reminds us, our very desire for justice in a world in which it manifestly does not exist is an indication of transcendence) – I am fully on board with his pitch to unify the quarrelling, death-dealing earthling, the human, around its only chance at global unity: the material common ground that is the earth. But I would approach this argument differently – not through immanentist politics and the mechanics of representation, but through logic and metaphysics.

Chapter 6

The Human Difference

To return to the Cassirerian line: a word *signals*, we recall, by pointing directly to the thing or state of affairs it represents, in the past, in the immediate present or in the future; a word *symbolises*, on the other hand, by virtue of its trans-contextuality. The difference between signals and symbols is not a difference in degree but a difference in kind, and it corresponds to a qualitative distinction between human and non-human thought. All thinking is sustained by signs, but some thinking, human thinking, deploys signs not merely to communicate, but also to conceive.

> If one has learned to use words not merely as mechanical signs or signals but as an entirely new instrument of thought . . . a new horizon is opened up. The principle of symbolization, with its universality, validity and general applicability is the magic Word, the Open Sesame, giving access to the specifically human world, to the world of human culture. (Cassirer, cited in Hamburg 1956: 133–4)[1]

Cassirer is not advancing a version of 'representationalism' here: symbols do not 'represent' an independent reality, merely standing for that which is already logically differentiated; rather, symbols *present* reality as such, differentiate it and establish relations among the differentiae, thereby rendering it a human reality. 'Symbolic forms are not indications, announcements, but "organs" of reality since it is solely by their agency that anything real becomes an object for intellectual apprehension and as such is made visible to us' (Cassirer, cited in Hamburg 1956: 119).

At this point, I will stand accused of speciesism. We are just animals, it will be said, no different and no better than cattle in the field, or jellyfish in the sea. If it is replied that this levelling reduction does no more justice to the distinctively bovine or jellyfish worlds than it does to the human world, the answer will come back: and how do you know what goes on there?

How do you know that the jellyfish does not use symbols? I reply, I do not know because I do not know how it thinks at all; I only know how humans think, and that is symbolically. I discern sign usage in the other animals, as in the human animal, but find no indication of symbolisation. That is, I find notably absent in the non-human environments the distinctive marks of symbolisation: art, science and religion.

One might ask if the pervasive underselling of reflection and human freedom among eco-critics – the denial of the human difference – creates more problems than it solves. The nineteenth-century assertion of the ideality of the human subject (the Scholastics spoke of 'the immateriality of the soul'), its unique capacity for moral responsibility, did not always result in aestheticisation, objectivisation and exploitation. We must be careful not to distort the truth in the interest of eco-politics: granted that the aestheticisation and objectification of nature – as something out there, over there, for our enjoyment, of use-value only (without spirit, et cetera) – is at the root of the current crisis, how can a disavowal of the human difference be the way forward? Do the ecologists who deny the human difference not recognise the contradiction involved in simultaneously asserting that (a) we are merely one species among many and have no unique vocation on the planet; and (b) we have a moral imperative to preserve, protect and shelter nature? No other species is held responsible (in the strong, moral, sense of the term) for the current state of the climate because no other species is morally accountable. To be responsible for something in a moral sense is not simply to be the efficient or relevant cause of a situation; it is also to be called to tend to the future of the situation.

Žižek asserts just this paradoxical quality of the human being, that it must be recognised as a material entity and as such dependent on the same life-giving conditions as all other earthly life and, at the same time, it must be regarded as not just one species among many. If the human being were only an animal, we would not be in the mess we are in. The ecological devastation wrought by the human being is in fact evidence that there is something else at work in us, something other than merely material forces or sophisticated animal instincts. We are split beings, to use his psychoanalytical idiom: one part of us is material and in that sense natural, but another part is 'spiritual' and transcends the material conditions of life. Because of this duality in the human, our relations to matter are never entirely balanced or natural. We tend toward merciless self-maximisation and exploitation of our material situation, a tendency entirely in excess of normal animal egotism:

> Suffice it to recall today's ecological crisis: its possibility is opened up by man's split nature – by the fact that man is simultaneously a living organism (and, as such, a part of nature) and a spiritual entity (and, as such, elevated above nature). If man were only one of the two, the crisis could not occur: as part of nature, man would

be an organism living in symbiosis with his environment, a predator exploiting other animals and plants yet, for that very reason, included in nature's circuit and unable to pose a fundamental threat to it; as a spiritual being, man would entertain toward nature a relationship of contemplative comprehension with no need to intervene actively in it for the purpose of material exploitation. What renders man's existence so explosive is the combination of the two features: in man's striving to dominate nature, to put it to work for his purposes, 'normal' animal egotism – the attitude of a natural-living organism engaged in the struggle for survival in a hostile environment – is 'self-illuminated,' posited as such, raised to the power of spirit, and thereby exacerbated, universalised into a propensity for absolute domination which no longer serves the end of survival but turns into an end-in-itself. (Žižek 1996: 63)

Žižek does not mention the flip side of this human duality. Because we are spiritual self-maximisers (and so never really fit into an ecosystem), we can also become, if we so choose, the servants of all. The very propensity for evil in us makes us potentially good. Schelling writes in his celebrated 'Freedom Essay':

Man [sic] can unfortunately only stand above or under animals and, even after having fallen below animals, he strives nonetheless to rule them from bottom up according to his disposition and for his purpose – as he actually should rule them from top down – and to misuse them. (Schelling 1809: 100)

The human difference in Schelling does not render the human being discontinuous with the non-human, as though it were of an entirely different substance (as in the Scholastic anthropology of the immaterial soul); rather, in the human being, the same powers at work in the non-human are active, but in a different arrangement. In Schellingian *Naturphilosophie*, ideality is a different ordering of a principle that in another configuration produces material reality. But the difference between the ideal and the real is not for that reason insignificant. The difference of the ideal from the real is the key to the discovery of their original unity, which is neither spiritual nor material. Where the real produces being necessarily, the ideal produces being freely, which means it is only on the level of the ideal that evil is possible, and only the ideal can be held accountable for what it produces. This does not so much elevate the human above the non-human (from a certain perspective, the non-human is in fact superior, for it does not deviate from the good) as establish an essential and dialectical relationship between the two. The ideal and the real do not differ in terms of the principles that constitute them; each contains what the other has, but in an opposed form. And the opposition between them is possible only on the basis of a common ground, equally constitutive of their respective modes of being.

At every period in his lengthy career, and in a wide variety of writing contexts, Schelling returns to the argument that difference is more basic than identity insofar as identity as such does not and cannot exist. For anything to exist, that is, to appear as standing out and apart from its causes, there must be duality and difference, which break identity apart into only relatively self-identical and internally related beings. And yet identity is the presupposition of difference; ergo, existence, being in space and time, does not exhaust reality. The argument proceeds as follows. Let the basic structure of difference be an opposition: A and not A, or A and B. In every act of predication, the basic form of opposition is assumed in the form of the difference between two modes of being, the being of a subject and the being of a predicate, and, paradoxically, for the sake of identifying the two. S is P (the form of all predication) presupposes some S that is not P in the sense of equivalence, but that it can in some respect be identified with P. S is P means S is not-S in some respect.[2] Take, for example, the proposition that has concerned us from the beginning of this essay, 'the earth is finite'. In this statement, we do not simply identify 'earth' and 'finitude' such that wherever we find finitude, we also find earth (for Mars too is finite, and Mars is not earth). Rather, we distinguish a subject, earth, from its predicates (finite, capable of life, et cetera) in order, partially, to identify them.

What does this have to do with nature as the common ground of all earthly differences? Everything. For, Schelling's argument continues, every act of predication is an act of opposition (of subject-being to predicate-being) and every opposition is possible only on the basis of a hidden common ground. S is P presupposes an X that is neither simply S nor simply P, but that is common to both, and can be in one respect S, and in another respect P. X can be, in a qualified way, identified with S or P only because it cannot be fully identified with either, for if it were, it would by virtue of the principle of non-contradiction preclude identification with its opposite. To illustrate this basic point: if S is *not* P, and X is simply identical to S, then X is *not* P. But if X is identical to S and different from P, then the proposition S is P is a contradiction. The 'is' in the basic form of predication cannot be identity. The 'is' is dialectical: it divides that which it identifies (S and P). S can be P if the 'is' is dialectical; the relation between them, then, becomes one of opposition, such that P is not only other than S, but its obverse (and can therefore be its predicate). If S and P are opposed in this way, then there must be some common ground between them that makes the opposition possible. This common ground will transcend the relation between S and P, thereby rendering the relation possible.

Let S be the human being, that being who takes responsibility for being (not only the being for whom being is an issue, as Heidegger puts it, but the being for whom being is a *moral* issue). Let P be the non-human animal, a being that lives without deliberation or moral responsibility. S is P would mean in this instance that a relation of reciprocal dependence obtains between the human (S) and the non-human (P). The human is animal. The human is non-human. The two, human and non-human, are indeed each the obverse of the other. But their otherness to one another does not render them unrelated and independent; rather, it renders them related or interdependent. Without the non-human, the human would not exist. Without the flora in our guts, for example, we could not eat. Without plants, we would have nothing to eat. Without technology, we could not sustain the numbers we now have. And now, in the Anthropocene, we come to realise that this relation of dependence goes both ways: without the human, the non-human (at least in its present form) is doomed. It is not, of course, that life could not succeed on the planet without us, for obviously it has and could again; but *now* the fate of every living being depends on what we will do. In the light of the foregoing, let us refine the now-familiar thesis of interdependence: without the goodwill of the human, the non-human is doomed. Without the goodwill of the human, the polar bear is doomed. Without the goodwill of the human, the fish in the sea are doomed. Therefore, the human and the non-human, which are opposed in a basic way about which I will now say more, are also identified in a relation of dependence. And their opposition and interdependence presuppose a common ground, which is neither opposed to either of them nor dependent on either of them. This common ground we can call 'nature' (the one that is not all).

Those who deny the opposition between the human and the non-human overlook or underplay the nature of human consciousness, the way it wounds us and places a gap between ourselves and our being, a gap that the non-human does not suffer. We long to be free of the gap, to be fully ourselves, like a mountain or a Labrador retriever. A non-human animal does not deliberate who or how it will be, and suffers no angst over what it is or is not. But every effort to forget ourselves, every descent into some pre-personal ersatz *unio mystica* – psychedelics, mosh pits, radical protests, war, sex, or just plain drunkenness – is followed by the painful return of the distance we thought we had abolished and, with it, moral anxiety, either in the form of regret or, even more simply, sorrow that the *unio* was so temporary, and to that degree a lie. We were promised more. As is well known, this is one of the reasons why the French call the orgasm the little death (*la petite mort*) – not only because in orgasm the man empties himself and merges with the species and so achieves the apex of his individuality, which is at the same moment the beginning of his decline (Schelling 1799: 35–6 – the analysis would have to be altered to describe the female orgasm) – but also because the orgasm, as the peak of earthly pleasure, is tragic, for it is neither sustainable nor all that satisfying, and the longed-for union with the beloved proves all the more illusory for being only temporary.

The move into a symbolically mediated environment that calls us to contemplate a plurivocity of sense raises a distinct set of not easily solvable problems for the animal. The *animal symbolicum* suffers in a distinctive way.

The human difference is brought out with powerful clarity in the 2015 novel *Fifteen Dogs* by André Alexis. The premise of the book is simple enough: if dogs were given human intelligence, would they be happier than humans? Or is human unhappiness a function of our intelligence? Apollo and Hermes are having a drink in a Toronto pub, discussing humans and what makes them so miserable. Hermes thinks it is something deficient in the human soul, something that makes them worse than animals. Give animals human intelligence, Apollo wagers, and they will turn out to be even more miserable than humans. Hermes takes the challenge, and through divine intervention fifteen dogs in a nearby kennel suddenly awaken with intelligence. The book describes the new forms of suffering that beset the pack as a whole and each of the dogs in its turn (for *individual* suffering increases exponentially with consciousness). The German shepherd suddenly begins to wonder what has happened to her last litter: 'It suddenly seemed grossly unfair that one should go through the trouble of having pups only to lose track of them' (Alexis 2015: 14). Another dog is dreaming about chasing squirrels, but at the very moment that ought to be the climax of pleasure, when he bites into the neck of the hapless creature, he suddenly experiences something he has never before experienced, a qualm of conscience: 'it occurred to him that the creature must feel pain. That thought – vivid and unprecedented – woke him from sleep' (Alexis 2015: 15).

The pack breaks out of the kennel and things become even more surreal. Their newfound consciousness prevents them from truly enjoying their freedom. They fall to squabbling and find it difficult to behave with the spontaneity and animal freedom of dogs. The real issue here is the transition from signalling to symbolising – the dogs become language users and discover, with equal parts wonder and horror, all of the things they can do with words. A poet arises among them and begins to beguile the pack with metaphors and symbolic expressions. The dogs feel their very consciousness transform at the sound of the strange things he does with his bark. A conservative movement emerges from the disgruntled dogs, who are now suffering in unprecedented ways, to clamp down on this new way of being and return to being dogs. The poet is driven out and a totalitarian regime enforced: all those who use language in this way will be expelled, or worse.

What follows is comic-tragic, as the dogs do their best to act like dogs, performing dogginess, barking rather than speaking – something that has never been a problem for them but that, in an image, sums up the human predicament. A dog does not act like a dog, but simply is a dog; a human being never simply is human, but is continually summoned by conscience to perform humanity, and to do so without ever really knowing what it is to be human. Let us not miss the point of this fable: Alexis is overturning one of the reigning assumptions of the post-humanistic era – that there is no qualitative difference between the human and other animals.

The take-home meaning of the Anthropocene, in my view, is that the human difference can no longer be denied. There is at least one feature of the human that distinguishes it from all other lifeforms: it is now responsible for the wellbeing of all. The Anthropocene has made explicit the nature of the ecological interdependence between the human and the non-human: they depend on one another as all opposites do. But the nature of this dependence is not identical: we depend on them for the material support of our lives; they depend on us for protection from the chaos at the heart of matter and the evil that slumbers within us. To say that the human and the non-human are, ontologically speaking, opposites is not to render them without relation to one another. It is quite the opposite, in fact: it is to render them *dialectically* related. The dialectical relation of the human to the non-human implicates both in each other's lives: the human being is not to be understood without the non-human being. And, most importantly, the opposition is made possible by a common ground that both hides behind the relation and expresses itself in it. This common ground, this hidden X, is nature. Nature is the one from which we have all come, but it is not the all; it is manifestly not divine. The Anthropocene reveals that nature is *not* absolute, and only *relatively* transcendent.

The earth transcends earthlings and does not depend on their existence, as its 4.5-billion-year history makes clear. And the earth points beyond itself just as much as we, in our dialectical relations to the other, point beyond ourselves. Even more disturbing to our dissociated sense of superiority, however, is that Anthropocenic nature is not only finite, but sick: sickened by our abuse, neglect and general disavowal of our special call to take responsibility for the relation. The non-human cannot do it, for that is not its calling. It is we, and we alone, who are responsible both for the mess and for cleaning it up.

I have summoned a set of unpopular tropes from metaphysics: transcendence, human difference, moral distinction, et cetera. The trend in recent decades is rather clearly in the direction of denying the human difference – Derrida's 'the animal that therefore I am', Deleuze's 'body without organs', Morton's 'mesh' and so on. Ecologists seem to take some comfort in asserting that we are just animals. But this assertion is as ideological as any, for we cannot be merely an animal and hold ourselves accountable for our animality at the same time.

Here, the Christian legacy still has something to offer. Christ, according to Paul, is the new *anthropos*. His divinised humanity is inclusive, not exclusive, and includes 'the whole created universe', which 'groans in all its parts as if in the pangs of child birth' to 'set our whole body free' (Rom. 8: 22–3). The Pauline idea of the redemption of matter through Christ, what we could call Paul's Christological materialism, was lost in the Middle Ages, and rediscovered in the Renaissance, with the fusion of the figure of Christ and the ancient idea of the human being as microcosm, or little world, within which every form of the larger world is recapitulated. If the human is redeemed in Christ, then so too must everything else be redeemed, from the most infinitesimal particle to the stars. Nicholas of Cusa was at the centre of this re-thinking of the theological destiny of matter. See Cassirer (1963: 40):

> In medieval thought, redemption signified above all liberation from the world, i.e., the uplifting of men [sic] above their sensible earthly existence. But Cusanus no longer recognizes such a separation between man and nature. If man as a micro-cosm includes the natures of all things within himself, then *his* redemption, his rising up to divinity, must include the ascension of all things. Nothing is isolated, cut off, or in anyway rejected: nothing falls outside this fundamentally religious process of redemption. Not only man rises up to God through Christ; the universe is redeemed within man and through him. The *regnum gratiae* and the *regnum naturae* no longer stand opposed to each other and to their common, divine goal. The union has been completed not only between God and man but between God and all creation. The gap between them is closed; between the creative prin-ciple and the created, between God and creature, stands the spirit of humanity, *humanitas*, as something at once creator and created.

Christ, as natural as he is supernatural, reveals the actuality of which we are the potency. His divinity reveals our potency for divinity, which will not exclude the earth – on the contrary. His uniqueness is communicated to all beings; he is the concrete universal, as Hegel says (Hegel 1827: 454–6). 'The religious destiny of the cosmos is, in a sense, decided within man' (Cassirer 1963: 64). The corporate nature of Christ, the new Adam, is the Hellenistic-Christian way of speaking of the spiritual substance of all that lives. It is the Christian analogue to the concept of Buddha nature in Mahayana Buddhism. But the roots of Paul's thinking on this are neither Platonic nor Eastern: they are Jewish. Messianism in the first century included a mystical-cosmological anthropology of 'the Son of Man', the archetypal human being, who dwells in eternity with God, and is progressively revealed in the prophets, until, 'in the fullness of time', he is manifest as the consummation of natural and human history.[3] At the centre of Paul's Christology lies the idea of corporate humanity, in solidarity with all creation. The individuality of each of us is underwritten – without compromising moral accountability, a paradox that Paul embraces – by a universality in which we participate, and which determines the shape of moral beings as it does the being of creation. This should not be misunderstood in a Platonic fashion: Paul's archetypal human being is historical, not timeless and eternal. The first corporate human being, Adam, at a specific moment in history, alters creation and disfigures human nature by refusing to recognise the holiness of God; the second corporate human being, Christ, at a second axis of history, redeems and transforms human and non-human nature through his unswerving obedience to the Father. Just as we were affected by Adam's sin without any choice on our part, so we are all caught up in the divinisation of nature in Christ, without doing anything to deserve it.

> Paul's Christ has had a history entwined with the history of man [sic]. Man was made 'in the image of God': that 'image' of God is Christ. There is in men a life derived from their natural progenitor, whom Paul calls by the Hebrew word for man, 'Adam.' But there is in men also a higher life, by which they are linked with God. (Dodd 1958: 95)

Christ's redemption of the world is *through* the human but *for* all that lives and suffers. Just so, the healing of the earth, should it occur, shall be through us but for all.

Notes

1. See Langer's account of Helen Keller, who transitions from signalling to symbolising under the extraordinary education of Anne Sullivan (Langer 1957: 62–3).
2. Schelling usually symbolises the structure as A=B, where the '=' sign does not simply *identify*, it differentiates and reidentifies in a qualified sense. A is B means that A is in one respect not-A, that is, that A has predicates with which is cannot be simply identified but to which it is related in a mode of relative identity. See Schelling (1809: 12ff).
3. See the Book of Enoch and 4 Ezra; Dodd (1958: 92).

Chapter 7

What's Really Wrong with Heidegger

Heidegger is one of the many figures taken to task recently for maintaining the human difference, albeit in a post-theological key. The animal, Heidegger writes famously, is 'world-poor', for to be in the world is to be 'thrown' into existence, with a past that is not available for alteration on the basis of which we project possibilities into the future (Heidegger 1927: 219–24). To exist is to be 'thrown' toward death, which, Heidegger argues, is a peculiarly human burden. Animals *are*, but humans *exist*, which means their being is never settled but always stands before them as a fundamental concern underwriting all other cares.

In the not so distant past, Heidegger was something of a poster philosopher for Deep Ecology. It would be churlish to deny that something changed for the better when environmental ethics in the US was overtaken by Heideggerians: superficial applications of deracinated ethical paradigms to the environment gave way to fundamental questions concerning the modern attitude to nature and the meaning of basic ontological concepts.[1] A new discipline came into existence: environmental philosophy.

But the time in which Heidegger could still be received as a breath of fresh air is long over. It is not only his complicity with Nazism that renders Heidegger's legacy suspect; the artificiality and pretentiousness of Heideggerian rhetoric becomes wearisome after a while. The Heideggerian history of being has been repeated so often that it has become banal. The frequent recycling of slogans such as 'onto-theology' and 'the metaphysics of presence' in graduate schools all over the planet only obscures the profundity of Heidegger's critique of technology. Because I wish to preserve something of the latter, let it be briefly repeated here.

Technology for Heidegger is forgetfulness of being, which, over the course of this career, he traces back to three principal sites: the eclipse of the pre-Socratic experience of *physis* by the Socratic–Platonic demand for grounding reasons; the Scholastic substitution of Greek aesthetic concepts for the dynamic historical categories of early-Christian discourse; and, finally, the Cartesian reduction of being to thought and extension. What are the relations of these three to each other? Do they constitute one movement, as the later Heidegger argues? Or are they three distinct instances of the capitulation of contemplation to calculation – concealing, as such, three different faces of the contemplative mind of the West? According to Heidegger, forgetfulness of being is a destiny: through these three transformations of thought, *Gestell* (enframing) became the modern default mode of experiencing beings (Heidegger 1954: 9). The future of human flourishing requires, writes Heidegger, the retrieval of a lost attitude of surrender to the unfathomable granting of being (*Gelassenheit*), a basic reversal of the attitude of control that has permitted us mastery over the emergence and withdrawal of beings.

Morton's Dark Ecology holds Heideggerian *Gelassenheit* to be as ineffective as Romantic poetry in the face of the eco-death-drive that currently grips us. Morton argues that *Gelassenheit* leaves us bereft of political discernment, placidly accepting 'the way things are'. Should we let the BP oil spill be? Should we let the decimation of the Amazon rainforest be (Morton 2010b: 210)? This is a cheap shot: *Gelassenheit* was never offered as a method of environmental practice; it meant to undermine techno-scientific-capitalist thought itself, to overturn its basic assumption that the human is or ought to be the master of being. To turn *Gelassenheit* into a method, a way of solving practical problems, is to leave the will to mastery at the root of our crisis unchallenged. *Gelassenheit* aims at undoing the will to mastery that Heidegger, among others, identified as the essence of technology. It is important to keep in mind that Heidegger's critique is not aimed at science as such; it is directed at a certain attitude toward being, an attitude that finds expression in all aspects of modern culture. The will to mastery is not only a drive to dominate matter, but a drive to master the human by reducing all modes of being to one: quantity.[2] Why have we been overtaken by this monistic ontology? What connects techno-science, the rise of capital, the ideology of consumerism and total quantification? Romanticism, Morton's favourite eco-abuser, is symptom, reaction and rebellion, but hardly the cause of our current problems. Something older is expressing itself in techno-scientific capitalism.

Heidegger's critique of technology hinges on his distinction between two basic kinds of thinking: 'calculative thinking' (*rechnendes Denken*) and 'meditative thinking' (*besinnliches Denken*). In his 'Memorial Address', delivered in 1955, Heidegger defines these two as opposites:

> Its [calculative thinking's] peculiarity consists in the fact that whenever we plan, research, and organize, we always reckon with conditions that are given. We take them into account with the calculated intention of their serving specific purposes. Thus we can count on definite results. This calculation is the mark of all thinking that plans and investigates. Such thinking remains calculation even if it neither works with numbers nor uses an adding machine or computer. Calculative thinking never stops, never collects itself. Calculative thinking is not meditative thinking, not thinking which contemplates the meaning which reigns in everything that is. There are, then, two kinds of thinking, each justified and needed in its own way: calculative thinking and meditative thinking. Meditative thinking is what we have in mind when we say that contemporary man is in flight from thinking. (Heidegger 1959: 46)

The above passage is taken from a lecture that Heidegger gave to the people of his hometown of Messkirch on the festive occasion of commemorating the achievements of their fellow Messkircher, composer Conradin Kreutzer, on the latter's 175th birthday. The distinction, however baldly stated so that the ordinary layperson could understand it, is the very heart of Heidegger's critique of technology, or, if you like, Heideggerian ecology. Technology is a destiny, not a choice – a sending of being that enframes human being, rendering it a calculator fixated on means–ends thinking or what the Frankfurt School calls 'instrumental reason', forgetful of 'the meaning which reigns in everything that is'. Modernity is characterised by the 'flight from thinking' (Heidegger 1959: 45), which is the forgetting of contemplation, the forgetting of the contingency, the gratuity, the gift-quality of being.

Calculative thinking is useful for changing a tyre or fixing a leaky nuclear power plant, but it has a fatal flaw: it is blind to the meaning of being. What this meaning is, Heidegger never directly discloses. In his early work, it is the pre-understanding of being that makes all local understandings of being possible, which can never be directly expressed in the terms that it produces, and that manifestly has something to do with time. In his later writing, it is 'the mystery' behind the play of concealment and unconcealment that determines our finite experience of truth (Heidegger 1930: 194). Or, even more cryptically, it is *das Ereignis*, variously translated by the neologism *Enowning* (in a clumsy effort to extract the etymological roots of the German word, which the later Heidegger makes much of) or, more prosaically, as 'the event' (Heidegger 1989).

Only by recovering the meaning of being will we remember how to 'dwell on the earth poetically', as Heidegger, citing Hölderlin, puts it (Heidegger 1951a). Dwelling (*Wohnen*) is what I have elsewhere described as living, thinking and building in such a way as to allow the beautiful to occur (McGrath 2003). A more orthodox Heideggerian would speak of recovering the rootedness (*Bodenstandigkeit*) so imperilled by technology.

All that with which modern techniques of communication stimulate, assail, and drive man [sic] – all that is already much closer to man today than his fields around his farmstead, closer than the change from night to day, closer than the conventions and customs of his village, than the tradition of his native world. . . . The *rootedness*, the *autochthony* (*Bodenständigkeit*), of man is threatened today at its core. (Heidegger 1959: 48–9)

When we authentically dwell, we enact the human essence by re-rooting ourselves in our historical and culturally specific existence. Dwelling is an act of resistance against the cultural homogenisation and self-abstraction made possible by technology. Technology in this sense is not machines or tools, but the collective attitude that has moderns in its grips. The alternative attitude, which comes into being when we authentically dwell and think meditatively, is *Gelassenheit*. This is a word with an immense history in German mysticism. It was coined by Meister Eckhart in the fourteenth century to explain how the soul overcomes its everyday sense of separateness from God and recovers the *unio mystica*, which is its essence, by returning to the ground of the soul, where there is no distance between Creator and creature, between subject and object, or between the soul and being. *Gelassenheit*, meaning literally 'letting-be-ness', is the attitude that stops frantically and futilely trying to *achieve* union with God, or holiness, or mystical bliss through a programme of self-effort (prayer, meditation, asceticism, good works). When we cease this activity – which is tantamount, Eckhart says, to unbelief, that is, not trusting – we see that what we long for is always already achieved (Eckhart 1941: 127).[3] The concept is developed by Eckhart's followers, Henry Suso and Johannes Tauler (the Rhineland mystics), and makes an appearance in the early-modern theosophy of Jakob Böhme. The word is, in short, saturated by the history of German theology, and by using it, Heidegger situates his later thought in a trajectory that begins with the very origins of the German language itself (in the vernacular preaching of the Rhineland mystics) and passes through theosophy and Pietism (McGrath 2008b), which are the immediate background of both Romanticism and German Idealism.

Heidegger retrieves *Gelassenheit* as the antidote to technocratic or re-ductively calculative thinking. It is not that the German mystics, the theosophists, or the German Idealists were innocent of calculative thinking; they were just as much in its grip as we are and also did not fully grasp the import of *Gelassenheit*. It is given only to us 'late-comers' (the heirs of the West, 'the evening people' or *Abendländeren*) to understand what the term really means. Where technology seizes beings and demands that they conform to a plan of its own – that beings reveal themselves in clear and distinct categories or submit to reduction to quantifiable terms so that they can be all the more amenable to the practical manipulation that is the essential motivation of technology – *Gelassenheit* is the opposite attitude. The *gelassene Mensch* forswears calculation and manipulation so that the essences of things are permitted to show themselves unmolested by human categories and aims. Notice, by the way, how Heidegger gives a mystical German term an atheological meaning (this is his *modus operandi* for all of the religious texts and themes that he retrieves from early Christianity, medieval Scholasticism and mysticism). Heidegger is the secular heir of German mysticism, realising purely immanent meanings of terms that originally referred to the transcendent. To be *gelassene* in the contemporary age is not to return to the Christianity or neo-Platonism of the past. It is not even to be religious in any recognised sense of the word. It is to be entirely *of* this world, equanimous in the face of death, released from the anxiety of self-assertion, and receptive to the wonder and beauty and depths of the things that are. Most importantly, the *gelassene Mensch* is free from the grips of enframing, free to say yes or no to technology.

Two generations of Heideggerian ecologists having taken pains to argue that the *gelassene Mensch* is not a Luddite rejecting technology as the work of the devil. She makes use of technology as necessary, but when the machines interfere with her experience of the depth dimensions of being, she leaves them be. She does not need to always and everywhere light up the night with electricity, but prefers to keep the rhythm of day and night and the repose and variety it offers. She enjoys simple living, and so might prefer, for example, to heat her home with wood that she harvests herself rather than use central heating. Morton excoriates this kind of ecology as the quintessence of the Romanticism that has dogged the environmental movement since its inception in the early twentieth century, implicating it in the very consumer-capitalist attitudes it professes to oppose (Morton 2007). The ecological aesthete basking in the bliss of unspoiled landscapes is no better than the mall-prowling window-shoppers for whom everything is a commodity to be enjoyed. Heideggerian ecology has achieved very little, according to Morton, if it has achieved anything at all. We have had several decades of *gelassene* ecology, he reminds us, and what has come of it?

Surely, Morton exaggerates here. We would have no national parks without 'Romantic' ecology. But Morton's point has a yet more political edge. What use is *Gelassenheit* in an age of accelerating climate change and mass species extinctions? What use is it in the race to the bottom that strives to capitalise on what few natural resources for survival the planet still mercifully possesses? What criteria does Heidegger offer to help us discriminate between beings that should be 'let be' and those that should not? Žižek is even more direct. This is not the time to let be. What we need is more calculative thinking, not less (Žižek 2008). The end-times are upon us and we need to change the course we are on or else perish altogether.

The change needs to be big and global, not small and local; political, even violent, not quietist or pacifist. And it could not be more urgently needed. It is not something we can afford to wait for 'from the Mystery'.

The Heideggerian must reply: urging action and big technological fixes (such as geo-engineering) to our problem only entrenches us more deeply in the calculative 'enframed' thinking that is the source of the present mess. The end result of such entrenchment will not be a saved but a ruined planet. The big technological fix can only bring about the apogee of the technological reduction of being to 'standing reserve': the planet itself become a giant battery, however rechargeable and sustainable, rejigged to supply limitless energy for human consumption. A geo-engineered future is one in which the essence of human being, which is fragile and hidden and shows itself only indirectly to the one or two with the courage to let be, will thereby be totally eclipsed.

It is easy to discern the stalemate in this dispute. Dark Ecology holds *Gelassenheit* to be an aestheticised and Romantic attitude to nature, and as such the very source of our present difficulties. Romantics, through an intrinsic logic, have become consumers. The neurotic repression of the messy materiality of our common existence is a disavowal of its ecological conditions, which are now biting back in the form of rising seas, desertified agricultural zones and barren, acidified oceans. To continue with the Romantic or Heideggerian agenda is to remain mired in a fatal fantasy. We need to break with it entirely, a break that has nothing to do with renouncing calculation; rather, it has everything to do with soberly coming to terms with the materiality and dys-teleology of human existence. As Žižek puts it, we are the product of a series of unimaginable catastrophes that can go wrong in any number of ways. On the other side, Heideggerian ecology calls, with equal insistence, for global attitudinal change, but the attitude at issue is calculation, ends–means thinking, instrumental rationality, will-to-power – an attitude the apogee of which expresses itself in such grandiose notions as geo-engineering. Both camps see the problem to be *fundamental*, not a problem of policy or design but a problem of attitude based on a misconceived understanding of the human being and its place in the universe. But each identifies an opposite paradigm as the problematic attitude: the Dark Ecologist says it is Romanticism; the Heideggerian ecologist says it is calculative thinking. The Dark Ecologist says the other side of Romanticism is calculation; the Heideggerian says the other side of calculation is forgetfulness of being.

The weakness of Heideggerian ecology (and it *has* failed us, as has Arne Naess's Deep Ecology before it and John Muir's Sierra Club ecology before that) lies elsewhere than in incipient Romanticism. It lies, rather, in Heidegger's abjuring of morality. I have written elsewhere on this fatal suspension of the ethico-political in Heidegger (so very different from Kierkegaard's 'teleological suspension of the ethical', which, far from deferring moral decision, renders the individual absolutely accountable), on his claim that ontology is prior to ethics and politics and clarifies in a neutral way the basic concepts of which ethics and politics make use (McGrath 2008a: 77–101). When this happens, this all-too-modern assumption of a view from nowhere, the ethico-political presuppositions of the thinker are smuggled in before the discussion has even begun, enshrined unchallenged as 'ontological principles'. True *Gelassenheit* is neither amoral nor apolitical. As Schelling puts it (and Levinas after him, in different words), every ontological concept is always already a moral concept. 'The first speculative concepts are also the first moral concepts, and a true philosophy cannot be conceived without morality' (Schelling 1831: 39). Moral decisions must be made; they cannot await the unveiling of beings, for the decisions will themselves determine the manner and form of the unveiling. If we do not make them deliberately, that is, in discussion with others, they will be made behind our backs, as it were.

A morally oriented *Gelassenheit* does not let everything be. On the contrary, it recognises that there are things that should not be and does not hesitate to act to rectify matters. There are indeed moral absolutes. Just as under no circumstances should a child be tortured, so too under no circumstances should a multinational capitalist entity be permitted to destroy the sea and the air upon which all living things depend. These things that should not be need to be destroyed, and the ecologist will find her capacity to discern what should and should not be precisely in her contemplative consideration of the situation. Heidegger, to be sure, has nothing to offer us in this regard, having given up politics after backing the wrong horse in the 1930s and never admitting it, persisting instead in his untenable deferral of morality. But the point remains: *Gelassenheit* is not opposed to just action; just action is its very presupposition. Without contemplation, the moral agent will lack the discernment needed to distinguish what he wants from what is in fact needed.

Regarding Romanticism, Morton himself admits that we are still Romantics (Morton 2010a). When all are equally guilty, there is no higher ground to be occupied. The best we can do is offer an internal critique of the Romantic mindset, recognising that it is still *our* mindset. In this regard, Heidegger makes some advances, for the *gelassene* attitude, which he identifies as the antidote to enframing, may be as simple as it is deep, even if it is not, for that reason, easy. Ask a Zen man or woman who spends whole days in seated meditation so as to break with the instrumental attitude that carves the world up into subjects and objects. Moreover, the notion of *Gelassenheit* brings into sharp definition the difference in the modern attitude to being, showing us in the same moment its own legitimacy as a counter-concept to the modern *Zeitgeist*.

What is truly remarkable about the late Heidegger is his insistence that a new form of *Gelassenheit* is possible still. It entails not a return to the past, which is never possible for Heidegger, but a new way of being modern, a modernity that has come to terms with the danger concealed in its origin, a danger that harbours a saving power. A *gelassene* modernity – what would that look like? Dark Ecology's vision of the future is all too easy to imagine, for, like all good science fiction, it is simply a hyperextension of the present: a trashed planet geo-engineered to postpone for as long as possible the inevitable extinction of our species, with some new, post-capitalist collectivisation of resources. Contrastingly, *Gelassenheit* refers to a *qualitative* shift in attitude, one that could indeed usher in a new world. To the charge that it has proven politically ineffective, we can and should reply, when was it ever truly ventured? At what point in the recent past was *Gelassenheit* an option as a politics? Should we not say of it what Chesterton said of Christianity to its critics? It is not that it has been tried and found wanting; it has been found difficult and so left untried (Chesterton 1910: ch. 1, part 5).

Notes

1. An early statement of the Heideggerian overhaul of environmental ethics is Bruce Foltz's *Inhabiting the Earth: Heidegger, Environmental Ethics, and the Metaphysics of Nature* (Foltz 1995).
2. Far more radical in his critique of modernity than Heidegger is René Guénon, whose 1945 classic *The Reign of Quantity* appears to be entirely forgotten.
3. On Eckhart's notion of *Gelassenheit* and its influence on Heidegger, see McGrath (2006: 130–48).

Chapter 8

Negative Ecology

Both Morton and Latour make the mistake of assuming that the modern understanding of nature as the other of the human (rendering the human unnatural and the natural unspiritual) is the last word on the concept. For this reason, they argue, political ecology must let go of nature altogether. But as we look more closely at what Morton and Latour object to – the aestheticisation and objectification of nature, respectively – we see the real problem more clearly. Neither position takes aim at the differentiation of the human from the non-human (although neither is particularly enthusiastic about it). They more specifically reject the notion of nature as *totality*, as something complete, real, eternally established – and to which nothing more can be added or removed. It is not nature in *any* sense that is the target of their critique, but nature as a static order unified prior to any deliberation about it. We should call this ideal that of normative totality. It is a notion one can certainly find as much at work in the ancient world (in, for example, Stoicism, neo-Platonism, Aristotelian Scholasticism) as in contemporary forms of eco-ideology. The source of the objection to it is twofold. On the one hand, the assumption of 'finishedness', the already-out-there-now-real quality of nature, is rejected in light of evolutionary theory: the universe does not start off complete, but begins in potency and evolves dynamically, with forms and species succeeding one another temporally. Put otherwise, we cannot point to 'nature' as an object because it is not stable enough, or clearly defined enough, to support such a designation. On the other hand, the conception of nature as static sets up a criterion of inclusion versus exclusion that makes neither political nor scientific sense. Within the parameters of such a perspective, we end up excluding from nature beings that are every bit as natural as the woods and the water: new chemical compounds constructed in a lab; new forms of matter artificially created but just as material as the substances out of which they are produced; or new forms of life that we are on the cusp of inventing. Nature as normative totality, then, is scientifically untenable in light of evolutionary theory and technological development, and politically untenable in light of how we can and already are deconstructing and reconstructing matter in new and unprecedented ways. Thus, Morton writes:

> There is no nature, never was, never will be. There is therefore no 'world' as such. Indeed, there is no ontology – no ontology is possible without a violent forgetting of the intrinsically incomplete, 'less than' level we have been describing. Thus no phenomenology is truly grounded in reality. Ecophenomenology therefore contains an internal limit caused by the humiliating paucity of the 'incomplete' ontic level. Science and capitalism have ensured that we are now directly responsible for what we see outside ourselves as Nature, if only in the negative. It is now the task of philosophy and politics to catch up with, and I hope surpass, this state of affairs. What has been called Nature (I capitalize it precisely to 'denature' it) is now on this side of history and politics. (Morton 2010b: 209)

Latour made this very same argument in his 2013 Gifford lectures (Latour 2017). Invited to join the likes of William James, Etienne Gilson and Charles Taylor, who preceded him as Gifford lecturers, and to speak on the topic of 'nature theology', Latour took the opportunity instead to deny any theology of nature whatsoever (Latour 2017). In place of nature, he offered his rejigged Gaia hypothesis. No middle ground is possible, in his view, between the two political theologies: the old political theology begins with an assumed unity; the new political theology begins with a multiplicity still to be (politically) unified.

But nature is a robust enough symbol to survive this level of demythologisation. There is nothing unnatural about an evolutionary view of the universe, nor is there any need for us to continue to assume, with premodern cosmology, that nature is eternally complete and already real and without any part for us to play in its evolution. Evolutionary models of nature were everywhere in the nineteenth century, and they played a decisive role in the development of the Romantic philosophy of nature (or *Naturphilosophie*). The nature that fascinated Goethe and the young Schelling was not a totality to which nothing more could be added, but a dynamic power of infinite productivity that never ceased overcoming any present state of manifestation it might have achieved. In *The Aphorisms on Nature*, wrongly ascribed to Goethe (it was written by Georg Christoph Tobler in 1783) and translated by T. H. Huxley for the first issue of the journal *Nature* (4 November 1869), we are presented not with a thing called nature, an organic whole with many integrated parts, but with a process that is never complete:

> NATURE! We are surrounded and embraced by her: powerless to separate ourselves from her, and powerless to penetrate beyond her.

Without asking, or warning, she snatches us up into her circling dance, and whirls us on until we are tired, and drop from her arms.

She is ever shaping new forms: what is, has never yet been; what has been, comes not again. Everything is new, and yet nought but the old.

We live in her midst and know her not. She is incessantly speaking to us, but betrays not her secret. We constantly act upon her, and yet have no power over her.

The one thing she seems to aim at is Individuality; yet she cares nothing for individuals. She is always building up and destroying; but her workshop is inaccessible.

Her life is in her children; but where is the mother? She is the only artist; working-up the most uniform material into utter opposites; arriving, without a trace of effort, at perfection, at the most exact precision, though always veiled under a certain softness.

Each of her works has an essence of its own; each of her phenomena a special characterization: and yet their diversity is in unity. (Tobler 1783)

The ideas of nature expressed in this poem – nature as subject, not object – as power of production, not product – as productive strife, rather than balance – were not unique to Goethe or Tobler, but everywhere in the air in German Romanticism. The Romantic concept of nature defined by Goethe, the young Schelling, and their many followers, just as emphatically breaks with the notion of nature as normative totality, or pre-established order, as does Dark Ecology. It was the signature feature of nature, according to the Romantics, always to *become* and never to arrive, to strive towards full actuality, but to never achieve it. In this way, nature exhibits a certain kind of endlessness, but not Hegel's 'affirmative infinite', outside of which there is nothing, or Spinoza's 'absolutely infinite', which involves no negation, but rather the endlessness which Hegel denigrates as the 'spurious infinite', that outside of which there is always something (Hegel 1831: 139, 149; cf. Spinoza, *Ethics*, I, def. VI). Aristotle called this 'the potential infinite', that which is never complete and to which another might always be added (Aristotle, *Physics*, Bk. 3, ch. 6). Rather than thinking this endless productivity of nature solely in terms of lack, Schelling thinks of it in terms of excess. Since nature cannot become fully embodied in a single being, the only manifestation adequate to it is an endlessly evolving, graduated series of finite beings. In this way Schelling identifies potency, dynamism, and non-actuality, with excess rather than lack of being; such excess is the very essence of the nature that we can perceive. 'The infinite can not even be presented in external intuition otherwise than through a finitude which is never complete, i.e., which is itself infinite. In other words, it can only be presented by infinite becoming, when the intuition of the infinite lies in no

individual moment, but is only to be produced in an endless progression'
(Schelling 1799: 15). The incompleteness of manifest nature renders our
empirical knowledge of it inescapably fragmentary. Nature as such ('unconditioned nature', in Schelling's idiom [Schelling 1799: 13]) is indefinable
because it is never finished becoming. As Schelling's contemporary, C. G.
Carus put it: 'For most of us, does not the idea of what we are supposed
to think by the word 'nature' lie totally in the dark? . . . For what is nature
other than that which is ever-becoming [*das stets Werdende*], that which
never comes to standstill, that which knows no persistent being' (Carus
1944: 14–15).

Naturphilosophie drew from a variety of sources, including the speculative Pietist tradition, which had preserved and transmitted neo-Hermetic
notions of nature from the Renaissance. Romantic nature was alive, even
ensouled, without, for all that, being divine. Nature was posited not over
and against spirit, nor as inert mechanism or external stuff, but as spirit itself
in unconscious form. This conviction united the new generation of artists,
scientists and philosophers who rejected eighteenth-century rationalism
and mechanistic science in favour of a more generous reading of nature, one
that could make sense of new advances in science and technology (especially
the breakthroughs exemplifying 'causality at a distance', chemistry, electricity and magnetism) without reducing nature to a dys-teleological theatre
of efficient causal collisions between otherwise unrelated entities. The key
was to understand nature through the human being, and the human being
through nature, and in so doing to avoid the disastrous eighteenth-century
dichotomies of human over nature, mind over matter.[1]

Schelling's *Naturphilosophie* appears in a series of densely argued if hastily
written treatises at the beginning of the nineteenth century in Germany.
His starting point is the rejection of the anthropocentric assumption of
eighteenth-century rationalism, which divided matter from mind and
nature from spirit and then related them to each other mechanistically. On
this view (for Schelling, untenable), nature is external to mind, impacting
it with sense data, which in turn stimulate ideas. Mind works, in turn, on
nature through practical action to make it a more suitable environment for
the human community – as though making alterations to something lacking
its own purposes and direction. Schelling's rejection of anthropocentrism
does not lead him toward any restoration of premodern cosmocentrism.
Rather, Schelling understands nature as an emergent and open system that
includes us as an integral part of the process of its coming into being.

At the centre of Schelling's fresh approach to nature is Kant's distinction
between organic causality and mechanistic causality. Two entities related as
cause to effect do not reciprocally influence one another; they are external
to each other such that the cause gains nothing from the effect and owes

nothing to it. Two entities related organically to one another, by contrast, are part of an organic whole within which they reciprocally determine one another. The twig causes the leaf, but the leaf in turn is the reason for the existence of the twig. The organic, as Kant puts it, is both cause and effect of itself, since the whole is dependent upon each of the parts but the parts are in turn dependent upon the whole, without which they would not exist.[2] Applied to the mind–matter relation, Schelling hypothesised that we can arrive at a more intelligible concept of nature if we assume an organic rather than mechanistic dependence of mind on nature. Mind then depends on nature in one way while nature in another way depends on mind. Mind belongs to nature as one of its constitutive parts, but so too does nature belong to mind as the whole belongs to each of its parts.

By rejecting the subject–object dichotomy, Schelling is able to think nature as a dynamic emergent order that includes the mind as its invisible completion. Nature is not a thing but a power that produces things; it is not that which is perceptible by the senses, but the drive toward perceptibility, which produces both the perceived and the perceiver. Nature is an impulse toward manifestation, which it achieves in the multiplicity of natural things and their variegated relations to one another – relations that are truly only graspable by mind. But whence this endlessly productive drive? What is the essence of that which is common to all, to both mind and matter – of that which flows through all things, from the molecular to the astral? The Renaissance Hermeticists borrowed from Plato and called this essence 'the world-soul'; Schelling liked the idea so much that he named one of his treatises after it (Schelling 1798). The world-soul is neither mental nor material, neither divine nor human, neither animal nor vegetal, but the spirit that animates all opposed forms of being, and which restlessly pursues exteriorisation through the emergence of the variety and plurality of things in the world. Among these products of the world-soul, a preeminent place is given to the human mind, which is uniquely capable of knowing itself and all things. Since the world-soul is not a thing, it can be considered absolute, or, better, unconditioned (*das Unbedingt*, literally, the 'un-thinged'). Since it is not something produced, but the producer, the origin of all products, it is not determined by anything prior to it, even if it receives determination in everything that it produces. Its goal is to be manifest in as rich a diversity of beings and levels of being as possible, and to have this diversity recognised as diverse expressions of one drive or power. This recognition occurs in human knowledge. We are nature become conscious of itself (Schelling 1800: 219).

Notice that the answer to the question of the transcendent is still undecided here. Is the natural drive to manifestation the expression of a deeper will to manifestation, as the speculative Pietists, drawing on Jakob Böhme, would say? Is God an *ens manifestativum*, a being toward revelation?[3] If this is so – and as Schelling develops his *Naturphilosophie* into a philosophy of spirit, he is increasingly inclined to believe it – then nature is the medium of God's self-revelation. The recipient of the revelation, the one to whom it is revealed, is the human being, the mirror of nature, who uniquely shares God's freedom and personality, his capacity to will and to love. Schelling will later pursue this line of thought to its logical conclusion in his great cycle of lectures (the crowning achievement of his career), the *Lectures on the Philosophy of Mythology and Revelation*. Here, Schelling explores the thesis that it is not only nature that makes God manifest; above all, human history reveals God, *sensus strictu*, as, if not *a* person, *personalising*, that is, acting and willing. For Schelling, God does not exist as a thing that first causes everything else; rather, God comes to exist as a personal, free and transcendent term of natural and historical evolution.

Nature as process, not product, is hardly a new thought, although it may be one that ecology needs to be reminded of continually. If nature is moving and never stable, mixed and never pure, and always unfinished, then it can never serve as a normative reference point for us. Moral and political life should have recourse to deeper, more ontologically nuanced points of reference: a fixed hierarchy of being will no longer do. By disabusing us of illusions that stand in the way of our thinking the being of that which is under consideration, Morton and Latour have made important contributions to what I call 'negative ecology'. As distinct from positive ecology, which proceeds from a defined and defended model of nature, negative ecology tears down concepts and images of nature – both traditional and contemporary – that can no longer be maintained in light of contemporary science and politics. Morton's and Latour's negative ecologies work in the interest of exposing the mutual contamination of the ontological and the ethico-political. When I venture to name the real, in the same moment, I am saying something about the ideal. To call being an ordered organic whole or, alternatively, a disordered continuum of matter, is to offer a range of answers to the question that is equiprimordial with the ontological question: the ethico-political question, *What ought we to do?* In 1927, Heidegger tried to separate the ontological from the ethico-political – with the embarrassing consequence that he found himself goose-stepping with the Nazis six years later. His analysis of being-in-the-world was so predetermined by ethico-political commitments that it left him little choice, if he was to be consistent, but to endorse National Socialism (McGrath 2008a: 89–101).

Ontological concepts are never pure, never free from being coded and shaped by the hands that constructed them; ontology is always over-determined by ethico-political commitments. The converse is also true: every ethico-political concept is always already an ontological concept – something early environmental ethicists, with their recycling of worn-out

Western ethical paradigms (utilitarianism, Kantianism, Aristotelianism) cut free of their political-ontological contexts (and thereby rendered less effective), were wont to forget. Contemporary science and technology studies offer us numerous demonstrations of the truth of this axiom (see Latour and Woolgar 1979). The presupposition that science proceeds disinterestedly, free of so-called 'value decisions', simply cannot stand up to empirical observation of what scientists actually do in their laboratories – namely construct, for a variety of social and institutional reasons, an ontology to explain what they have *chosen* to observe – an ontology that is inescapably nested in the ethical-political concerns of the community of scientists conducting the research.

Is negative ecology a version of negative theology? Here caution and qualification are necessary. In negative theology, the infinite is denied predicates on the grounds that they are drawn from the finite and used, at best, analogously or metaphorically. The *modi significandi* of the divine names are unknown to us. Therefore, the predicates we use to speak of the infinite – good, first, one, et cetera – are to be negated at the apex of theology, leaving the theologian standing wordless before the mystery of divine infinity. As Augustine puts it in the famous Sermon 52, if you can comprehend it, it is not God (*Si comprehendis, non est Deus*). At this point, if the negative theologian speaks at all, he no longer uses words to define and demonstrate, but rather to pray. Clearly, to apply this logic to ecology without qualification would be to risk re-divinising nature, which is precisely what the Anthropocene forbids us to do. Negative ecology is not needed because *no* predicates apply to nature, as though nature were the infinite that in principle exceeds human comprehension; negative ecology is needed, rather, because the traditional predicates we have applied to nature (whole, eternal, stable, moral order, et cetera) have ceased to be tenable. Nature has changed for us. It now reveals itself to be more elusive and quixotic than previously believed. We can, perhaps, say with Heidegger that nature withholds the secret of its being: it is 'earth' in his 'Fourfold', the dark, self-withholding other of unconcealed truth (Heidegger 1951b: 352). Schelling calls it 'ground', a being that *is not* in the definitive sense but always *yearns* to be, the maternal womb in which the spirit gestates and out of which it is born.

> Man [sic] is formed in the maternal body; and only from the obscurity of that which is without understanding (from feeling, yearning, the sovereign mother of knowledge) grow luminous thoughts. Thus we must imagine the original yearning as it directs itself to the understanding, though still not recognizing it, just as we in our yearning seek out unknown and nameless good, and as it moves, divining itself, like a wave-wound, whirling sea, akin to Plato's matter, following dark, uncertain law, incapable of constructing for itself anything enduring. (Schelling 1809: 29–30)

However inscrutably productive, nature is manifestly finite, not infinite; it is potency, not act; longing for being, not substance; a mode of nothingness. One might ask, what is new about this? In Christian theology, nature is indeed finite, set over and against its infinite source. In Schelling – and in the Anthropocene – however, finite nature manifests itself as finite not in virtue of being divinely produced, but because it is horizoned by nothingness. At the quantum level, we find indeterminacy that can be expressed only in contradictory statements, and we seem to be peering into the very abyss of nothingness out of which all things have arisen. Hence the source of nature is now in question in a way that it was not in an early-modern or late-medieval context – or, for that matter, in ancient cosmology.

The no longer tenable Aristotelian-Stoic-Scholastic notion of nature as *nomos*, created moral order, is the product of divine goodwill: thus it shows us how to act, how to treat one another, how to govern ourselves, how to use our sexual organs – all is decided in reference to natural law, revealed in the things God has made. The equally untenable Platonic notion of nature as *kosmos* emanates from the divine mind and can be distinguished from it only by abstraction. Stoic nature (the *logos spermatikos*) and neo-Platonic nature (matter animated by the world-soul) both *express* the divine mind in a multiplicity of forms that are at bottom reducible to one infinite, and so incomprehensible, principle of intelligibility. Nature is a sign in this key, a sign that directly and unambiguously points to the divine: it can thus be legitimately regarded as divine, with qualification. Negative theology is needed – in Stoicism, in Aristotelian-Scholasticism and in neo-Platonism – to avoid misapplying to the divine predicates drawn from (and according to their *modi significandi*, applicable only or primarily to) the finite. God is not good in any sense of the word that we understand, and nature is only relatively good, the negative theologians never tire of repeating.

In *negative ecology*, the logic is different. Here, negation or *remotio* is needed to avoid misapplying predicates from an earlier epoch of nature to the new form nature takes in the Anthropocene. Nature, I have suggested, reveals itself as gift, as the good that need not be. But to speak too quickly of the source of the gift – to speak of the divine giver, the divine mind or the divine will – or, alternatively, of the primal accident – is to say more about nature than we are now warranted to say. We are, to put it rather crudely, under a far darker cloud of unknowing than were the mystics of the Middle Ages. But uncertainty goes both ways: just as we are forbidden from declaring what the source of nature is, so too are we forbidden from saying what it is not. We cannot with any certainty declare the source unintelligent, and so the foundations of atheist scientism are taken away.

Negative theology, it should be said, in its most extreme forms, also applies *remotio* to the finite. The essences of things are unknown to us,

Aquinas writes, *formae substantiales per se ipsas sunt ignota* (*Quaestio disputata de spiritualibus creaturis*, a.11, ad 3).

> It is part of the very nature of things that their knowability cannot be wholly exhausted by any finite intellect, because these things are creatures, which means that the very element that makes them capable of being known must necessarily be at the same time the reason why things are unfathomable. (Pieper 1953: 60)

Clearly the point here is neo-Platonic in origin. Because the true essences of things are the divine archetypes, ideas in the mind of God, because God's primary attribute is simplicity (God or infinite being excludes not only all potency but all duality) and because our reason is discursive (bound to the basic duality of subject–predicate logic), we can only think of any given essence as differentiated from another. We are compelled by the structure of cognition to think things as they are not, as separate from one another and multiple in their origin, where they are essentially and in their origin one. To properly think the being of any creature, its *forma substantiale*, we would need to think the divine being, and such a thought is not possible for us prior to the *visio beatifica*, when, Aquinas believes, we shall be rendered capable of seeing God face to face.

But negative ecology is not based upon neo-Platonic presuppositions, although it is perhaps inevitable that there will be something neo-Platonic about whatsoever we say on this point. It is not because of what we believe we *must* say about the source of nature (to follow Aquinas – or, why not, Plotinus – that it is absolutely simple and cannot be thought discursively) that we deny predicates. It is because *we do not know what to say* about the source of nature that we must deny all predicates on offer, so strange has nature become to us. And we cannot fully think the being of nature without thinking its source – this is true of anything (you cannot understand water without understanding oxygen and hydrogen; you cannot understand an acorn without understanding an oak; you cannot understand a chair without understanding the biped that made it to support his or her frame in the sitting position) – but it is preeminently true of *natura*, that being that was not from eternity but that has by some means and from some source been born. To say of nature, to take one predicate, that it is *order*, is to say of its source that it is *orderer*, and this is to say something incorrect, for we know that nature, for all of the order that it spontaneously manifests, is in equal measure disorder; it gives itself to us as that which is *to be* ordered and reordered. To say of nature, to take the opposite predicate, that it is *accident* is to say more than we know. We know, of course, that the universe is in some sense the product of a series of accidents receding back into deep time, a series of events that could have been otherwise and that exhibit no *telos* or obvious design. The asteroid that hit the earth 65.5 million years ago and wiped out the dinosaurs, making possible the evolution of mammals, of which we are the high watermark, could have been otherwise: It might have missed the earth, and thinking nature (we humans) might not have been (assuming that the reptiles would not have evolved into consciousness – not a bad assumption, since they certainly have had long enough to do so). The chemical transformations in the make-up of the earth that made possible the Great Oxygenation Event 2.3 billion years ago could have been otherwise, and if they had been otherwise, life as we know it would not have evolved on the planet at all, for it would not have had an atmosphere in which to evolve. The size and position of Jupiter in our solar system, massive and perfectly situated to divert most of the comets and asteroids flying randomly through space and routinely demolishing the surface of other planets, could have been otherwise, in which case the earth would look more like the moon, a pockmarked, lifeless wasteland. I could go on. But we cannot say, indeed *we cannot even think*, that the beginning of everything, the reason why there is something rather than nothing, is an ur-accident. An ur-accident is not a reason for there being something rather than nothing, but rather the denial of a reason.

What we are left with after negative ecology is the unfathomable and terrifying contingency of nature, that is, the contingency of order itself. Nature divested of most of our cherished predicates is, at the very least, that which need not be, that which could have been otherwise. Nature is the one from which all that we know and can know has come, but it is not the all; it is the one that is not all. It takes only a shift in perspective to see contingency in a positive light, not as the logical absence of something (necessity) but as the factical presence of something (being). Contingency, conceived positively as the factical presence of being, illuminates nature in its sheer gift-quality, the fact, terrible to comprehend, that nature is to some degree good and that it need not be. It is given to us – we may not, therefore, claim it as our product, and we will never be able to proclaim ourselves lords of nature, despite all our technological progress. Even the most unimaginable and fantastic advances to come in science and techno-logy will never render nature something that is entirely ours to command. Nature will always remain gift, that which we do not command and without which we would not be. Even an apparent overcoming of death through the prolongation of physical presence, either through the continual substitution of new bodily parts for old ones, or the 'uploading' of memories into a silicon chip – even these fantasies of calculative reason remain humiliated before the one fact that cannot be undone, the absolute fact: that time is not ours to stop. We may not be able to say what nature is for us now, but at its core, it is transience: it comes and goes of its own accord and its passage may not be stopped or reversed. The moment that has just passed as you read this sentence was, in this sense, a thing of nature, a thing that comes to be of its own secret, and once having become, may be neither undone nor exactly repeated.

It might be pointed out that nature, particularly in its transience, is also a source of suffering and pain. That nature is not unequivocally or absolutely good or bad only confirms the point: it is a *contingent* good and, for us, the source of most if not all our pleasure and happiness. It is not impossible to use the same reasoning deployed here to justify the opposite conclusion to the one we have come to, to reject nature, as did Schopenhauer, and say that because it is such a mixed thing, because it takes with one hand what it gives with the other, and because it gives us nothing permanent upon which to base our hopes or even our existence, we ought to reject it entirely. Such a conclusion is as rational as the opposite one, which I have asserted, because neither judgement is a simple deduction: both are *decisions*, decisions to live in nature in a certain way. I have decided otherwise than Schopenhauer, and if I have other reasons motivating this decision, theological reasons that do not, strictly speaking, have a place in negative ecology, so too did Schopenhauer have his religious reasons for rejecting nature and the human being's dependence upon it. Negative ecology is not a complete and self-sufficient system, and it does not lead us to certainty but to a question, a question that demands an answer of us. The answer will not be a merely theoretical or detached observation but will, rather, put our entire existence at stake. By deciding for or against nature, we decide for or against our earthly existence. The Schopenhauerian rejection is not new: it was the same decision made by the ancient Gnostics, who competed with the early Christians for winning over the religious imagination of the Roman Empire (which was in many ways more cynical than our time), and the dignity of the option must be recognised even if I here choose otherwise.

Notes

1. As Louis-Claude Saint Martin, 'the unknown philosopher', put it, '*Il ne faut pas expliquer l'homme avec les choses mais expliquer les choses avec l'homme*'. Cited in Baader (1851–60: XI, 233). On Saint Martin and Martinism, see Bates (2000).
2. See the first part of Kant's 'Third Critique' (Kant 1790: paras 64 and 65). See also Schelling (1797: 192).
3. On Böhme and speculative Pietism see McGrath (2012: 44–81; 2018b).

Chapter 9

The Road not Taken

The proximate background of early-modern science and technology is not Scholasticism – not even Scholastic nominalism – but, as I, and others, have argued, Renaissance Hermeticism. The latter is distinguished from the former in its combination of two ideas that are found in neither the Scholastic nor the ancient world: that the human is self-made, and that time is open-ended, inspiring us to direct our own destinies. Both ideas, of Biblical origin, definitively shaped modern science and politics, and gave rise to the cult of progress and the politics of revolution that reshaped European science and culture over the course of four centuries. In the context of Renaissance Hermeticism, the self-made human thrown into an emergent universe was aligned with a non-reductive and contemplative attitude to nature (the ancient ideal), which came to be replaced by the more familiar modern goals of critique, control and calculation. Nature in Renaissance Hermeticism is easily mistaken for a modernised ancient *kosmos*, for the Renaissance humanists were fascinated by all things ancient, including, ancient cosmology, astrology and anthropology. However, neo-Hermeticists approached nature as a finite, emergent order, that is, as *creatio*, and not, as did the ancients, as an infinite and complete totality. The task of humanity is to perfect nature and thereby fulfil the human vocation to be a co-creator.

I have coined the term 'neo-Hermeticism' to distinguish the Renaissance revival of Hermeticism – spearheaded by Ficino's 1471 Latin translation of the *Corpus Hermeticum* – from the ancient philosophy that produced the body of writings ascribed to the legendary figure of Hermes Trismegistus. This field of study is not well known. French philosopher of religion Françoise Bonardel calls it 'Christian Kabbalah and Theosophy' and describes it as follows:

Under the influence of Ficino (1433–1499) and Pico della Mirandola (1463–1494), people began to seek out in the Hermetic teaching the most widely 'comprehensive' vision of the world, one that could unite the Judeo-Christian and Platonic traditions, root the nascent science of modern times in some ancient wisdom (*prisca theologia*), and thus safeguard 'the vocation of man' (Pico della Mirandola), in danger of fragmentation from the very explosion of knowledge. Thus the movement of the Christian Kabbalists was born, for whom alchemy, through its unique art of transmutation, can join forces in striving for the assumption of the glorious body of the resurrection. (Bonardel 1992: 79)

Several elements differentiate neo-Hermeticism from its Hellenistic sources. First, the *Corpus Hermeticum* belongs to a family of Hellenistic religious philosophies, including, among others, Gnosticism; these philosophies developed independently of Christianity and, to some degree, in competition with it. Neo-Hermeticism, however, was deeply informed by the Christian humanism of the fourteenth century and brought to the Renaissance revival of alchemy a set of Christian and Jewish assumptions foreign to ancient Hermeticism. Chief among these were the doctrine of the dignity of the individual, and, related to that, the sacred duty to perfect the earth through labour, which came to mean through science and technology.[1] Without these two theological additions, Hermeticism would never have given rise to modern science. Remarkably, the neo-Hermetic magus did not regard the contemplative attitude as incompatible with technology; indeed, she recognised contemplation to be the latter's precondition. In this sense, Hermeticism brought together two attitudes that have not since been thought complementary: contemplation and the will to improve the world. The ancients had a contemplative science grounded in a doctrine of the eternity of *kosmos*, but no technology in the modern sense of the term. They were content to describe the world as it was given to the mind to know. Early medieval thinkers understood creation to be finite and imperfect, but they did not produce technology either, for they lacked the humanistic optimism, focusing their contemplative gaze instead on the eternity that extended beyond the sensual world. The Renaissance Hermetic shared the medieval presupposition about the non-totality of *natura* and the primacy of contemplation, but he was able to break through the ancient quietism, which still constrained Scholasticism, into a radically new ethical context in which the human being was understood to be called to co-create the world, not simply receive it readymade from the hands of God.[2]

Neo-Hermeticism is only one aspect of the Renaissance, of course, and much could be said, and perhaps should be said, about the relation of this perplexing period to the modern.[3] It was a period full of paradoxes – perhaps unsurprisingly, given that it was one of the virtues of 'Renaissance man' to be capable of uniting opposites within himself. One of the more popular definitions of God to emerge from the Renaissance was that of the *coincidentia oppositorum*, the coincidence of opposites – as the most important Renaissance theologian, Nicholas of Cusa, referred to it in his 1440 treatise *De Docta Ignorantia* (Cusanus 1440: 49–51). The infinity of God excludes nothing, since to exclude something is to be to that degree finite, and therefore all things are predicable of God, including opposed properties. God is therefore incomprehensible to the human mind, which, bound as it is by the principle of non-contradiction, must conceive of things according to exclusionary categories: God is either present or absent, either existent or non-existent, and so on. The Renaissance revelled in the inclusionary logic of infinity and sought to approximate this generosity in everything, from science to culture. Is it any wonder, then, that contemporary interpreters have no trouble seeing whatever it is they want to see in the Renaissance? It is for some a conservative age that looks back to ancient Greece and Rome for the expansive and generous aesthetic rejected by medieval theologians (Culianu 1987). And it is for others a progressive age that looks forward to developments in science, architecture and art, and sets to work emancipating humanity from its traditional forms of servitude (Yates 1964). It is in one way a religious age, intuiting the presence of God – the sphere whose centre is everywhere but whose circumference is nowhere (Cusa again) – in all things. For others, it is an atheistic age, an age capable of producing corrupt popes, Machiavellian princes and the capitalist Medici – and of elevating the human to the place of God. But no one can deny that, whether religious or atheistic, it is a *Christian* age, one that interiorises the external forms of medieval Christianity, thus laying the groundwork for the Reformation. And yet, if Christian, it is also a neo-pagan age that revels in the stories, values and colourful sensuality of ancient polytheism. It is idealist and cynical at the same time. Hillman sees in the Renaissance the freeing of the polytheist 'soul' from its confinement within monotheistic medievalism (Hillman 1975). Culianu sees in the Renaissance a return to the life-affirming bacchanalia of pre-Christian European paganism (Culiano 1987). And Merchant, we recall, sees in the Renaissance the last expression of the enchanted cosmos of a more integrated civilisation: an ecological holism that sadly succumbed to the mechanistic thought of the seventeenth century (Merchant 1980).

I am as guilty as any of finding what I need for my argument in the Renaissance, namely, a humanism that is not at the expense of nature, and a naturalism that is not at the expense of the human. But before going into more detail, it is worth reflecting on why this age is so fertile for its interpreters. One thing one cannot find in the Renaissance is the reductionism so characteristic of the form of modernity that followed it. Nothing is 'just' molecules in motion for the Renaissance; nothing is just self-interest; nothing is just hunger for power. The Renaissance image of the human is too complex for such formulae. When we describe the Renaissance, therefore, we need to be sensitive to our own intolerance and try not to impose it on people who were in many ways more generous in spirit than we. Ficino, Pico and Paracelsus may have been pluralist in their approach to questions of nature and spirit, but they were also Christian. They may have insisted on the animate character of nature, but they did so without denying transcendence. They may have looked to the future, but they did not relinquish the past.

Without question, the Renaissance was the first flush of modernity in Europe – a beginning – but it is not clear that what we experience today is a continuation of what was begun in the Renaissance. The Renaissance was a time of possibility, and among the possibilities that opened up were directions for the development of European civilisation that were ultimately not taken. We see the hallmarks of modernity make their first appearance in the Renaissance: the globalising spirit, the future-oriented appetite for discovery and invention, the affirmation of the secular. But we also see a certain emphasis on virtue, on the care of the soul, and on the contemplation of the natural and the divine – an emphasis notably absent in the mainstream philosophy and science of the seventeenth and eighteenth centuries. In many ways, the Renaissance seems to have successfully pursued certain modern ideals without having fallen prey to their correlated modern ideologies. The Renaissance was pluralist without being relativist. It extolled the practical arts and human self-making without being reductionist or technocratic. It was secular without being irreligious. As critical, calculative and controlling in their own way as the seventeenth-century rationalists who succeeded them, Renaissance thinkers were also *contemplatives*, and rooted their many scientific, cultural and political activities in a nuanced account of the multifaceted nature of human intelligence and of the capaciousness of our concepts of nature, God and human being. Logic and theory were not elevated above feeling and intuition, for, to return to the coincidence of opposites, the infinity of the divine being and the open-endedness of creation were held to always exceed the reach of a certain kind of univocal thought. Analogy and metaphor were regarded as necessary to science as are definition and deduction. The imagination was held to be as valuable to science, if not more valuable, as the intellect. To return to where I began in this essay, the Renaissance was comfortable with the richly overdetermined symbolic quality of thought and experience and refused to reduce culture or nature to that which could be calculated and controlled. The Renaissance looked to the ancients for a subtler and more aesthetic approach to life, and extolled the arts of rhetoric above logic for precisely this reason – because rhetoric left intact the subject matter under discussion as opposed to cutting it to fit a procrustean bed of human presuppositions. A fresh enthusiasm for public life, for politics and for great works of art and architecture was allied with an entirely new emphasis on private life, on the secular pleasures of friendship and family, and on possibilities for self-cultivation and transformation latent in the ordinary. A lively feeling for the dynamic and evolving nature of the physical and the human world was the horizon of Renaissance humanism.

The Florentine Academy established by Ficino in 1462 under the patronage of Cosimo de Medici was a school of philosophy unlike any other before it: not Scholastic, not cloistered, but a centre for the *studia humanitas* emerging at this time – the study of classical writers who had been neglected by the Scholastics, in conjunction with an attention to spiritual life such as could only be found in the cloister thitherto. Ficino not only trained scholars, but cultivated virtue in his disciples, enjoining upon them a dedication to contemplative pursuits and the practice of altruism for the sake of the transformation of society. Rhetoric, literature and art were on the menu – but alongside science, theology, magic and alchemy. The boundaries between disciplines, between religions, between eras of history were exuberantly overstepped in an unparalleled celebration of the totality of the human experience.

> Renaissance *humanitas* began among readers and writers as a *care* for the *contents* of the *intellectual imagination*. This *humanitas* was in fact an exercise of imagination, an exploration and discipline of the imaginal, whether through science, magic, study, love, art, or voyage. (Hillman 1975: 194)

Michel Foucault describes the abrupt turn from Renaissance Hermeticism to calculative science in the seventeenth century not as an *evolution* but as a cultural *revolution*, the rejection of one paradigm of nature in favour of another for predominantly political purposes (Foucault 1966: 19–50). In the culture wars of the late Renaissance, the Cartesian subject won out over the neo-Hermetic magus. The latter paradoxically fused the Christian attitude – to moral reform, technical progress and the duty to perfect what God has left imperfect – with the ancient idea of the primacy of contemplation. Where the neo-Hermetic magus contemplated an emergent order not entirely of his making and endeavoured to understand it as far as possible to be able to participate productively in it, the Cartesian subject did not find himself in any order, but rather ordered what it recognised as inherently disordered. The implication of this world-generating responsibility is that the subject itself finds itself without a place in the order that it has produced. The power of the Cartesian subject is contingent on its homelessness in the universe: only that which wholly transcends extended being, which is in no way part of the being it orders, can ultimately control it.[4]

For the neo-Hermeticist, total control is neither achievable nor desirable: nature is wondrously incalculable because all things mirror each other in an infinity of correspondences. 'The universe was folded in upon itself: the earth echoing the sky, faces seeing themselves reflected in the stars, and plants holding within their stems the secrets that were of use to man [sic]' (Foucault 1966: 19). And yet there is nothing quietist or passive about Hermetic contemplation; on the contrary, Renaissance *contemplatio* folds itself naturally toward making and doing.

It is worth reflecting, in this light, on who the Renaissance magus was. He was not a fallen angel who really belonged somewhere else, and nor was he the sovereign subject of idealism, concealing in his *a priori* nothingness the mechanism by which the order of things is generated. He was, rather, the node in the network of spiritual–material relations that suture together the finite and emerging order of nature, the connecting point in the currents of desire that animate the macrocosm. He was, in fact, not far from Deleuze and Guattari's schizoid nomad (no accident here, since Western esotericism was one of Deleuze's early fascinations) (Kerslake 2007): 'Not man [sic] as the King of Creation, but rather as the being who is in intimate contact with the profound life of all forms or all types of beings, who is responsible for even the stars and animal life' (Deleuze and Guattari 1983: 4). The modernity that won out over Hermetic *techne* relegated contemplation to an aesthetic sphere defined by its lack of practicality. The task of science in this non-contemplative key was not to understand the world so much as to change it.

We must be careful not to misunderstand neo-Hermeticism as a strategy for re-enchantment designed to counteract medieval nominalism and its reductive ontology. Since it is often misused in support of esoteric programmes of re-enchantment, it will do us well to keep in mind that neo-Hermeticism was an ethos of world transformation as rooted in the Bible (and its original disenchantment of nature as *creatio*) as it was in the *Corpus Hermeticum* and the Kabbalah. I make this point because I see no hope for the re-enchantment industry to be politically effective in ecology, if for no other reason than that it is plainly ideological, and it runs counter to scientific trends and consensus. There is no reversing disenchantment, just as there is no possibly genuine re-enchantment of the world – at least not at the level of any large-scale collective. For us moderns, nature is not divine and never will be again. The world grew grey when God was located beyond it. But the effect was not all negative: as I have been arguing, as nature lost its magical aura, the human being was set free.

But just because there is no going back does not mean that there is only one way forward. Consumer-capitalism is not only ecologically and economically unsustainable; it is also morally and spiritually bankrupt. The reverence for nature that I will urge us to embrace cannot be found by reverting to pre-Christian patterns of living; it will be acquired only through a revolution within the disenchanted world itself. Far from being at odds with living in a disenchanted world, reverence in fact depends on disenchantment. We need first to dissociate from the object, separate ourselves from it, to really see and value it. The ethos of participation – enchantment – is too unconscious to enable true reverence for nature, too sunken into the object without any sense of self apart from it. The enchanted self can be overwhelmed and possessed by nature, but it cannot truly revere it. Just as only a person deserves respect in the Kantian paradigm, so too can only a person, one who grasps herself as distinct from the things around her, revere nature. To stand in reverence of something is neither to identify oneself with it (as, for example, in magical thinking) nor to dissociate it entirely from one's personal being, as when we objectify it; it is to recognise its value in relation to oneself and to the other things upon which it depends and that depend on it. Above all, it is to recognise two constitutive features of the thing: that it need not be, and that it is good that it is. Reverence is not magical thinking, for it presupposes the power to objectify. It is the attitude of one who, having objectified the thing, has passed through the crisis of calculation and control. Reverence decapitalises the thing, undoing its reduction to both use-value and exchange-value, and thereby setting it outside the domain of the commodified. It is what we participate in when we deploy public funds and legislation to set aside a tract of land for the use of non-human animals and the flourishing of unbuilt forms. A national park, properly conceived, is not there for recreational purposes – that would simply be a different form of commodification, as though Jasper National Park were worth more to the economy as alpine recreational area than as a source of natural resources. This is why the protection of wilderness areas must always be at the expense of public revenue: here, we say, in effect, the market ends.

Reverence is on the other side of objectification; that means we who would revere a thing must pass through objectification first. Only a disenchanted consciousness, one that has fallen from the *participation mystique* into duality and consciousness of self – that is, only a person – can revere things.[5] Similarly, only one who knows the advantages to the human community of the capitalist reduction (advantages that Marx himself did not deny but rather presupposed in his dialectic of history) can set limits to the market. The nostalgia of those who pine for a return to the cosmocentrism of the ancients contains a contradiction within it. Those who truly participate in the cosmos have no sense of themselves as participating in it. Rather, they are wholly lost in it, lacking the critical distance presumed in the act of valuation. 'The so called primitive does not live at one with nature, he is unacquainted with it; they rather do not recognize the distinction' (Latour 2004: 44–5). What is called for, then, is not a return to enchantment – that could only be ideology. What is needed is a new kind of relation to the thing (or the revival of an older one in an Anthropocenic key), one that is no longer calculating or controlling, but reverential.

For a brief moment in the history of modernity, reverence was held up as the moral attitude to nature proper to the modern scientist. We have observed that in the neo-Hermetic idea of creation – nature as a living being created by God, the medium of his self-revelation – Renaissance humanists found a theologico-metaphysical ground for the rapidly developing experimental sciences of the time and, on the basis of this groundwork, blended science with political considerations while rendering science itself a moral obligation. It bears emphasising again that neo-Hermeticism (like its older sibling, Jewish Kabbalah) was not a return to pre-Mosaic cosmology. The neo-Hermetic universe is not a totality of eternal form endlessly cycling through matter, but a finite and emerging order. The finitude of creation was the Renaissance alchemist's entry point into an active and transformative appropriation of the power animating all natural processes.

Neo-Hermeticism was also a spirituality, informed and determined by the Renaissance sense for the dignity of the person and the duty of the individual to cultivate his or her self (Gillespie 2009: 78). Renaissance alchemical work was not only carried out on the things of nature; it was, we have seen, simultaneously an internal work, the transmutation of the basal elements in the alchemist's personality into moral power, which was believed to lead not only to the betterment of the alchemist but also to the socio-political transformation of the alchemist's community, and in turn the restoration of the human race to its prelapsarian perfection. In this regard, neo-Hermeticism differs significantly from, on the one hand, the circular cosmocentrism of ancient philosophy – for which time and progress do not exist – and, on the other hand, the eliminative materialism of modern science – for which personality and soul do not exist. Most importantly, Renaissance alchemy had a political edge. The work was for the sake of perfecting an incomplete nature in all respects: materially, psychologically and socio-politically.

A figure like Paracelsus (1493–1541) combines in himself the paradoxical attitudes that fuse in neo-Hermeticism: on the one hand, he is a pious Catholic and his religious views belong in the Middle Ages, but, on the other, he is inspired by the Reformers to correct the systemic injustices of the Middle Ages and the corruption of the Church.[6] The eschatological edge of his thinking inclines Paracelsus to radical politics and social utopianism, making him dangerously intolerant of existing and traditional social hierarchies. Alongside other early-modern theologians (such as Calvin and Zwingli), Paracelsus takes a heterodox swerve away from the Augustinian political theology that had determined the Church's political thought throughout the Middle Ages; he sought in its place an early-Christian, this-worldly eschatology. The first Christians, it has often been pointed out, embraced a radical politics that called them to work tirelessly toward the realisation of the Kingdom of God 'on earth as it is in heaven' as Jesus himself had commanded them (Matt. 6: 10), without for a moment arrogating to themselves the power to bring it about unaided: the *eschaton* promised by Jesus and Paul was assumed to be a transformation of *this* world, not, as in Augustine's doctrine of the two cities, its annihilation and replacement (Moltmann 1967: 37–45).[7] Paracelsus's political eschatological faith, then, explains to a certain degree his unstoppable and at times self-destructive zeal to transform the existing conditions of science, medicine and society.

As a scientist and a scholar, Paracelsus was fearlessly experimental and progressive. He vehemently denied the Scholastic distinction between theory and practice, a distinction that, he never tired of pointing out (at the expense of his own professional advancement), had delayed the advance of medicine for centuries. Raised alone in the Swiss Alps by his grandfather, who was a kind but solitary herbalist who first taught the young boy the 'virtues' of plants, Paracelsus left Switzerland and wandered back and forth across Europe, practising and learning medicine wherever he could and treating people for free. He earned the reprobation of every university he worked in for refusing to continue to support Scholastic science, which was indeed holding medicine back (more interested as it was in maintaining Aristotelian scientific presuppositions than in advancing according to the new empiricism). He styled himself an iconoclast and debunker of Scholastic charlatanism, and thus is no doubt an early modern, a humanist and a reformer. And yet there is nothing reductionist about Paracelsus's view of the universe: he understands nature to be creature, not created, but a special kind of creature that has the potency to make spirit manifest in matter (and not just by means of analogies). The task of the alchemist was not quietist contemplation but tireless activity in the service of creation, making perfect in all respects what God had left unfinished – taking the raw materials of physical things, of the personality and of society itself, and disassembling them for the sake of isolating their constitutive elements so that they might be recombined or transmuted (*transmutio*) into new and higher forms.

If we are coming to the point at which we need to recognise that technology is not a tool we use but a dynamic, emerging, self-organising system that evolves on its own, it is because we are compelled in the Anthropocene to see that spirit, that which enlivens matter, is active in it too. Jacob Böhme describes Mercurius, the spirit of nature, as 'fiendish and poisonous', but paradoxically also 'the primal cause of life and stirring'. 'This form [Mercurius] is agitation (*Unruhe*) but also the seeker of peace (*Ruhe*); with his search he creates agitation' (Böhme 1997: 524). Without this stirring, there would be no opposition, no struggle in nature, and God would never be revealed. 'If this [agitation and opposition] were not, there would be no nature, but rather an eternal stillness . . . so would an eternal peace reign in the divine nature, but this nature would not be revealed, only in struggle is it revealed' (Böhme 1997: 519). Mercurius, for Böhme, is not only the one who unifies opposites; s/he also generates opposites, dividing and creating the conditions that make new unifications necessary. S/he is the perennial disturber of the peace, introducing creative chaos into stagnant situations, but s/he is also the restorer of peace, bringing peaceful resolutions out of conflicts but always in a way that does not simply return to a previous state but also produces something new and unprecedented.[8]

Remembering the role of Mercurius in the constitution of the modern spirit allows us to address a certain trend in eco-criticism, namely a kind of fascination with the agency of the non-human. One need not look far for examples, in such criticism, of the liveliness of so-called 'inanimate' matter: 'actants' (Latour), 'vibrant matter' (Bennett), 'hyperobjects' (Morton), 'assemblages' (Deleuze/Guattari). These are things that act like people – and people who are really made up of things. Eco-critics compete with one another to see who can venture more deeply into the dystopian reality of the Anthropocene. They compose panegyrics to the trash piles and landfills they praise for being self-organising systems no less than are forests and rivers. They offer a poetics of waste, ostensibly to wean ecologists from their persistent fantasy of wilderness – to bring ecology down to earth, as it were, to the reality of the planetary situation. This aesthetic bottoming out does not issue into nihilism, however, but rather – surprisingly – in a return of wonder, a surge of amazement over the diversity and strangeness of the technosphere. Humans are no longer privileged with agency, the eco-critics explain. Humans, too, are assemblages of actants, products of novel and unnamed systems of self-organisation, which include the toxic waste our civilisation produces in planetary proportions.

One notices a distinctive emphasis, in this literature, on the blurring of the classical distinction between the animate and the inanimate. Aristotle laid the foundation for this distinction with his argument that living things are 'ensouled' (literally animated), whereas non-living things are not. How else, he asks, are we to explain birth and death, or the difference between a living body and a corpse? It was clear to Aristotle that in death some principle – the soul (*psyche*) – has left the body (be it human or non-human), which is for that reason transformed into a corpse. The soul, far from being immortal, is in some sense *immaterial*, Aristotle explains: for the soul is the act that activates the potencies of the body, and the principle of act, in his view, always transcends any material it actualises. But, the object-oriented ontologist counters, rocks and minerals, oceans and glaciers, and piles of discarded steel are no less alive than plants and animals. The preference for the one over the other – that vitalist privileging of the living over the non-living – is, the object-oriented ontologist cautions (with some justice), a significant source of environmental abuse. We are worried about our forests and rivers but pay little mind to airplane graveyards in Africa or to the trash manifestly not decomposing in our landfills. If we could only recognise that all of this matter is of ecological concern, that all of this matter matters, our environmentalism would become less sentimental, less romantic and less dishonest – and with that turn to the real, more effective. Environmentalists who lavish their affections on pet wildernesses ought to show as much care for their nearby landfills – as Žižek argues in a hilarious video.[9]

Choosing but one author from the rush of eco-critics joining this anti-humanist armada, let us consider Jane Bennett for a moment. In *Vibrant Matter: A Political Ecology of Things* (Bennett 2010), she argues that a more honest assessment of the activity of non-living things can lead to a more ecologically just society. The chief obstacle for ecology, in Bennett's view, is our persistent separation of the living from the non-living, and the organisation of resources in terms of the subordination of non-living things to the needs of living things:

> The quarantines of matter and life encourage us to ignore the vitality *of* matter and the lively powers *of* material formations, such as the way omega-3 fatty acids can alter human moods or the way our trash is not 'away' in landfills but generating lively streams of chemicals and volatile winds of methane as we speak. I will turn the figures of 'life' and 'matter' around and around, worrying them until they start to seem strange . . . to encourage more intelligent and sustainable engagements with vibrant matter and things. A guiding question: How would political responses to public problems change were we to take seriously the vitality of (nonhuman) bodies? By 'vitality' I mean the capacity of things – edibles, commodities, storms, metals – not only to impede or block the will and designs of humans but also to act as quasi agents or forces with trajectories, propensities, or tendencies of their own. . . . How, for example, would patterns of consumption change if we faced not litter, rubbish, trash, or 'the recycling,' but an accumulating pile of lively and potentially dangerous matter? (Bennett 2010: vii–viii)

I will leave aside for a moment the more obvious philosophical objections to Bennett's argument – her failure, for instance, to attend to the difference between analogy and metaphor.[10] Such objections would lead us into interesting but nonetheless tangential disputes in the history of philosophy. As with much of eco-criticism, Bennett's point is a pragmatic one: her aim is not so much to attribute moral responsibility or other attributes of personhood to inanimate things as to encourage those who are morally discerning to attend more responsibly to the material conditions that make life possible on this planet. She urges us to offer a soberer assessment of the cost – measurable in material processes we like to ignore – of consumer civilisation. I do not wish here to continually catch the new breed of materialist eco-critics in their own performative contradictions, or to repeatedly critique their desire to have their cake and eat it too ('we are nothing but things, but we should treat things better than we do').[11] Rather, I want to affirm this challenge to the Aristotelian distinction between the ensouled and the inanimate. I want to do this, not by jumping on the latest European graduate school bandwagon, but by pointing out that the Aristotelian distinction has already been challenged – namely by neo-Platonists and Hermeticists two millennia ago. And it was this very challenge to the distinction, this insistence on the distribution of soul (or 'vibrancy' if you prefer) among both the living and the non-living (indeed across all that is) that impelled the modern experiment. Again, we have forgotten so much. The patron saint of modern science and technology, Mercurius, was called the *anima mundi*, the world soul because he enspirited everything, the animate *and* the inanimate. This Renaissance retrieval of an ancient trope was not deployed in the service of re-divinising the earth, but rather in the interest of making sense of the surprising things humans had begun to discover about the material world – things Aristotle never seemed to have suspected existed and so never bothered to look into. Matter was underwritten by an invisible order of objects interacting with one another in law-like fashion, and the same laws were working in living being as in non-living being. Chemistry revealed that the same principles interacted to constitute the stomach of an animal as were at work in the soils of a swamp. Magnetism and electricity, manifestations of 'causality at a distance', demonstrated that beings were communicating with one another much in the way humans speak to each other, by exchanging information and responding accordingly. The diverse universe, composed of the living and non-living – and on another level, of the rational and non-rational – was revealed to be one homogeneous order of matter animated by a living spirit who integrated it all into one lively system capable of continual diversification and productive of the most surprising singularities.[12] Historians of science tell us that Aristotle ignored this dimension of being because he, residual Platonist that he was, was locked onto the universal – the repeating and the regular (that is, natural generalities as opposed to singularities). For assorted reasons (some of which were theological), the early moderns had the opposite focus: it was the strange and unexpected singularity that promised to be the key to understanding the invisible order. To understand a piece of nature was to understand (or possess the key to understanding) all of it. Understanding was power – not sovereign power but the power of one able to work with nature because she had become obedient to it.

Mercurius is not only the one who makes an organism come alive; s/he is also the one who initiates the decomposition of that same organism into its component non-organic parts. The central work of the alchemist, the *transmutio*, involved isolating a piece of matter in a hermetically sealed container, an alembic, and gently 'agitating' it with heat to accelerate the process of decomposition. With each stage in the process, different potencies of matter would be released. The process was not held at a safe distance, for the alchemist herself was affected by it. The alchemist patiently and methodically participated in the process at every level of engagement (intellectually, aesthetically and psychologically) and expected to feel distinct changes in mood at each stage. Some alchemical treatises even prescribe the playing of music appropriate to a given stage, as this was thought to intensify psychological identification with the matter in the alembic. In the *nigredo* stage, the moment when the thing begins to decompose, the alchemist descended with the rotting matter into the abyss, which was not nothingness but rather pure potency, the *massa confusa* from which order emerges, the *prima materia* out of which all things come, and which therefore pre-contains all possibilities. To create something new, one needed to descend into these dark depths of the not-yet real. The putrefying matter in the alembic was itself returning to the primordial chaos out of which the composite structure had first emerged; therein lay the possibilities and ingredients for the new form that was desired. There was no avoiding the abyss, so the alchemist did not try to – and one of the indications that a given stage had reached its crisis point was the psychological depression that would so often suddenly take hold of the alchemist with the onset of *nigredo* (some would indicate this with a remark in their lab reports, 'the black crow had arrive') – a gloom that was not a passing feeling but a sign that the dark depths had been entered.[13] Only by going through such a descent could one break through to the more euphoric phases: to the *albedo* or white stage of purification (in which the components of the being to emerge are cleansed of former associations) and the *rubedo*, the red stage, in which something new begins to take shape and pulses with the vitality, the blood, of life.

Mercurius was understood to be active at all stages; s/he was always the agent who governed the transformation, whether it involved the death and decomposition of the old or the birth and emergence of the new. It was precisely this Mercurial power that was sought in 'the work': to be able to effect transformations in matter by studying how they naturally occur. But one did not arrive at such insights equipped with Promethean arrogance or the pretence of mastery; one only got there by letting down defences and letting go of prejudices, including moral objections. It was said of Mercurius that s/he was 'found in filth' (*in stercore invenitor*). Just as spiritual alchemical work was hardly for the prudish or morally repressed – it was not enough to *know* of the morally degenerated; one had also to participate in it (or, rather, acknowledge the degree to which one already did participate in it – the degree to which one's virtues depended upon one's vices, for example) – so too was no form of materiality to be overlooked. Indeed, the lowest forms of matter (among the metals, lead) were the most valuable because in them, in seed, could be found the ingredients of the higher forms.

The contemporary reductionist ecology of things is rife with Mercurial preoccupations. The landfill is lively with Mercurial transformations, and since Mercurius is good with the good and bad with the bad (not to be trusted), we would do well to pay particular attention to such repressed sites of material transformation, where the real of our idealised consumer lifestyle can no longer be denied. Let us indeed recognise that things are doing things to other things and to us, irrespective of our best-laid plans. Bennett cites Robert Sullivan's minor ecological classic, *The Meadowlands: Wilderness Adventures on the Edge of a City*, to illustrate her point. Sullivan's book is a powerfully poetic expression of the non-discriminatory Mercurial life that inhabits all things, even those things that we find least appealing. Sullivan is a freelance journalist who spent years exploring the landfills beyond the New Jersey Turnpike, the '32-square-mile wilderness, part natural, part industrial, that is five miles from the Empire State Building and a bit bigger than Manhattan' known locally as 'the Meadowlands' (Sullivan 1998a). He ventures into this derided and scorned outpost of civilisation with canoe, hiking gear, pick and shovel, like an early explorer, full of childlike curiosity at the sheer size of the thing. He climbs the highest peak and surveys the area.

> Snake Hill is cragged and denuded, a 150-foot tall, all-but-removed casualty of a gravel company's demolition work. But what's left of it is still the only real hill in the Meadowlands. The rest of the hills are garbage hills, the Meadowlands having once been the largest outdoor garbage can in the world. Snake Hill is to the Meadowlands what the Empire State Building is to New York or the Space Needle to Seattle, only instead of looking out on a living city, it looks out on the world's great postindustrial landscape. (Sullivan 1998b)

On the other side of the eight lanes of traffic pouring without interruption across the turnpike, Sullivan discovers with amazement that creatures have adapted and even thrived in this wasteland: 'It is now a good place to see a black-crowned night heron or a pie-billed grebe or 18 species of ladybugs, even if some of the water these creatures fly over can sometimes be the color of antifreeze' (Sullivan 1998b). Industrial waste becomes sublime, in the technical sense of the word – massive enough to threaten the ego and simultaneously fill it with the kind of pleasure Kant describes as the thrill of awe. Sullivan recalls:

> Once, on a canoe trip I got stuck in a body of water so polluted that when I touched the paddle to the bottom, huge cabbage-like clumps of garbage floated

up to release a scent that I thought for sure was going to cause me to throw up. Another time, I paddled over a radio tower that had fallen and was submerged. It is thought to be the first in the world to have transmitted the voice of Frank Sinatra, and when I looked down on the tower, with its accompanying submerged control-room building, I felt as if I were over an Atlantis. (Sullivan 1998b)

Bennett is right: ecology must spend less time on birding adventures with the Audubon Society and more time following the likes of Sullivan on his tour of trash piles around New Jersey. For if any matter requires our urgent attention, it is our waste. The landfill is the quintessential psycho-analytical rationalisation, the solution to a problem solved by concealing from consciousness what we refuse to know. How many of us have ever visited one? Usually we cannot get near it because it is hidden from sight. What we see instead, typically, is our trash neatly sorted into bins before it magically disappears. Our waste does not cease to exist, however; rather, it is buried in the ground and homes and communities are built on top of it. Some of this waste will remain 'active'; it will not decompose for thousands of years. Such places have a strange life of their own, and we would do well to pay attention to what is going on there. If we follow the logic of alchemy, it will be precisely here, in the place of the discarded, the disavowed and the filth, that the new form of society, the ecological civilisation so dearly needed, will be discovered.

> The . . . garbage hills are alive . . . there are billions of microscopic organisms thriving underground in dark, oxygen-free communities. . . . After having ingested the tiniest portion of leftover New Jersey or New York, these cells then exhale huge underground plumes of carbon dioxide and of warm moist methane, giant stillborn tropical winds that seep through the ground to feed the Meadowlands' fires, or creep up into the atmosphere, where they eat away at the . . . ozone. One afternoon I . . . walked along the edge of a garbage hill, a forty-foot drumlin of compacted trash that owed its topography to the waste of the city of Newark. . . . There had been rain the night before, so it wasn't long before I found a little leachate seep, a black ooze trickling down the slope of the hill, an espresso of refuse. In a few hours, this stream would find its way down into the . . . groundwater of the Meadowlands; it would mingle with toxic streams. . . . But in this moment, here at its birth, . . . this little seep was pure pollution, a pristine stew of oil and grease, of cyanide and arsenic, of cadmium, chromium, copper, lead, nickel, silver, mercury and zinc. (Sullivan 1998a: 96–7; cited in Bennett 2010: 6)

A Mercurial rather than Promethean focus in ecology, a humble and realistic descent into matter, one that is fully modern – indeed, more originally modern than the will to mastery vilified by Heidegger – could lead us into a more responsible assessment of the truth of our situation. My prescription for ecological conversion: start composting. The sight and smell of our organic refuse returning to earth is an intensely sensual lesson in the economy of life. Consumer culture is often critiqued as 'materialistic', but in fact it is as deeply idealist as you can get, substituting worlds of the imagination for the real. Ecology is, or could be, the healthy dose of realism that could leaven the idealism of our age. One need not return to ancient wisdom to dismantle reductionism. The ecological attitude is right beneath the surface of modern consciousness. It is nothing other than the Mercurial genius of the modern that is needed.

A full-blown Hermeticism such as Böhme's holds that God needs matter to know himself, and thus creates not arbitrarily but strategically, so as to come to self-consciousness through it. Böhme might have ventured into the heretical, as his Lutheran contemporaries noted (they forbade him to continue writing, but it was too late – his hand-written treatise *Aurora* [Böhme 1997] was going viral in Amsterdam, circulating and copied by the Kabbalists and theosophers who flourished in the tolerant Dutch Republic), but he did so on the basis of an uncommon sensitivity to the dignity, the spirituality and the truth of the body. Böhme was no academic theologian, and the privileged life of the seventeenth-century cleric was denied him. He was a shoemaker with an intense spiritual life, an autodidact in a time of troubled religious pluralism. He wrote his treatises in hours stolen away from his trade. Engravings show him sitting at this workbench, writing, with the tools of his trade lying nearby, hammer, nails, leather. Even if it is found wanting as a theology, Böhme's thesis concerning the necessity of matter for divine self-knowledge might be salvageable as a psychology. Indeed, Böhme freely admits that he has modelled his theological speculations on his own psychological introspection, what we might call, with Freud, his self-analysis (perused on the solidly Biblical assumption that, as the *imago Dei*, the human self ought to be able to tell us something about the divine). Without matter, embodiment, sensation, physical suffering, the recalcitrant other of the self, as Fichte will put it later (the not-I), there is no self-consciousness. Human consciousness is in every way dependent on consciousness of materiality. The reverse follows: the denial of matter is the deliberate refusal of consciousness, that is, repression. Böhme's eighteenth-century follower Friedrich Christoph Oetinger developed this insight into a theology of the body that is almost Nietzschean in its refusal of a certain kind of Christian Platonism. For Oetinger, any philosophy or theology that denigrates the body, or makes it a means to a spiritual end (as Augustine could be said to have done), is to be rejected. Drawing freely on Böhme and the Kabbalah, Oetinger rethinks spirit not as the opposite of body but as its most perfect expression. 'Spirit does not exist without body' (Oetinger 1776: pt 1, 223); 'To be embodied is no imperfection, as commonly believed, but a perfection' (Oetinger 1776: pt 1, 131–2). The incarnation of Christ is at the centre of this spiritual materialism; the *Logos* becomes flesh not solely to save a fallen material order: the manifestation of God to Godself, which sets the absolute in motion, is fully achieved only when God stands forth in time and space, at a particular moment in history, bodily, in Christ. Only when God has thus become absolutely other to Godself, finite, embodied, localised in space and time, only then is God fully revealed. Oetinger finds the Jewish Kabbalists too other-worldly on this point. Böhme alone seems to have grasped, not just the dignity of the body, but its glory. While the tradition has tended to read Böhme as crudely materialistic because he lacks the distinctions necessary for a more sophisticated spiritual vision, Oetinger sees Böhme's materialism as his great advantage over his predecessors. The sum of Böhme's vision, in Oetinger's view, is the intimacy of spirit to matter: 'Embodiment is the end of all God's work' (Oetinger 1776: pt 1, 223).

Note that this dialectical relationship between divinity and materiality is not the *Deus sive natura* of Spinozistic pantheism: crucial for the neo-Hermetic understanding of nature is God's transcendence of it. But God's transcendence of nature does not render it meaningless or accidental: rather, nature plays a catalytic role in the inner life of God, one that is progressively realised through human science. On the assumption that God needs us to individuate, to become God, the Creator, the neo-Hermetic empiricist has a moral duty to lend his or her powers to the transformation of matter, so that it might become more perfectly the image of divinity. This is no doubt a heterodox position. The medieval Scholastic concept of creation is not so intimately tied to the life of the Creator as the created universe is to the God of neo-Hermeticism. Although a revelation of God's mind, material nature is not held to be essential to God's own experience of Godself in orthodox Christianity. In a theology of creation such as Augustine's, matter is to some degree arbitrary, and it is true that medieval ascetical-mystical theology habitually directed the soul beyond and above it. Matter was good, no doubt, but not *that* good, and in its tempting quality it posed a grave threat to the soul: best to have as little to do with it as possible. The neo-Hermetic model of nature, by contrast, required that the philosopher / theologian / natural scientist (ideally the same person) contemplate the material structure of nature, not in an theoretically oriented, objectifying state of detachment, but immersively; for matter was understood to be our primary mediator of the divine mind. This contemplative approach was not passive but productive: it was 'the work' (the *opus alchemicum*); alchemy alternated between patiently contemplating the secret at play in natural transformation, and reproducing and accelerating that transformation through technical means. Renaissance Hermeticism was, I repeat, *alter-modern*, another way of being modern, and as the history of science would go, the road not taken by the West. The neo-Hermetic scientist did not enjoy the show of nature from a safe distance (he was not an aesthete); rather, she got her hands dirty, for nature was an emergent order that needed our help.

Neither did the neo-Hermetic subscribe to the fact–value distinction (which was already taking hold in other areas of modern inquiry): the work was both scientific and ethico-political. The first entity to be transmuted (decomposed down to its base elements or *prima materia* and reconstituted at a higher level) was the alchemist himself, and through this transformation society itself was to be perfected. Dovetailing with the Renaissance-humanist revival of the Hellenistic practice of care of the self, neo-Hermetic science was simultaneously a technique for working with matter and a practice of virtue. This was possible because neo-Hermetic *natura* was conceived to be intimate with the human: when we contemplated nature, we contemplated ourselves, and vice versa. When we operated on it, we operated on ourselves. When we profaned it, abused it or denigrated it as a means to some utilitarian end, we profaned, abused and denigrated ourselves. Human works, the moral character of the self, the products of culture, and technology itself are as natural as fungi or sexual reproduction; they would be all the more successful the more in accordance they remained with the deep spiritual patterns at play in both matter and mind. Here is Paracelsus on the relation of nature to art:

> Q. Give a concise definition of nature.
> A. It is not visible, though it operates visibly; for it is simply a volatile spirit, fulfilling its office in bodies, and animated by the universal spirit – the divine breath, the central and universal fire, which vivifies things that exist.
> Q. What should be the qualities possessed by the examiners of nature?
> A. They should be like unto nature itself. . . .
> Q. What matters should subsequently engross their attention?
> A. The philosophers should most carefully ascertain whether their designs are in harmony with nature. . . . If they would accomplish by their own power anything that is usually performed by the power of nature, they must imitate her in every detail. . . .
> Q. What is the object of research among philosophers?
> A. Proficiency in the art of perfecting what nature has left imperfect. (Paracelsus, *Alchemical Catechism*)

Note the paradox in this passage: on the one hand, the Paracelsian scientist is to look to nature as to an archetype; on the other hand, he is to perfect nature by technical means. The archetype that governs the work is not simply given but is in part constructed, by the ingenuity of the scientist, in the work itself. Not only is alchemical *techne* conceived here as *physis* by other means, but nature itself, being incomplete and imperfect, simply cannot be the standard – this was not nature, rejected by Latour as 'outside', 'unified' and 'indisputable'; it was a nature that was inside us as much as outside us, as disordered as it was ordered, requiring discernment and moral decision so that the imperfect might be progressively cut away. The nature with which the alchemist worked was within him as much as it was without him, as immaterial as it was material; hence the alchemist had to combine spiritual and moral practice with scientific know-how. For what he was called to perform was nothing less than an act of magical co-creation. The nature that was his guide in everything he did was not an object or the totality of objects; it was an order emerging simultaneously with his own efforts to bring it into being. No question, the magus's participatory transformation of the base into the sublime promised him immense power over natural processes, but the assumption that such power was his to command at will was a temptation to be resisted.

From this ethical imperative to direct nature for human betterment while resisting the will to mastery arises the curious blend of traditional Christian piety with scientific discipline in alchemical engravings. The alchemist was dependent upon power that, in the end, she could not possess, for it was the privilege of Mercurius, the created spirit of nature, to initiate the alchemist into knowledge or leave him bereft with his failed experiment. *Aurum nostrum non est aurum vulgi*, 'Our gold is not the ordinary gold', the alchemists claimed, but the kings and queens upon whose patronage they depended paid no attention, and so alchemy became known for its more utilitarian possibilities.

In the famous engraving (opposite) from Heinrich Khunrath's 1609 book *Amphitheatrum sapientiae aeternae*, the alchemist kneels in prayer in his laboratory before beginning his work. In the book itself, Khunrath divides the work of the alchemist into three parts – alchemy, magic and Kabbalah – and holds that one cannot proceed without the other.[14] One part of the book deals with physical alchemy, a second with the spiritual psychology of the alchemist and a third with theology, which Khunrath understood in a devoutly Lutheran, if heterodox, way. The room in the engraving depicts the plurality and multifacetedness of the alchemists' work. It is divided in two: on the left side, the *oratorium*, where reading, meditating and prayer take place; and on the right, the *laboratorium*, where work with matter occurs. Neither contemplation without work, nor work without contemplation, but both are required of the alchemist. Proverbs and sayings from neo-Platonism and the Christian mystical tradition adorn the right side: *Sine afflatus divino, nemo unquam vir magnus*, 'Without Divine inspiration, no man is great' (from Cicero, *De natura deorum*); *Hoc hoc agentibus/nobis aderit ipse Deus*, 'When we attend strictly to our work, God himself will aid us'; *Ne loquaris de Deo absque lumine*, 'Don't speak of God without light'; *Disce bene mori*, 'Learn how to die'. Above the central arch, leading presumably to the alchemist's sleeping chamber, is inscribed *Dromiens vigila*, 'While sleeping, be vigilant' (Khunrath, like other 'spiritual

An engraving from Heinrich Khunrath's *Amphitheatrum sapientiae aeternae*, Frankfurt, 1609

alchemists', looked to his dreams for revelations). So far, reading these instructions, we could be in the cell of a medieval monk. But on the right side of the room, a set of different commandments is inscribed: *Nec temere, nec timide*, 'Neither rashly, nor timidly' – enjoining the alchemist to dare to tamper with nature, but to do so with reverence. *Sapienter retentatum, succedet aliquando*, 'That which is wisely tried, will succeed sometimes'. *Ratio / experientia*, 'Reason / experience' – a Paracelsian emphasis on following one's own reason and experience (as opposed to slavishly relying on tradition). And perhaps the most fascinating paradox, which sums up the attitude of alchemical contemplative science as a whole: *Festina lente*, 'make haste slowly'. This is the very essence of the contemplative critique, control and calculation that was lost in the beginning of modernity: to work and simultaneously to wait; to objectify while allowing oneself to become the object; to analyse without presuming to master the power of synthesis; to deploy reason as an instrument, while remaining open to the way things reveal themselves of their own accord.

On the table in the centre of the room lie scattered musical and scientific instruments. Lining the walls are substances in glass vials, the materials of the work. A still sits on the floor beside the table. In the right-hand corner, one can see the oven in which the fire of transformation is stoked, the bellows lying on the floor nearby.

When the adages and proverbs are read rightly, the position of prayer in which the alchemist is depicted will not be misunderstood: this was not quietist contemplation; it aimed at results. It was not enough to contemplate nature in a passive way. Contemplation needed to be active and productive, for the human being was called to participate in the emergence of natural order and bring it to even more effective fruition in ways that could be of direct benefit to humankind. And yet, in the end, the participatory perfection of natural processes was embraced for the sake of the moral transformation of the magus and the betterment of society: to become himself holy, individuated, a Mercurius incarnate and a servant of the good – this was the true gold sought at the end of the work (Abraham 1998: 145–8).

There were complex ethico-political reasons for the rejection of the neo-Hermetic philosophy of nature by mainstream science in the seventeenth century. But it was not, as Culianu would have us believe, a rejection of paganism by Reformed Christianity that killed the Renaissance; it was, rather, the triumph of one sense of nature over another.[15] Nature as dead mechanism, out there, waiting for our instrumental reason to do something about it, triumphed over living nature. A sense of the *anthropos* as master rather than magus, as one who needed a greater control over matter than Hermetic science offered, overtook us in the seventeenth century, even if it was a stance made possible by attitudes endemic to Christianity (the disenchanted universe, one-sided monotheism, other-worldly eschatology). The neo-Hermetic epistemology of resemblances (the signature of things), with its penchant for infinity, was unmanageable, limitless, but admitting no certainty, 'plethoric yet absolutely poverty stricken' (Foucault 1966: 33–4). A knowledge that proceeded by infinite accumulation of confirmations could never attain the degree of mastery demanded by techno-science. In Foucault's account, Faustian man had to reject Hermeticism if he was to succeed in subordinating all things to his control. For the alchemist, this rejection could only mean mistaking the means for the end. The end was not to rule as sovereign over nature, nor to elevate oneself above matter as controller and calculator, but to become oneself an expression of the same productive power emerging in nature. The technological power that the work made available to the Hermeticist was not to be deployed for the purposes of self-aggrandisement (the production of the common gold, *aurum vulgi*), but for the sake of moral and political transformation.

Notes

1. See especially Cassirer (1963: 24–45); Gillespie (2009: 44–68); Yates (1964: 144–56).
2. This is the so-called Yates thesis of the genesis of modern science from Hermeticism. See Yates (1964). Isaac Newton's fascination with alchemy is well known, but similar arguments can be made for Shakespeare, Leibniz, Spinoza and, later, Goethe, Novalis and Schelling. Where I disagree with Yates concerns her presupposition that Hermeticism was a primitive form of the science and technology that would come out of it. I will argue, with Culianu and Foucault, that Hermeticism was an *alternative* form of modern science and technology, one that was rejected for ethico-political reasons and not because it was bad science.
3. Dating historical periods as multivalent as the Renaissance is always contentious, especially as there are those who say the Renaissance itself is a pure construct of nineteenth-century historians. If dates are needed, then we could say that the Renaissance was well underway when Petrarch was crowned poet laureate in Rome in 1341, and it was more or less over by the time Giordano Bruno was burned at the stake in the same city in 1600.
4. Bonardel sees this triumph of the reductionist spirit in the decline of alchemy in the seventeenth and eighteenth centuries. While more and more alchemical texts were printed in this period, their emphasis changes and a literalism creeps in which was allied with a much greater emphasis on the utilitarian manipulation of matter. 'One finds a decline of symbolism in the service of allegory, a pedagogical desire to strip away the veils, a socialisation of spiritual preoccupations, and finally, above all, an insidious slide from the prerogatives of Hermes to those of Prometheus: one no longer assists Nature; one takes it by force and competes against it' (Bonardel 1992: 80).
5. The French anthropologist Lucien Lévy-Bruhl coined the term 'participation mystique' to describe the characteristic feature of the so-called 'primitive mind': the psychological identification with objects typical of magical thinking. The 'primitive mind' does not distinguish itself from the object but is bound to it by a direct and magical relationship. See Lévy-Bruhl (1926). See also Jung (1971: para. 781). Lévy-Bruhl's language is outdated, colonial and perhaps offensive, but the epistemological point is still valid. To be identified with an object is typical of magical and mystical consciousness; to be differentiated from an object is the condition of the possibility of knowing it, indeed, of having an object to know in the first place.
6. On Paracelsus, see the definitive biography by Weeks (1996).
7. N. T. Wright argues repeatedly and in many books that the point of the resurrection in early Christianity was the socio-political and material transfiguration of *this* world, not escape from it. See for example Wright (2008). On Paul's understanding of the socio-political relevance of the resurrection see Wright (2017: 41–59).
8. It should be clear from this that Hegel's notion of spirit is a development of the Hermetic symbol of Mercurius. Hegel is not alone in turning with enthusiasm to what I have called 'the road not taken', that is, Renaissance Hermeticism, neo-Hermeticism, Kabbalah and the occult; so too did Oetinger, Hölderlin, Schelling, Schlegel, von Baader and Novalis (to mention only German Romantics). Hegel turns

to the Renaissance and the alchemical symbolic in order to master the discourse, to convert the esoteric into exoteric logic, and so remove the threat it poses to rationality and science. See Magee (2001).

9. See <https://www.youtube.com/watch?v=j_K_79O21hk> (accessed 16 October 2018).

10 When we speak of a 'healthy' climate, we use an analogy; when we speak of the 'agency' of a heap of compost, we use a metaphor. There is a genuine sense in which climates can be healthy, namely as productive of health; but compost does not in any genuine sense of the term act or produce agency. On the Scholastic distinction between analogy and metaphor, see Hochschild (2010).

11. I also set aside the objection that one cannot very effectively encourage moral responsibility in people by denying their capacity for it (and what else is the claim that a person is no more of an agent than a heap of garbage but a denial of moral responsibility?). I have already to some degree addressed this problem. Spinoza was the most honest of anti-humanist philosophers, and he had no difficulty in following through with his reduction of human striving and moral life to the desire (*conatus*) that all things possess to persist in being (he was above all consistent): the conclusion could only be that humans are not morally responsible in the strong sense of the word 'responsible', because they are not free. The corollary of this conclusion is that there is no real distinction between good and evil; there is only the relative distinction between good and bad, between that which increases the power of a mode and that which impedes or decreases it.

12. The recent revival of the theory of panpsychism among some philosophers of mind (Brüntrup and Jaskolla 2017; Nagel 2012; Chalmers 1996) signifies a return to the Renaissance philosophy of a unified nature, which was in part material, in part mental. The one world (*unus mundus*) of the Renaissance philosophy of nature resonated with sympathies that could at best be accounted for through the use of analogies. Magic was not the product of an intervention or instrumental domination of natural processes but of a psychic identification with them. On Renaissance panpsychism, see Cassirer (1963: 148–52).

13. The alchemist's depression at entering the *nigredo* stage is the likely source of the Renaissance tradition of celebrating *melancholia* as the pre-condition for scientific and artistic inspiration, a theme immortalised in Albrecht Dürer's 1514 engraving *Melancolia I*. To create is to first of all enter into *meontic* nothingness, the empty space of possibility, and the condition for this entrance is death, the loss of the actual, of what one knows, what one is, and what one loves, to the inevitable process of decomposition. On Dürer's engraving and the cult of melancholia in the Renaissance, see Yates (1979: 57–70). The theme was also popular among the Romantics. On Schelling's interpretation of melancholia see McGrath (2014b).

14. On this engraving see Forshaw (2012).

15. The thesis of Culianu's well-known study of the Renaissance, *Eros and Magic in the Renaissance*, is that Hermeticism did not die out because its science was superseded by Newtonian mechanics; it rather died out because of the Reformation prohibition on images (Culiano 1987). Culiano is certainly correct that at the heart of Renaissance Hermeticism is a robust, non-subjectivist and ontological theory of the imagination and its role in the production of knowledge. But his antipathy for Christianity gets the better of him, and his otherwise excellent book ends with the banal opposition of the pagan Renaissance and prudish Christianity. For one thing, many of the greatest figures in the neo-Hermetic movement were not pagan at all but Christians.

Chapter 10

Contemplative Politics

Among the philosophers and students of philosophy to whom I speak about environmental matters, I frequently meet with a kind of frozen horror when the situation of the earth comes up. Everyone knows how bad things are. Everyone knows that the course we are on now is sure to make things worse. We stare into the future of eco-collapse like a deer into the headlights of an onrushing vehicle; we are paralysed by the apparent impossibility of the situation. Much more rarely do I encounter any intention to do anything about it. Philosophers, it seems, are, as Marx noted, more inclined to interpret the world than to change it – even, or perhaps especially, if that interpretation leads to nihilism and despair. More than once have I concluded a seminar in environmental philosophy with a sense of defeat in the face of students' cynical indifference to the situation I have endeavoured to describe. It is not that climate-change scepticism is present in significant numbers among students of philosophy. Rather, eco-anxiety has mostly replaced the existential angst that was once so characteristic of young students of philosophy. There is no shortage of fear or apprehension in my seminars; there is, however, a notable absence of political will. I have also noticed how few of my students are politically involved in the governance of their society in any way, and how few of them bother to vote. Eco-anxiety has rendered many millennials politically impotent.

The situation is different outside the philosophy classroom. In the world of ENGOs and climate-change activism, of which I am also a part, it is precisely the generation who are doomed to inherit the earth who are most up for the fight to save the future. So, what is it about the study of philosophy and the prevalence of quietism? Why does reading Aristotle, Descartes and Heidegger seem to render students politically inactive?

This is an old problem, and it addresses the central thesis of this essay, that the apparent dichotomy between contemplation and action is false. In Christendom, these two ways of life were differentiated, institutionally, in the functional separation of contemplative and active religious orders – the latter assigned the tasks of education, preaching and caring for the poor and the sick, and the former endowed with the intellectual and liturgical work reserved for the cloister. The same dichotomy determined also the class distinction within the monastery between lay brothers, who worked the fields, and choir monks, whose day was dedicated to liturgical and contemplative prayer. Quietist contemplation has hardly since gone out of fashion, and not only among philosophy students. Žižek has argued somewhere that the perfect accomplice for global capitalism is the exploding industry of Western yoga, which offers the consumer a spiritual life to supplement his or her other rounds of consumer enjoyments, a spiritual life whose central tenet is a superficial appropriation of the Buddhist doctrine of *anatta*, the denial of the existence of a self. The Western yogi dedicates his time to outfitting the meditation room with exotic items and designer *zafus*, punctuating the working year with exclusive retreats in the tropics, and is too busy 'deepening' himself to bother with something as pedestrian as the daily news, or even the sorry state of his city. Nicely aligned with this spiritual narcissism is devotion to a fulfilling career and a certain elevated, even green form of consumerism. Bad conscience is assuaged by vegetarianism and mindfulness exercises. Whether or not that is a correct interpretation of yoga is not the point. Rather, his claim is that capitalism is facilitated by the political quietism of the consumer class, and this is promoted rather than challenged by a superficial approach to the practice of mindfulness.

One point that no one can deny is the disproportion between the increase in our knowledge of the scale of ecological disasters developing in the Anthropocene – from the irrefutable evidence of climate change (even if the anthropogenic causes can still be disputed, the rising temperatures and melting ice cannot) to the glut of ocean plastics that are choking sea birds and poisoning not only fish but the humans who consume them – and the political will to correct the course. Few believe that we will reach anything like the controls on emissions the 2015 Paris Agreement declared to be necessary to avert the worst effects of climate change. The defection of the United States from that agreement in the wake of the general rise of xenophobic populism in Western democracies has encouraged other dissident voices to rise up in protest against carbon taxes and UN-sanctioned programmes aimed at weaning the developing world from fossil-fuel consumption. The battle against climate change is quickly becoming ideological in the strict sense: we continue to talk the talk but have no intention of walking the walk. Anthropogenic climate change is the lie we tell ourselves to maintain the status quo, that is, we need to *say* we are doing something about the situation, but that does not imply we are actually doing anything at all.

On the other side of the spectrum, activism becomes more and more desperate, and ENGOs more and more militarised and even fanatical, willing to endorse any philosophy and politics so long as it supports the cause. I have heard public talks by well-known environmentalists advocating the virtues of Xi Jinping's authoritarian rule in China because it is preferable to the sluggishness of Western democratic responses to the emergency. We have to stop lecturing China about human rights violations, the distinguished speaker insisted, and instead encourage radical green energy policies. More disturbingly, he continued that we might learn something about governance from China, which seems to have found the solution to the atomistic individualism that neuters every environmental movement: namely, old-school police-state authoritarianism. Here the opposite problem to contemplative quietism rears its head: not lack of will to change, but neglect of philosophical critique and interpretation, which has caused many environmentalists to lose the plot. A world state with police power to enforce environmental policy could be, in some technical respects, a greener world, but who would want to live in it?

Before we run headlong into eco-fascism, we would do well to think a little harder about the deep roots of ecological ruin – not only the technical and natural side of the crisis, but its political and spiritual dimensions as well. My argument for a return to consideration of the religious precursors of ecological crisis (with due acknowledgement of Lynn White Jr) could, from an activist perspective, be considered a form of navel-gazing – a rearranging of deck chairs on the *Titanic* – when what is required now more than ever is action. But without genuine understanding of the origins of ecological crisis in certain ethical and spiritual attitudes – a body of values that is far from universal and the emergence of which is specifically locatable in history – our action will at best be superficial, and at worst a perpetuation of the problem that leaves untouched the fundamental assumptions engendering it beneath the surface. It would be like pulling out weeds without digging up their roots: the gardener condemns herself to long and continual defeat.

Between the indifference of the graduate seminar and the blind activism of some ENGOs, there is a middle way. But it will be maintained only by refusing to oppose both interpretive analysis and political change while simultaneously rejecting an older source of the problem, the false dichotomy between contemplation and action. (Qualified) critique, control and calculation remain the way forward – the sheer logistical feat required to feed the more than 7 billion humans who call this planet home demands it.

Technology helped create such a population boom, and technology remains essential to supporting and controlling it before it gets out of hand.

To work *with* the biosphere, rather than against it, to imagine a technosphere become mutually symbiotic with the biosphere, and to come up with environmental solutions that are also social solutions – these are Herculean tasks. They will require more than capital and technology, although they will certainly require plenty of both. We know that ecological civilisation is the only possible future for humanity on earth, but we do not know how to get there. The development of the ecological civilisation to come (and we have a duty to hope for it, however impossible it seems from our current perspective – indeed, we must hope for it precisely because it appears both impossible and necessary) requires deep contemplative penetration of the interconnectedness of things. Morton is surely right: interdependence *is* the ecological thought, but genuinely thinking this thought requires a degree of wisdom that few if any now possess. We might well remember that insight into interdependence is the core of Buddhist enlightenment. Whatever else it might be, the Buddhist realisation of *paṭiccasamuppāda* is hardly a *technical* achievement. If interdependence is to be more than a theory, if it is to become a value that governs policy and decision-making, we are going to need to leaven our one-sidedly calculative modernity with contemplation. Environmental activism is not enough; we also need environmental contemplation. And we need the eco-activist and the eco-contemplative to be the same person: we need contemplative environmental activism and contemplative environmental politics so that the ecological thought can sink in and become ecological *practice*.

Here I take a page from Meister Eckhart, the busy religious administrator who first defined *Gelassenheit* as the way to divine consciousness. Against the quietism of the Brethren of the Free Spirit and allied fourteenth-century movements, he insisted that the active life that is also a contemplative life is higher than the contemplative life without action. Where the one-sided contemplative can find God only in special times and places, the active contemplative sees God everywhere and in all things. She does not divide herself between prayerful and non-prayerful states of minds but prays when she works and works when she prays.

> Because truly, when you think that you are acquiring more of God in inwardness, in devotion, in sweetness and in various approaches than you do by the fireside or in the stable, you are acting just as if you took God and muffled his head up in a cloak and pushed him under a bench. (Eckhart, in McGinn 1981: 183)

Eckhart's frustration with what we could call contemplative fetishism drives him into a reversal of the traditional reading of the story of Martha and Mary from the Gospel of Luke (10: 38–42). Jesus is visiting friends in

Bethany. The story describes two sisters in the household and their alternative reactions to Jesus' presence. Martha quickly gets to work preparing a meal for the honoured guest. Mary, by contrast, sits at Jesus' feet in rapt attention, hanging off of every word that comes out of his mouth. Frustrated by the non-cooperation of her sister, Martha complains that Mary is doing nothing to help out with the housework. 'Lord', she says to Jesus, 'do you not care that my sister has left me to get on with the work by myself? Tell her to come and lend a hand' (Luke 10: 40). Jesus' answer to Martha had always been interpreted to mean that the contemplative life is higher than the active life: 'Martha, Martha, you are worried and distracted by many things; there is need of only one thing. Mary has chosen the better part, which will not be taken away from her' (Luke 10: 41–2). The Latin version is *sollicita es, et turbaris erga plurima*, which is rendered in Luther's German as *du hast viel Sorge und Mühe* – which could be translated as 'you have many cares and concerns'. On the basis of the Germanic reading of the Latin, Eckhart is able to reverse the meaning of the story. He argues that in fact Jesus is praising Martha for her advanced state of consciousness: so confirmed is she in her devotion to him that she can be with him in the housework. Her 'many cares and concerns' indicate an elevated consciousness, for she is genuinely concerned with the one-sidedness of Mary's attitude. Where Mary must distinguish contemplation from action and needs to remove herself from the ordinary duties of daily life in order to be with the Lord without distractions, Martha does not separate the two, and is able to do both, and listens to Jesus in the housework. Martha's consciousness is higher than Mary's for she can contemplatively act and actively contemplate.

> He [Jesus] affirmed that she [Martha] lacked nothing of all that is necessary for eternal happiness. Hence he said, 'You are careful' [*du hast viel Sorge*] by which he meant 'You stand in the midst of things, but they do not reside in you; and those are careful who go about unimpeded in all their daily pursuits. . . . Such people stand in the midst of things, but not *in* things'. (Eckhart, Sermon 86, in McGinn 1986: 340)

On this extraordinary work of Biblical deconstruction, Caputo comments:

> To Eckhart, Mary symbolized the *merely* contemplative life, a sheltered life of prayers, visions and consolations, devoid of concrete works. . . . Martha on the other hand is a spiritually more mature personality, ripened and 'exercised' by the years. Martha is not the opposite of Mary, viz., action without contemplation. Martha could work and in the midst of activity preserve her inner silence and unity with God. Mary's union with God, on the other hand, was so fragile and untested that she had to rest at Jesus' feet in order to preserve it. . . . Eckhart held that inner silence is entirely compatible with other activity. Indeed, we need look no further than his own life for an example of this unique compatibility. He offered a good illustration of what he meant: a wheel moving on its own axis is fully in motion even while its center is still. (Caputo 1978: 204–5)

However dodgy Eckhart's scriptural interpretation of Luke 10: 38, theologically the Dominican is on solid terrain. From the divine perspective, divinity and creation are not two, for one simple reason: they cannot be two, for the infinite God has no other. Divinity and creation are not separate (even if not-identical), but one continuous outflowing being. Martha, who does not distinguish between work and prayer, between action and contemplation, sees things as God sees them, as one. The human perspective that refuses to separate contemplation and action, divinity and humanity, Creator and creature, or spirit and matter, is therefore higher than the perspective that prefers the former over the latter; because it participates in divine consciousness, it can see God and world as one and find divinity in the ordinary. I touch here on a theme in Eckhart that Hegel picked up on and that might contain a clue to how to contemplatively critique, calculate and control a situation – namely, Eckhart's identification of identity and non-identity. It is not that the distinction between God and creation is unreal, as in certain forms of philosophical and theological monism; rather, the distinction is essential to the rich identity in difference that constitutes divinity. One must be able to say that creation is both divine and not-divine; its non-divinity mediates its divinity, and vice versa. Eckhart makes the point psychologically. He distinguishes the knowledge of the 'self in God' granted us by the 'eternal light' – the experience of mystical union – from the knowledge of the self 'apart from God', the self in its historical individuality, in its separateness or *haecceity*, as Scotus would put it, which is, to be sure, a variety of nothingness, but not simply nothing. Such finite knowledge is not to be discounted, Eckhart says, but can be had only through 'life'. The knowledge of the self in God, on the one hand, is a knowledge in which the self cannot be distinguished from God, and the rapt soul declares, 'The eye with which I see God is the same eye with which God sees me. My eye and God's eye are one eye, and one vision or seeing, and one knowing and one loving' (Eckhart, Sermon 57, in Walshe 2009: 298). The knowledge of self that life grants us, on the other hand – and here Eckhart means practical life, the life of housework and service – discerns the individual virtues 'clearly in God through images' (Eckhart, Sermon 86, in McGinn 1986: 339). What is seen as one in God is seen as multiple apart from God – a standard neo-Platonic point. But what Eckhart does with the point is anything but standard. Far from devaluing the ordinary perspective that sees things as many, he argues that it, too, has its role, and that without it our consciousness is less than divine. In order to truly participate in divine consciousness, we have to be both divine and non-divine, one and many, identical with God and different from God – for difference and multiplicity is God's will. It pleases God to share being through diversity rather than to remain inured in identity, and for the human being to renounce this diversity is just as counter to God's will as for the human being to forget the original identity of things. It is not enough, Eckhart says, to disappear into the contemplation of the Godhead, to lose sense of self and time in the eternal oneness of the divine birth. We need also to reappear in the separateness of historical life; we need to descend into time, as God himself descends in the incarnation; to lower ourselves into matter and suffer the differences; to affirm by immersion the goodness of creation.[1] Unlike other neo-Platonist authors, pagan and Christian, Eckhart does not deny ordinary dualistic consciousness as nothing, illusion, error – something that ought not to be and should be somehow transcended. Rather, in his insistence on creaturely nothingness, on poverty and detachment, even from divine things, Eckhart maintains the identity of identity and non-identity: the identity of the finite standpoint of dualistic consciousness and the infinite standpoint of non-dual consciousness, an identity in which the finite does not disappear but is preserved as the mediator of infinity. Like Luther, whom Eckhart anticipates and influenced, the soul must simultaneously be regarded as nothing and everything, simultaneously Godless and divine, or, in Luther's famous phrase, simultaneously sinner and saved, *simul justus et peccator*. The simultaneity of opposites in the Christian life does not allow the Christian to elevate his or herself above ordinary flawed and divided consciousness or to enjoy some form of existence beyond sin; rather, it is only in sin that she is saved, and so sin or dividedness must persist, for salvation and divinity depend upon it. This is surely what Eckhart meant when he said 'because in some way or another it is God's will that I should have sinned, I should not want not to have done so' (Eckhart, *Benedictus*, cited in McGinn 1981: 216) (and not what the Inquisitor's attributed to him, namely teaching licence to sin).[2]

Eckhart's experience of finitude as God's own experiencing of himself is, according to Hegel, nothing exceptional, but rather the ordinary experience of the Christian at prayer (Hegel 1827: 189–97). To pray is both to performatively recognise the distance that separates the finite from the infinite and, in that act, to abolish the distance in a bodily and psychological expression of divine intimacy. The Christian prays to a God who is both distant – for why else pray? – and near; both transcendent, to be adored on high, and immanent, so close to the soul that she can speak directly to God in her heart. Herein for Hegel lies the advantage of the cultic observation of religion over the abstract theoretical or metaphysical approach: in the *cultus*, the finitude of the human standpoint is not left behind in an effort to raise one's consciousness to the divine (as it is, for example, in certain forms of mysticism). The Christian claim to know God in prayer is inseparable from the Christian's knowledge that he is *not* God. But in one's not being God, one is *also* God, for our knowledge of God can only be God's knowledge of

Godself, since God has nothing outside of the divine being and cannot be related in any other way to the praying consciousness than non-dualistically. There is therefore no such thing as a *merely* human knowledge of God; knowledge of God is possible only through God. This does not mean that we ought to endeavour to transcend the conditions of human knowledge; rather, it means the reverse: we are to recognise that these limitations – the suffering body, the desiring psyche, the yearning will – far from being an obstacle to divine knowledge, are the conditions of its possibility. A finite experience of the infinite is affirmed on the assumption that this is no human achievement, but a divine one: it is not the *mystic* who knows God through his finite faculties but *God* who knows Godself through the mystic's finite faculties. In this divine act of self-knowledge, God posits God's other, the finite, in order to know Godself by means of it, and both the finite or dualistic standpoint and the infinite or non-dual reality are simultaneously affirmed and identified, without confusion.

What does all this have to do with contemplative ecological politics? Everything. The phrase itself, contemplative politics, is a *coincidentia op-positorum*, for politics is not contemplation, and contemplation is not political – at least not in their everyday sense. And it is precisely this coincidence of opposites that is required right now. We know that frenetic and unconscious development has brought about the great acceleration and the destruction of countless eco-systems upon which we depend. All of the plastic in the ocean and most of the indecomposable waste mouldering in overflowing landfills all over the world was created in my lifetime. We literally did not know what we were doing as we moved from more traditional forms of storage and construction to producing and packaging everything in the miracle substance, plastic. This was non-contemplative development. We could have known better – and some spoke of the danger, Cassandra crying in the streets – but we willed not to know and frenetically aligned ourselves with a certain unreflective ideal of modernism. We know now that further development of this kind will spell disaster for the planet. But we also know that 'doing nothing' is not on: something must be done, but what? Contemplative politics means listening deeply to the situation and searching the motivations of the political action pursued, uprooting concealed agendas and ruthlessly unmasking rationalisations. It unites a Marxist critique of ideology with a Christian trust in being, for not everything depends on us, and to believe that it does is disastrous. Contem-plative politics alone can break with past patterns and give birth to the new form of modernity even now struggling to emerge. We need to distance ourselves from the one-sided pursuit of critique, control and calculation that has brought us to the edge of the apocalypse – and yet soberly recognise that there is no way back to older patterns of cosmocentrism. The new thinking will be ecological and modern; the chaosmos is not a meaningless abyss, even if it is not teleologically oriented to human flourishing. The universe is not a cosmos to nest in, nor a machine to manipulate. And we, thinking nature, are the nature at issue. Who we will be depends entirely on who we understand ourselves to have been.

All that is well and good, my critics might say, *a charming tribute to a faded European sensibility, an attempt to restore the* philosophia perennis, *since the coincidence of the opposites of contemplation and action you articulate is hardly unique to Europe, but is nothing other than a European version of the Hindu Prakriti/Purusha, or the Chinese yin/yang. But what, after all that, is to be* done? A fair question. Over 7 billion humans are struggling to enter the consumer class on a planet that cannot possibly sustain the pace of such development. The seas are acidifying and rising faster than feared. The release of methane from thawing permafrost in the north seems to have rendered as wishful thinking even the most alarming predictions of global warming. The plastics that saturate our oceans are showing up on all the shores of the world, and there is no end in sight to their proliferation. Oil production continues without pause as global demand refuses to capitulate to climate science and UN policy. The breakdown of international order – Trump, Brexit, the rise of populism and the decay of democracy before the clamour of a working class hungry for jobs that no longer exist in our increasingly automated economy – has not only rendered the UN impotent but has practically installed consumer-capitalism as the only system upon which humans seem to agree. From the US to China, the majority readily assent (whether theoretically or performatively) to the proposition that freedom equals liberty to acquire mass-produced goods and to experiment with identity in endless pursuit of novel experiences and narcissistic enjoyments – the very ideology responsible for making the twentieth century the most environmentally ruinous in human history to date. What in the face of this, it bears repeating, is to be done? What does the contemplatively political ecologist have to offer?

Here there can be no programme, no comprehensive political position that could mobilise under the banner of 'contemplative political ecology', but only the *ad hoc* efforts of diverse individual political ecologists and the communities to which they belong. The contemplative qualifier of political ecology precludes the drafting of monolithic policy and the writing of manifestos to be imposed on the unwilling. Contemplation is irreducibly individual – if not, for that reason, individualist. Contemplation refuses the imposition of ideals and judgements on those who do not experience its truth, even if the contemplative nonetheless believes that, given the right conditions, the truth she sees can be communally experienced. If the contemplative does not hesitate to try to persuade, to preach or to teach, she never coerces, but openly invites. She offers a standing invitation to *look and see* – not a dogma enshrined by definitions, but the true, the good and the beautiful.

Contemplative political ecology can be neither left nor right, then, since it is in principle dis-identified from ideological categories. But this does not mean that it presumes to rise above the political debates of our time. By being so *dis-identified*, contemplative political ecology is able to *identify* with what is ecological on both sides of the political spectrum. It can affirm, with the left, internationalism, globally coordinated state control of resources and development, and state-enforced policy to mitigate global warming, protect the remaining wilderness, defend threatened populations of non-humans and more equitably distribute not only wealth but also the environmental burden of living in the Anthropocene. But at the same time, and for the same reasons, contemplative political ecology can, with the right, support the smallest forms of government insofar as participation in governance promotes active love of land and sea, of the local and regional, and above all of the preservation of rural life too often neglected by centralised authority. Contemplative political ecology brings together what conventional politics has torn asunder because it refuses false dichotomies (for example, internationalism versus local governance, ecology versus economy, sustainability versus development).

This is an alchemical work, for the Mercurius released in the alembic is the spirit of nature and our own spirit, and there is no way to work on it without simultaneously working on ourselves. This, to conclude, is the paradox of environmental philosophy: the future of nature is the future of the one who thinks nature, *thinking nature*. Contemplative politics is materialistic idealism. It is the union of science and art (another disjunction in the modern of which we have not yet spoken, but which is the heart of the matter) in the production of a technology that allows the beautiful to occur. I have argued for a dismantling of the consumer-kitsch machine via a theological deconstruction of consumerism, but I am not advocating a return to Christendom any more than I am advocating a re-enchantment of the world. If I do not know the new form thinking nature will take in the advanced Anthropocene, that is because it is has not yet existed.

Notes

1. Eckhart's denial of a hierarchy of being, in which a particular time, place or being could be closer to God than another, was taken up by Cusa. This elevation of the individual above the universal, which follows from the maximisation of God's transcendence of creation in Eckhart's mysticism, and following him, in Cusa's homogeneous universe (every point in the finite universe is equally distant and near

to the infinite One), does not denigrate but rather ennobles the finite. Every time and place, every individual thing, offers a unique viewpoint on the One, and each is as such precious and necessary for making up what is lacking in the other. The ecological significance of this thought is worth reflecting upon. The extinction of the golden toad of Coast Rica (extinct since 1989) would be, according to Cusa, the loss of an irreplaceable manifestation of the divine. Conservation becomes a theological work. See Cassirer (1963: 32): 'The true sense the divine first discloses itself when the mind no longer remains standing at *one* of these relationships, not even at their simply totality, but rather collects them all in the unity of a vision, a *visio intellectualis*. Then we can understand that it is absurd for us even to want to think the absolute in itself without such a determination through an individual point of view. But we also understand that none of these points of view has any priority, because only the concrete totality of them can mediate a true picture of the Whole for us. In this whole, every single viewpoint is included and recognised both in its accidentality and its necessity.'

2. This passage was cited in proposition 14 of the 1329 Papal Bull 'In agro dominico' condemning many of Eckhart's teachings as heretical. See McGinn (1981: 79).

Chapter 11

Anthropocenic Nature

Contemporary interdisciplinary ecology, especially the new field of 'environmental humanities', is wise to eco-ideology: armed with an armada of French theorists, the environmental humanities survey the charade of early environmentalism as a parade of hippies in denial about the reality of modern life and their own complicity in it. But environmental theory, especially insofar as it stands under the influence of Continental philosophy, suffers from another, even more persistent and problematic, form of modern ideology. It has (not always, to be sure, but for the most part) already decided the question concerning transcendence – and done so in the form of a negation. From Deleuze to Stengers, Latour to Žižek, a consensus has formed that the thought of transcendence is the enemy of ecology. Whether in the form of the traditional devaluation of matter (a certain form of Platonism, but certainly not Plato) or of Christian instrumentalism, transcendence is rejected for allegedly affirming the being of the beyond at the expense of the being of the here and now. Ecology must let go of the transcendent at the same time that it lets go of nature; ecology is immanentism. With Nietzsche, it must abjure the beyond to remain faithful to the earth.

> Let your will say: the overman *shall be* the meaning of the earth! I beseech you, my brothers, *remain faithful to the earth*, and do not believe those who speak to you of otherworldly hopes! Poison-mixers are they, whether they know it or not. Despisers of life are they, decaying and poisoned themselves, of whom the earth is weary: so let them go. (Nietzsche 1882b: 13)

Immanentism in eco-criticism is not usually presented as the conclusion of an argument or a thesis presented for dispute: it is a basic presupposition, and so meets with little objection from the educated public. If the assumption is thematised – that is, if it is presented as a metaphysical position and not, as is usually the case, a self-evident truth – it is advanced (at least in Continental circles) on the questionable presupposition that Heidegger successfully unmasked the history of philosophy as 'onto-theology'. The tacit assumption of the ideology of the day renders many forms of inter-disciplinary ecology less than radical, for they do not challenge our age in its most fundamental ideological core, wherein we casually defect from the religious and hold ourselves to be wiser and more honest than every human civilisation that preceded us (insofar as every civilisation prior to the contemporary age was a religious civilisation, that is, understood itself in the light of transcendence). With the denial of transcendence, the socio-political inflates to the compass of the universe, for it is no longer bounded by anything. In the absence of the transcendent, there is nothing but us and what we do. 'If nature known by the sciences is no longer the ultimate referee able to settle conflicts, then politics has to take over and the common world has to be composed' (Latour 2017: 8). Latour assumes that when nature, as the already unified 'outside' to the political, is debunked by science studies, which exposes the social, institutional and political context of scientific knowledge, so, too, is all transcendence proven to be untenable. Religion is assumed to be the original version of the de-politicisation of nature: insofar as the transcendent is held to anchor human norms in an eternal order, it stands outside the political, and privileges certain speakers (priests and prophets) above others, in exactly the same way that a depol-iticised nature as an order of value-free facts privileges the scientist above others. Now, free of the myth of transcendence, we can get down to the messy work of assembling and disassembling the collective.

Things are not so simple. Transcendence cannot be so easily done away with, for immediately after it is dispensed with, it returns in other forms. Denied, transcendence returns as Nietzsche's overman, as the apotheosis of 'the collective' in Latour, as the absolutisation of 'the mesh' of interdepend-ent beings in Morton – even as, simply, the infinite continuum of matter ('the plane of immanence') in Deleuze. The god will be worshipped, in one form or another. Nature, however, is not the transcendent, and Latour is right: *this* is the truth of the Anthropocene. Nature, which in a political eco-logical context can only really mean the nature that makes possible our lives (nature-for-us, *umwelt*, the world around us, environment), is as fragile and contingent as we are, the contingent product of a series of contingencies. It needs our care if it is to continue to shelter and support human life. That which shelters us must itself be sheltered by us – this is the precarity of living in the Anthropocene (Serres 1995: 11). In short, nature, however massive in comparison with the human, is no less a creature than we are – no less vulnerable to the vicissitudes of time, transformation and decay.

Latour is surely right in asserting that the Anthropocene is not the exaltation of the human but its humiliation. The Anthropocene means a separation is no longer possible between natural and human history. Nature and culture, fact and value, fold in on each other like two ends of a Möbius strip. We are, from a certain reductionist perspective, like bacteria in the Petri dish that continue to reproduce in limited space until poisoned by their own waste. In the Anthropocene, humanity wakes up from its dream of transcending the material conditions of its own existence. This dream did not always accompany the human race; it was the fundamental fantasy of modernity. The fact–value distinction, with its corollary, the separation of nature from culture, is not found in the early Renaissance, the Middle Ages or the ancient world. It is in this sense that the Anthropocene is, or could be, a genuinely postmodern moment. We have now awakened from the delusion of our separateness from nature, of our superiority to all other earthlings: we now know ourselves to be *another* earthling alongside all the others, dependent, like they are, upon this fragile and singular planet that has evolved uniquely to produce a delicately balanced habitat suitable to all our lives, and of which no known parallel exists. We speculate about finding another home for ourselves in the stars, but all the evidence points to the futility of such a dream: if there is another planet with a climate like ours, it is so far away that we will never reach it. The best we can hope for is setting up a colony on a barren planet like Mars, where colonialists will be forced to live the entirety of their lives indoors (sign up for the Mars One project if you can imagine spending the length of your existence inside a mall), with the necessities of life shipped from earth. As Latour puts it, we should not speak of space exploration, but of space transportation:

> You may still spend huge budgets on what used to be called, ironically, the 'conquest of space,' but it will be to transport, at best, half a dozen encapsulated astronauts from a live planet to a few dead ones. Where things will happen is down here and now. Don't dream any more, you mortals. You won't escape to outer space. You have no other abode than down here, the shrinking planet. (Latour 2017: 54)

But the Anthropocene need not mean the death of nature. If we are right that nature is a symbol and not a technical term, its fate is not bound up with the demise of one of its meanings. The Anthropocene certainly means that the modern notion of nature as object – spiritless stuff available for manipulation, a means to the end of human flourishing, the already unified outside of the political – is no longer tenable. But in its absence, other senses of nature emerge, and older, forgotten meanings of nature take on new significance. We need to move into a new era of thinking nature, an era of Anthropocenic nature.

One of the historical associations that the Anthropocene has reactivated is the sense of the finitude of nature, a finitude that does not stand over and against us, which is not finite by virtue of being delimited by human freedom, but which in fact includes us. The Anthropocene is an opportunity to rethink nature as *creature*, that is, as a being like ourselves, one that does not bring itself into existence but for whom existence is unnecessary and accidental. Žižek is right, at least on this point: there is something vaguely religious about the way the symbol of nature functions in contemporary environmentalism. Ecology is the new site of the sacred for us. But the nature held sacred by some ecologists is manifestly not infinite. One of the many tensions in early ecological discourse (Thoreau, Muir, Naess) involves the way this discourse overburdens nature with a sense of divinity that we can no longer reasonably sustain. Disenchantment is not reversible. We do not have access to lost pagan attitudes any more than the child who discovers the real secret behind Santa Claus is able to return to the magic of the Christmas he enjoyed before he learned the devastating truth. We cannot forget the scientific and religious history of the West. The fantasy of a re-enchanted nature must be destroyed to free from its ashes a genuine attitude of *reverence*.[1]

What I have in mind by reverence for nature is analogous to the attitude with which we spontaneously 'respect' (*Achtung* – Kant's word) the humanity of the other. To respect another person is to adopt a posture of 'non-interference' in order to leave them free 'to pursue ends and goals they have chosen for themselves' (Seidler 1986: 19). In Kant's moral theory, one need not mistake the other person for the infinite or for a deity in disguise if one is to respect him. Nor does respect mean that in certain instances a more utilitarian attitude will not be necessary. Kant, for example, recognises that we must routinely use one another, and for this reason 'contracts' are required. The other consents to being used by me so long as my use is conditional and reciprocal (Kant 1797: 62). But the contract is based upon respect. By respecting the other, I recognise in her a spontaneity and destiny that is uniquely her own, just as my path is also my own. Respect is the attitude that sees in the other another self. We respect other persons because we recognise in them the same freedom (or better, responsibility) that we know in ourselves. We should respect such responsibility wherever it is found. This is the solution to the question of the moral worth of artificial intelligence, should one prove possible, or of the cloned human, as soon as we create one. If it shows itself to be morally responsible, that is, if it shows itself to possess freedom, the capacity for good and evil (Schelling 1809: 23) – that is, if it can author itself in the moral sense of the word 'authorship' – act such that we would be compelled to hold it accountable for what it does – then we will have to respect it. To deny it such respect would be to deny it of ourselves, for the AI, the clone, the whatever-it-is-that-we-have-summoned-into-being, will have proven itself indistinguishable from us. To deny humanity to that which proves itself not merely capable of suffering, but of choosing in the moral sense, is inhuman.

But what attitude remains for the non-human? We *worship* the divine, we *respect* persons and we *reverence* the earth and all that thrives upon it. Reverence is not respect; there is a breach of continuity between the human and the non-human earthling that is acknowledged in acts of reverence: we are free; they are not. To deny this is to deny that we have responsibility for reversing the mess we are in – whereas they do not. And yet we do not gaze at them as though they were alien to us. We are opposites, yes, but opposites have origins in common or else they could not be opposed. We see in the non-human something that is also in us, something that we hold sacred and revere in ourselves. If we were to deny them reverence, we would in that same act deny that deepest part of our earthly being. Reverence for nature need not, then, be tied up with a programme of re-enchantment or the spurious adoption of a non-Western or pre-Christian mysticism. Nor do we need to be instructed in it. Rather, it is spontaneous wherever the experiential conditions for its possibility are present. We need regular direct experiences of the dynamic and emerging order of the non-human world. Reverence for nature requires, as Czech philosopher Erazim Kohak argues in his 1984 classic *The Embers and the Stars*, a 'bracketing' of the technological attitude that assumes that everything has meaning only in relation to human beings and their needs.[2]

We must disenchant ourselves once again, if only for the sake of awakening a genuine reverence for nature. Nature is not our God; nature is not infinite. A certain measure of anthropocentrism is, for environmentalism, insurmountable. The very term 'the environment' references one environment among innumerable possible environments, and one for whom that environment environs. Without for a moment denying von Uexküll's multiplicity of worlds, which are as varied as the organisms that constitute and are in turn constituted by them (Cassirer 1944: 23–5), environmentalism concerns nature-for-us, or the world *for* human beings, as it is and might be in the future.

The Anthropocene does not so much give the lie to the nature–culture distinction (Latour's contention) as it does to the modern idealist separation of nature and culture. To distinguish is not to separate, write the Scholastics. I can distinguish my body from my mind even though I may not be able to separate them. Aquinas distinguishes the essence of a tree from its existence without asserting thereby that its essence could float free of its existence (Gilson 2002: 42). If we can no longer cleanly separate natural history from human history, then we are no longer in the Cartesian moment in which a separation of the human from the natural was assumed.

But neither are we back in the pre-Christian cosmology of belonging. We agree with Dark Ecology that neo-Romanticism *is* a problem: disenchantment cannot be reversed. The romance of return that fuels much popular ecology is not helpful: we cannot at this moment in our history legitimately describe ourselves as contained by a *kosmos*. Latour brings this point home trenchantly in his demythologisation of Gaia. The point of Lovelock's hypothesis is not that it uses climate science to refurbish ancient holism, but exactly the opposite: Lovelock uses climate science to disabuse us of the myth of belonging to a universe that is predesigned to host beings such as us. The delicate fine-tuning of temperature, climate and molecular substructure that makes life possible on this planet alone in the solar system, if not in the universe, is not prior to the emergence of life, as though it were a stage set for us to act upon, but emerges simultaneously with life itself. Looking at the barren wastes of other planets, Lovelock asks why an atmosphere uniquely develops on Gaia that keeps water from evaporating into space and produces the oxygen necessary for photosynthesis. He answers that it is life itself, apparently the product of an accident, that produces the gasses that keep the climate warm and oxygen-rich enough for it to flourish. 'Gaia inflicts upon humans a narcissistic wound by bringing them back from an infinite universe to a tiny cosmos' (Latour 2017: 79).

If the ancient paradigm of containment in *kosmos* is no longer viable, neither is the *modern* paradigm of mastery. The Anthropocene means that we cannot continue to think of ourselves as transcendent spirit that floats over the material conditions of existence – we know too clearly that this dissociation from matter will have its revenge upon us. It may be our destiny to be the only bright point of reflection and judgement in the expanse of space-time that surrounds us, and if so, a disavowal of this vocation cannot be the way forward. We have reached a point where natural history and human history merge without collapsing into one another. We cannot say, at least not with any certainty, that the future of nature will be decided politically and not naturally, although much depends on what we do today about anthropogenic climate change. The two sides of being – traditionally distinguished as nature and culture – are in fact one interconnected and twisting surface. It is one history now, since what human beings have done and will do will affect all life on earth. And we share this history with all other earthlings, with the polar bears, the reptiles, the sea and the atmosphere. Our reverence for nature will come, if it will come at all, from this recognition of origins in common.

We need to find a new way of thinking nature without disavowing the human. Deleuzian rhizomes will not do the trick: species egalitarianism also perishes in the Anthropocene since *someone* is clearly responsible, or at lease *has* to *take* responsibility for the future. It has been noted before that it is not just a war of humans versus non-humans that typifies the Anthropocene; it is also a war of certain privileged humans against others who are less privileged and who are destined to bear the worst repercussions of climate change. Our thinking of nature in the Anthropocene needs revision, not jettisoning; we must move toward thinking the coincidence of opposites revealed to us in the Anthropocene, the coincidence of nature and culture. This is the function of a concept of Anthropocenic nature. The Anthropocene is reversible only by means of an unthinkable catastrophe; if we are to imagine a future of nature, and if this imagining is to have political power, it needs to be an Anthropocenic future. In this regard, we might ask: why indeed is it easier for us to imagine the end of the world than the end of consumer-capitalism? Answer: we lack imagination. The failure of the environmental movement is a failure of imagination. If we cannot imagine a planet of 11 billion consumers – if the only outcome of that trajectory is total ecological and (with it) economic collapse – can we at least imagine a planet of 11 billion humans who are no longer consumers? This last point is the thesis for a new discussion, one that no longer separates economy from ecology. For this much can be said with some certainty: one way or another, consumerism *will* come to an end in the Anthropocene.

Like goodness, truth and beauty, nature is one of those dialectical concepts that is meaningless without an opposite. In the ancient world, the opposite of nature (or *physis*, the totality of things that come to be and pass away) was eternity, that which neither comes to be nor passes away. In the Middle Ages, nature was creation and, picking up on the ancient distinction between that which comes to be and passes away, and that which never comes to be and never passes away, the Scholastics spoke of that to which existence is always accidental, *ens finitum*, by distinction from that which *is* eternal, being itself, *ens infinitum* or *ens necessarium*. Thus the opposition advanced in medieval Jewish–Christian cosmology was between nature and the transcendent, a conception that survived into the Renaissance, when it was overturned by the Promethean substitution of the false opposition between human and nature. The Jewish world *interrupts* the ancient world, bringing it to an end, and to fail to see this is to miss the epochal significance of the Hebrew Bible. Something decisive for the birth of the modern happens in the Jewish–Christian context, which underscored the difference in kind between time and eternity. The ancient was inclined to see time as illusion, the play of light eternal on our finite faculties of perception, or, as Plato put it in a memorable phrase, the moving image of eternity (Plato, *Timaeus* 37d). The dialectical opposition between time and eternity was ultimately appearance, not reality. If we could see things as they really are, we would see that sensible nature does not exist; there is only eternal nature, which is its archetype. In the Jewish–Christian context, the dialectical relation of time to eternity, of nature to divinity, is rendered real: sensible nature is not just a copy of eternal nature; it really is other than eternity, and while it depends on eternity for its essence and existence, it is, no less, set free from eternity and rendered, in the act of creation, a thing in its own right.

We have seen how, with the medieval move from emanation to creation, nature suffers a first disenchantment: divested of spirit, it becomes a contingent thing, dependent upon something other than itself for its existence. In Platonic and Aristotelian philosophy, nature's materiality, its implication in processes of coming to be and passing away, does not disenchant it in the least, even if it breaks with primitive forms of nature worship, for what comes to be and passes away in nature are nothing other than the eternal forms of being that constitute the divine. Nature (even for Aristotle) was thus participation in eternity, or emanation of divinity, a dramatisation of a plurality that truly exists as a unity. Without a sense of *creatio ex nihilo*, the ancients did not separate eternal spirit and contingent nature; the latter was a manifestation of the former, as the colours streaming from a prism are refractions of the one light that enters it from the other side. With the theological notion of *creatio*, and only with it, nature is set apart from the divine and at the same time given a definite boundary. All that happened in nature was expressive of divinity, but nature itself was not the divine: it was set apart from divinity so that it might be something for itself. Nature thus had an opposite, and its other was God.

It bears restating that it is hard to pinpoint an exact beginning of modernity. (The invention of the printing press? The rise of the mercantile class in the late Middle Ages? The Renaissance? The Reformation?) But we can say this: modernity is found wherever the dialectical opposition between nature and God is replaced by a dialectical opposition between nature and humankind. For the modern, nature's other is 'man', who now arrogates to himself the claim to being 'spirit' exclusively. Because he alone is spirit, nature is there for him to use – as in Fichte's philosophy, where nature is understood to be something produced by spirit as its other, that being posited by spirit through which spirit realises itself by overcoming and domesticating it. Descartes, of course, is the more typical culprit in this regard, and when he defines the human as *res cogitans*, over and against *res extensa*, he denies cognition, consciousness and sensitivity of every extended being – everything that is *essentially*, rather than accidentally (like the human being), material. He is most vilified for the dualism he introduces into anthropology, with the body now an instrument of the mind and, as such, accidental to human identity (Descartes ought to be declared, for this reason, the patron saint of VR), but he might also be remembered as the one who most emphatically denies spirit of nature. Cartesian arguments were used to justify vivisection in early modernity: since the animal was not genuinely, that is, spiritually alive, there was no reason not to slice it open and peer into the machine of its inner workings. In Kant, the spirit–nature opposition is compounded by the notion of freedom as transcendence of the network of cause and effects that constitutes nature, an inexplicable transcendence, to be sure, but for Kant, an undeniable one, and evidence that we have our roots and our destiny in another world. Schelling rebelled and insisted that nature, too, was spirit, albeit in unconscious form, but it is not clear whether he succeeded in extricating anthropology from this modern hubris. After all, the 'Freedom Essay' ends with a retrieval of the noumenal nature of freedom: to be free is to have one's genuine being self-authored in eternity (Schelling 1809: 49f.). With the Anthropocene, the bubble bursts: we are manifestly not the kind of transcendent spirit that could lift itself at will above matter – we are of matter and vulnerable to its history.

But why should this humiliation be understood as the negation of transcendence? Is it not in fact the opposite? Is Anthropocenic humiliation not the rehabilitation of an authentic notion of transcendence? *We* are not the transcendent; rather, we belong on one side of the boundary, along with everything else that exists in space and time. The Anthropocene is a return to a theological sense of nature, as Pope Francis makes clear in his intervention into the climate-change debate, the encyclical *Laudato si'* (Francis 2015). With the return to a theological sense of nature, we move *ahead* into a new era of thinking the finitude of the creature, one unknown in previous ages of the Church. The Christian theological sense of the term 'nature' had a distinct advantage over the modern sense: it neither idealised the human nor divested the natural of 'values'. Nature as God's 'other' could never be good or bad in any human sense. It is better described as awesome, terrible, worthy of equal parts fear and reverence. It is what Rudolf Otto called the numinous, the *mysterium tremendum et fascinans* (Otto 1950). Such a coincidence of feelings would make good sense of the conflicting emotions bound up with the varieties of eco-anxiety prevalent today. Nature, our dreams are telling us, is both homey and horrific, both comfortable and cruel. Insofar as it is created, every entity in the cosmos necessarily reveals the Creator, but in so doing, it reveals the non-necessity of creaturely existence and thus the Creator's terrible freedom.[3]

Those unfamiliar with the long and venerable tradition of Catholic social teaching are prone to misplace the radicality of *Laudato si'*. It is not radical to have a Pope speak informedly and critically on economy, politics and social justice. So did Leo XIII, Pius XI, John XXIII, Paul VI, John Paul II and Benedict XVI. *Laudato si'* belongs alongside *Rerum Novarum*, written by Leo XIII in 1891, an encyclical that broke down the barriers between the armies of underpaid and angry workers indentured by industrialism and the Church. It belongs with *Quadragesimo Anno*, the 1931 encyclical of Pius XI, which critiqued the immorality of keeping economic control in the hands of the few. It belongs alongside the 1991 encyclical *Centisimus Annus* written by John Paul II, which reminded the world that before politics was reduced to an either–or between two equally reductionist modern alternatives, capitalism *or* communism, a third way was possible, which neither denied the individual the right to property nor delivered up humanity to the mechanics of the free market, but, rather, freed the individual to seek his fulfilment and moral perfection through his work while placing restrictions on the power of capital to level social institutions and dissolve communities. Francis has contributed to this long if little-appreciated tradition of papal teachings on social justice. What is truly innovative about *Laudato si'* is that, at a stroke, it connects the social crisis of late capitalism, the amassing of wealth in the hands of the few, the disenfranchisement of whole populations of humans, to the environmental crisis, and in particular to climate change. Ecology is not only about the interdependence of species on the ecosystems that make them possible. It is also about the interdependence of social injustice and environmental injustice.

Pope Francis has connected the two ends of the Möbius strip, just as surely as has Latour. The human predicament can no longer be separated from the ecological predicament, but not because the human being is nothing, but because the degradation of the earth is essentially connected to the degradation of human society. The demise of the one is the demise of the other and vice versa. Interdependence, the Pope argues, is to be understood theologically: care for our fellow human beings and care for the environment are the same thing. This point can be interpreted in a purely secular key: we must not talk about preserving wilderness and biodiversity and reducing pollution without also talking about a more just distribution of the finite resources of our common earth. Otherwise put, we will not have a sound ecology until we also have a sound anthropology: environmentalism needs to be grounded in an authentic humanism if it is to become a global politics. However academically sophisticated, the anti-humanist ecology on offer has little political power to influence policy or ordinary people. Put it this way: how are you going to get people to care about something in which they have no part?

Most importantly, Pope Francis wishes to assert, against modern dualism, the solidarity of creation, the home common to humanity and all life. Nature is not our other; we are of nature; we are thinking nature. In the face of the Anthropocene, we need to recognise that our home is in peril and that the purely scientific fixes on offer are not enough. The ecological crisis facing the world requires a degree of collaboration and integration of theory and practice never before seen in human history. If it is to happen, it will come about not through the universal adoption of a single unified theory of ecology and economy. Rather, we will be united in response to a common threat. The destruction of the other's habitat will be known to be our loss also. Only thus will the recognition dawn on us that, however diverse we may be in ethnic origin, religion, economic class, political view, or even species, what we have in common – this delicate garden called planet earth – is more important than what divides us. In a deft retrieval of a misused term, Francis calls the mobilisation of all human knowledge and practice in the service of the health of the earth 'integral ecology': all academic disciplines, all human endeavours, from palaeontology to poetry, from sociology to spirituality, are needed now for the sake of collaboratively producing a programme of care for our common home.

This, then, is Anthropocenic nature: nature as creature, not Creator; immanent, not transcendent; as contingent and dependent as we are; full of beauty and ugliness; good and evil; in part organic and in part artificial; in part habitable and in part uninhabitable; in part alive and in part non-living; in part material and in part immaterial; and everywhere in need of us as much as we are in need of it. Nature is gift, and as gift, it has a fearsome contingency about it. No gift need be given; the gift that must be given is no gift. To be gifted is to be the contingent recipient of a contingency. To use an excellent theological term, it is to be graced. Nature profiled against the *anthropos* is not wilderness (which was too easy to mistake for divinity) but a cultivated garden made habitable for over 7 billion human and non-human lives. This is nature, for us, now. As Saint Francis says in his Canticle, nature reminds us of God in its glory and beauty, but nature is not God. It is of the same substance of which we are made: it is sister and brother. As such, it deserves better than we have offered it of late.

To revere the earth in the Anthropocene is to acknowledge, in a new way, its sacredness. But no sense of the sacred is possible in the absence of transcendence. Sacredness is the very feeling of transcendence; it is the phenomenality of the transcendent. I feel the sacredness of a gift because I recognise how the freedom out of which it was given transcends the order of necessity that otherwise governs human relations. The gift is horizoned by the unfathomable freedom of the other. It has a 'beyond' quality. So too does the earth. We need to use it to live, but the use of a thing does not preclude reverence for it and its origin. I may indeed use a gift and continue to reverence the gift-act that makes it a gift. My claim to ownership of a gift does not divest it of its giftedness. Only this can politically unite the earth community: a sober recognition of our common origin and a universal (and legally binding) acknowledgement that these material conditions (air, land, water) are the very limits of life itself and so should not be commodified: they are neither possessions nor rights, since without them one cannot possess or claim any right at all. They are beyond the relations that rule all other interactions on earth. We revere the earth because it is the very gift of life itself. And because we are all equally the receivers of the gift, the earth makes us one. We revere the earth, then, also because its ultimate gift is not only life under any circumstances, but sustainable life, life at peace with itself. We revere the life-giver and the peacemaker. I don't think Jesus would mind if we added to the Beatitudes, for in the Anthropocene we have come to recognise that peace is not an option but a necessity if the human race is to continue – and that it will not be produced by a merely human collective but must be given by the earth that gives us everything. Blessed be the earth, the peacemaker; revere her, for without her you shall perish, and with her all things are possible. Blessed be the earth, the peacemaker, for it shall be called child of God.

Notes

1. The term 'reverence' has a history in ecology. Albert Schweitzer received the 1952 Nobel Peace Prize for his concept of a universal ethic based on 'reverence for all life' (*Ehrfurcht vor dem Leben*). On a boat trip on the Ogooué River in French Equatorial Africa in 1915, where he was travelling to set up the Albert Schweitzer Hospital, Schweitzer became obsessed with the question of what principle was sufficiently universal and secular to found a global ethic. He hit upon the phrase 'reverence for all life' one evening as the barge passed by a herd of hippopotamuses at sunset. See Schweitzer (1931: 154–5). We revere life, according to Schweitzer, because 'we are life that wishes to live and are animated by a will in the midst of other lives animated by the same will' (Schweitzer, cited in Brabazon 2000: 271). My use of the term 'reverence' differs in two important ways from Schweitzer's: first, I do not limit reverence to life, and so disentangle it from vitalism and the ethics of a will to live. I would rather attach it to the gift-quality of the earth, and so extend it to water, air, minerals, molecules, et cetera. Second, I do not hesitate to argue that reverence should be accompanied by moral judgement such that we recognise among 'the things that are' those things that should not be (and that we ought to destroy – for example, the Aids virus).

2. Kohak built himself a house in the woods of New Hampshire 'beyond the power-line' in the 1980s, not to flee civilisation but to conduct an experiment. He wanted to see what would happen to his sense of value when he was momentarily removed from the artificial environment (Boston) in which he passed his workdays. What he discovered is that the things that grow, thrive and die without our interference have an agenda of their own. In the 'radical brackets of the forest clearing', an affirmation of value that was not possible, or very difficult, in the city, became spontaneous for Kohak, the 'radical opening of our life and thought to the world of others, human, animate, inanimate, in the integrity of its otherness and the meaningfulness of its being' (Kohak 1984: 207).

3. Pope Francis's encyclical gains its title from Saint Francis's 'Canticle of the Sun', which begins with an affirmation of the creatureliness, the finitude, of nature. 'Be

praised, my Lord [*Laudato si*], through all your creatures, especially through my lord Brother Sun, who brings the day; and you give light through him. And he is beautiful and radiant in all his splendour! Of you, Most High, he bears the likeness. Praise be You, my Lord, through Sister Moon and the stars, in heaven you formed them clear and precious and beautiful.' It is worth remembering that Lynn White Jr finishes his breakthrough essay with a plea to remember Saint Francis (White 1967).

Bibliography

Translation of scripture used: The New English Bible. Oxford: Oxford University Press, 1961.

Abraham, Lyndy. 1998. *A Dictionary of Alchemical Imagery*. Cambridge: Cambridge University Press.

Alexis, André. 2015. *Fifteen Dogs*. London: Serpent's Tail Books.

American Psychological Association. 2011. *Psychology and Global Climate Change: Addressing a Multifaceted Phenomenon and Set of Challenges. Report of the Task Force on the Interface Between Psychology and Global Climate Change*. Washington, DC: APA.

Anderson, Fulton. 1960. Editor's introduction. *The New Organon* by Francis Bacon, pp. vi–xxxviii. New York: Prentice Hall.

Anthers, Günther. 2007. *Le Temps de la Fin*. Paris: L'Herne.

Aquinas, Thomas. 1485. *Summa Theologica*. Trans. Fathers of the English Dominican Province. New York: Benzinger Brothers, 1948.

Augustine. 426 *City of God*. Ed. David Knowles. Trans. Henry Betterson. New York: Penguin, 1972.

Baader, Franz von. 1851–60. *Sämtliche Werke*. 16 vols. Neudruck der Ausgabe Leipzig. Ed. Franz Hoffmann and Julius Hamberger. Scientia Verlag Aalen, 1963.

Bacon, Francis. 1620. *The New Organon*. Ed. Fulton H. Anderson. New York: Macmillan, 1960.

Badiou, Alain. 2003. *Saint Paul: The Foundation of Universalism*. Trans. Ray Brassier. Palo Alto: Stanford University Press.

Bates, David, 2000. 'The Mystery of Truth: Louis-Claude de Saint-Martin's Enlightened Mysticism'. *Journal of the History of Ideas*, 61: 4, 635–55.

Belloc, Hilaire. 1912. *The Servile State*. New York: Cosimo Books, 2007.

Bennett, Jane. 2010. *Vibrant Matter: A Political Ecology of Things*. Durham, NC: Duke University Press.

Benz, Ernst. 1965. *Evolution and Christian Hope: Man's Concept of the Future, From the Early Fathers to Teilhard de Chardin*. Trans. Heinz G. Frank. Garden City: Anchor Books, 1968.

Berdyaev, Nicolai. 1965. *Christian Existentialism: A Berdyaev Synthesis*. Selected and trans. Donald A. Lowrie. New York: Harper and Row.

Berman, Joshua A. 2008. *Created Equal: How the Bible Broke with Ancient Political Thought*. Oxford: Oxford University Press.

Bigg, Charles. 1886. *The Christian Platonists of Alexandria*. Oxford: Oxford University Press.

Blanco, Carlos. 2013. 'God, the Future, and the *Fundamentum* of History in Wolfhart Pannenberg'. *Heythrop Journal*, 54:2, 301–11.

Bloch, Ernst. 1954. *The Principle of Hope*. Trans. Neville Plaice et al. Cambridge, MA: MIT Press, 1986.

Blumenberg, Hans. 1966. *The Legitimacy of the Modern Age*. Trans. Robert Wallace. Cambridge, MA: MIT Press, 1983.

Bohm, David. 1980. *Wholeness and the Implicate Order*. London: Routledge.

Böhme, Jakob. 1997. *Jacob Böhme Werke*. Ed. Ferdinand van Ingen. Frankfurt: Deutscher Klassiker Verlag.

Bonardel, Françoise. 1992. 'Alchemical Esotericism and the Hermeneutics of Culture'. In *Modern Esoteric Spirituality*, pp. 71–100. Ed. Antoine Faivre and Jacob Needleman. New York: Crossroads.

Bonhoeffer, Dietrich. 2009. *Letters and Papers from Prison*. Ed. Eberhard Bethge. Minneapolis: Fortress Press.

Brabazon, James. 2000. *Albert Schweitzer: A Biography*. Second edition. Syracuse: Syracuse University Press.

Bradley, James. 2012. 'Philosophy and Trinity'. *Symposium*, 16:1, 155–78.

Brassier, Ray. 2007. *Nihil Unbound*. London: Palgrave Macmillan.

Brüntrup, Godehard and Ludwig Jaskolla. 2017. *Panpsychism: Contemporary Perspectives*. Oxford: Oxford University Press.

Burkhardt, Jacob. 1860. *The Civilization of the Renaissance in Italy*. Trans. S. G. C. Middlemore. London: Penguin, 1990.

Campbell, Colin. 1987. *The Romantic Ethic and the Spirit of Modern Consumerism*. Oxford: Basil Blackwell.

Cammaerts, Emile. 1937. *The Laughing Prophet: The Seven Virtues and G. K. Chesterton*. London: Methuen.

Caputo, John D. 1978. 'Fundamental Themes in Meister Eckhart's Mysticism'. *The Thomist*, 42:2, 197–225.

Cassirer, Ernst. 1944. *An Essay on Man: An Introduction to the Philosophy of Human Culture*. New Haven: Yale University Press.

—. 1963. *The Individual and the Cosmos in Renaissance Philosophy*. Trans. Mario Domandi. University of Pennsylvania Press.

Chadwick, Owen. 1964. *The Reformation*. Harmondsworth: Penguin.

Chakrabarty, Dipesh. 2009. 'The Climate of History: Four Theses'. *Critical Inquiry*, 35:2, 197–222.

Chalmers, David. 1996. *The Conscious Mind: In Search of a Fundamental Theory*. Oxford: Oxford University Press.

Chesterton, G. K. 1910. *What's Wrong with the World*. San Francisco: Ignatius Press, 1994.

Cloots, André. 2008. 'Modernity and Christianity: Marcel Gauchet on the Christian Roots of the Modern Ways of Thinking'. *Milltown Studies*, 61, 1–30.

Collingwood, R. G. 1940. *An Essay on Metaphysics*. Oxford: Clarendon.

Coward, Harold and Toby Foshay, ed. 1992. *Derrida and Negative Theology*. Albany: State University of New York Press.

Culianu, Ioan P. 1987. *Eros and Magic in the Renaissance*. Chicago: University of Chicago Press.

Cunsolo, Ashlee. 2012. *Lament for the Land: On the Impacts of Climate Change on Mental and Emotional Health and Well-Being in Rigolet, Nunatsiavut, Canada*. Online <http://hdl.handle.net/10214/3545> (accessed 20 September 2018).

Cusanus, Nicholas. 1440. *Of Learned Ignorance*. Trans. Germain Heron. London: Routledge & Kegan Paul, 1954.

Danowski, Déborah, and Eduardo Viveiros de Castro. 2017. *The Ends of the World*. Cambridge: Polity Press.

Deleuze, Gilles, and Felix Guattari. 1983. *Anti-Oedipus: Capitalism and Schizophrenia*. Trans. Robert Hurley, Mark Seem and Hele R. Lane. Minneapolis: University of Minnesota Press.

Derrida, Jacques. 2007. 'No Apocalypse, Not Now: Full Speed Ahead, Seven Missiles, Seven Missives'. In *Psyche: Inventions of the Other, Vol. 1*, pp. xx–yy. Ed. Peggy Kamuf and Elizabeth Rottenberger. Stanford: Stanford University Press.

Dilthey, Wilhelm. 1883. *Introduction to the Human Sciences*. Trans. Ramon J. Betanzos. Detroit: Wayne State University Press, 1988.

Dodd, C. H. 1958. *The Meaning of Paul for Today*. London: Collins.

Dupré, Louis. 1993. *Passage to Modernity: A Hermeneutics of Nature and Culture*. New Haven: Yale University Press.

Eckhart, Meister. 1941. *Meister Eckhart: A Modern Translation*. Trans. Raymond B. Blackney. New York: Harper and Row.

—. 1965. *Deutsche Predigten und Traktate*. Ed. Josef Quint. Munich: Carl Hanser.

Edenhofer, Ottmar, et al. 2014. *Climate Change 2014: Mitigating Climate Change*. Intergovernmental Panel on Climate Change. New York: Cambridge University Press.

Ellenberger, Henry F. 1970. *The Discovery of the Unconscious: The History and Evolution of Dynamic Psychiatry*. New York: Basic Books.

Faivre, Antoine. 1992. 'Ancient and Medieval Sources of Modern Esoteric Movements'. In *Modern Esoteric Spirituality*, pp. 1–70. Ed. Antoine Faivre and Jacob Needleman. New York: Crossroads.

Fancher, Hampton, and David Peoples. 1981. *Bladerunner: A Screenplay*. Online <http://www.dailyscript.com/scripts/blade-runner_shooting.html> (accessed 20 September 2018).

Fenech, Adam, Jay Foster, Kirk Hamilton, and Roger Hansell. 2003. 'Natural Capital in Ecology and Economics: An Overview.' *Environmental Monitoring and Assessment*, 86, 3–17.

Fink, Bruce. 1995. *The Lacanian Subject*. Princeton: Princeton University Press.

Foltz, Bruce. 1995. *Inhabiting the Earth: Heidegger, Environmental Ethics, and the Metaphysics of Nature*. London: Humanities Press.

Forshaw, Peter. 2012. 'Infinite Fire Webinar I: The Alchemy of the Amphitheatrum'. Online <http://www.ritmanlibrary.com/2012/10/infinite-fire-webinar-series-i-the-alchemy-of-the-amphitheatrum> (accessed 20 September 2018).

Foster, Jay. 2003. 'Between Economics and Ecology: Some Historical and Philosophical Considerations for Modelers of Natural Capital.'*Environmental Monitoring and Assessment*. 86.

Foucault, Michel. 1966. *The Order of Things: An Archeology of the Human Sciences*. London: Routledge, 2002.

Francis I. 2015. *Encyclical on Climate Change and Inequality: On Care for Our Common Home*. Brooklyn: Melville.

Fritsch, Matthias. 2017. '"La Justice Doit Porter Au-Delà de la Vie Présente". Derrida on Ethics Between Generations'. *Symposium*, 21:1, 231–53.

Gascoigne, John. 2010. 'The Religious Thought of Francis Bacon'. In *Religion and Retributive Logic. Essays in Honour of Garry W. Trompf*, pp. 209-228. Ed. Carole Cusack and Christopher Hartley. Leiden: Brill.

Gauchet, Marcel. 1985. *The Disenchantment of the World: A Political History of Religion*. Trans. Oscar Burge. Princeton: Princeton University Press, 1999.

Gilbert, Bruce. 2017. 'Hegel and the Imperatives of Love'. *Symposium*, 21:1, 18–37.

Gilding, Paul. 2011. *The Great Disruption: Why the Climate Crisis Will Bring on the End of Shopping and the Birth of a New World*. London: Bloomsbury Press.

Gillespie, Michael Allen. 2009. *The Theological Origins of Modernity*. Chicago: University of Chicago Press.

Gilson, Etienne. 1955. *History of Christian Philosophy in the Middle Ages*. New York: Random House.

—. 2002. *Thomism: The Philosophy of Thomas Aquinas*. Trans. Armand Mauer. Toronto: Pontifical Institute of Medieval Studies.

Gogarten, Friedrich. 1953. *Verhängnis und Hoffnung der Neuzeit: Die Säkularisierung als theologisches Problem*. Stuttgart: Friedrich Vorwek Verlag.

Grant, George. 1987. 'Thinking about Technology'. In *Technology and Justice*, pp. 11–34. Notre Dame: University of Notre Dame Press.

—. 2002. *Collected Works of George Grant, Vol. 2: 1951–59*. Ed. Arthur Davis. Toronto: University of Toronto Press.

Guénon, René. 1945. *The Reign of Quantity and the Signs of the Times*. Trans. Lord Northbourne. Hillsdale: Sophia Perennis, 2001.

Haff, Peter K. 2014. 'Technology as a Geological Phenomenon: Implications for Human Well-Being'. *Geological Society of London: Special Publications*, 395, 301–9.

Hall, Calvin S. 1999. *A Primer of Freudian Psychology*. New York: Meridian.

Hamburg, Carl H. 1956. *Symbol and Reality: Studies in the Philosophy of Ernst Cassirer*. The Hague: Martinus Nijhoff.

Hawken, Paul, Amory B. Lovins and L. Hunter Lovins. 1999. *Natural Capitalism: Creating the Next Industrial Revolution*. Little, Brown & Company.

Hegel, G. W. F. 1827. The Lectures of 1827. In *Hegel's Lectures on the Philosophy of Religion*. One-volume edition. Ed. Peter C. Hodgson. Berkeley: University of California Press, 1988.

—. *Hegel's Science of Logic*. Trans. A.V. Miller. London: George Allen & Unwin Ltd, 1969.

—. 1832. *Lectures on the Philosophy of Religion. Vol. 3*. Trans. R. F. Brown, P. C. Hodgson and J. M. Stewart with the assistance of H. S. Harris. Oxford: Clarendon Press, 2007.

Heidegger, Martin. 1927. *Being and Time*. Trans. John Macquarrie and Edward Robinson. Oxford: Blackwell, 1962.

—. 1930. 'Vom Wesen der Wahrheit'. In *Wegmarken*, pp. 177–202. Frankfurt am Main: Vittorio Klostermann, 1967.

—. 1951a. 'Dichterisch wohnet der Mensch'. In *Vortraege und Aufsaetze*, pp. 181–98. Pfullingen: Neske.

—. 1951b. 'Building Dwelling Thinking'. In *Martin Heidegger: Basic Writings*, pp. 347–63. Ed. David Farrell Krell. Trans. Albert Hofstadter. London: Harper, 2008.

—. 1954. 'The Question Concerning Technology'. In *The Question Concerning Technology and Other Essays*, pp. 3–35. Trans. William Lovitt. New York: Garland Publishing, 1977.

—. 1959. 'Memorial Address'. In *Discourse on Thinking*, pp. 43–57. A translation of *Gelassenheit*. Trans. John M. Anderson and E. Hans Freund. New York: Harper and Row. 1966.

—. 1989. *Contributions to Philosophy (of the Event)*. Trans. Richard Rojcewicz and Daniela Vallega-Neu. Bloomington: Indiana University Press, 2012.

Henry, John. 2002. *The Scientific Revolution and the Origins of Modern Science*. Second edition. New York: Palgrave Macmillan.

Hillman, James. 1975. *Re-visioning Psychology*. New York: Harper and Row.

Hochschild, Joshua P. 2010. *The Semantics of Analogy: Rereading Cajetan's* De Nominum Analogia. University of Notre Dame Press.

Horkheimer, Max. 1947. *Eclipse of Reason*. New York: Seabury Press, 1974.

Joyce, James. 1939. *Finnigan's Wake*. London: Faber and Faber.

Jung, C .G. 1948. 'The Spirit Mercurius'. In C. G. Jung, *Alchemical Studies*, pp. 191–250. *The Collected Works of C. G. Jung*, Vol. 13. Ed. Herbert Read, Michael Fordham, Gerhard Adler and William McGuire. Princeton: Princeton University Press, 1967

—. 1961. *Memories, Dreams, Reflections*. Recorded and edited by Aniela Jaffé. Trans. Richard and Clara Winston. New York: Vintage Books, 1989.

—. 1971. *Psychological Types*. Trans. H. G. Baynes. Princeton: Princeton University Press.

Kahn, Brian. 2015. 'Scientists Predict Huge Sea Level Rise Even If We Limit Climate Change'. *The Guardian*, 10 July. Online <https://www.theguardian.com/environment/2015/jul/10/scientists-predict-huge-sea-level-rise-even-if-we-limit-climate-change> (accessed 20 September 2018).

Kant, Immanuel. 1784. 'What is Enlightenment?' Trans. Carl J. Friedrich. In *The Philosophy of Kant: Immanuel Kant's Moral and Political Writings*, pp. 132–9. Edited by Carl J. Friedrich. New York: The Modern Library, 1949.

Kant, Immanuel. 1790. *Critique of Judgment*. Trans. Werner S. Pluhar. Cambridge: Hackett, 1987.

—. 1797. *The Metaphysics of Morals*. Trans. Mary Gregor. Cambridge: Cambridge University Press, 1996.

Kerslake, Christian. 2007. *Deleuze and the Unconscious*. New York: Continuum.

Kierkegaard, Soren. 1843. *Fear and Trembling*. Trans. Howard V. Hong and Edna H. Hong. Princeton: Princeton University Press, 1983.

—. 1844. *The Concept of Anxiety*. Ed. and trans. Reidar Thomts and Alber B. Anderson. Princeton: Princeton University Press, 1980.

Klein, Naomi. 2014. *This Changes Everything: Capitalism vs the Climate*. New York: Simon and Shuster.

Kohak, Erazim. 1984. *The Embers and the Stars: A Philosophical Inquiry into the Moral Sense of Nature*. Chicago: University of Chicago Press.

Kolbert, Elizabeth. 2015. 'If We Burned All the Fossil Fuel in the World'. *New Yorker*, 11 September.

Lacan, Jacques. 1973. *The Four Fundamental Concepts of Psychoanalysis*. Ed. Jacques-Alain Miller. Trans. Alain Sheridan. London: Vintage, 1998.

Langer, Susanne K. 1957. *Philosophy in a New Key: A Study in the Symbolism of Reason, Rite, and Art*. Third edition. Cambridge, MA: Harvard University Press.

Latour, Bruno. 2002. *Rejoicing or the Torments of Religious Speech*. Cambridge: Polity, 2013.

—. 2004. *The Politics of Nature: How to Bring the Sciences into Democracy*. Trans. Catherine Porter. Cambridge, MA: Harvard University Press.

—. 2011. 'Waiting for Gaia: Composing the Common World Through Arts and Politics.' Lecture at the French Institute, London. Online <http://www.bruno-latour.fr/sites/default/files/124-GAIA-LONDON-SPEAP_0.pdf> (accessed 15 October 2018).

—. 2015. 'The Other State of Emergency'. Trans. by Jane Kuntz. Oped published in *Reporterre*, 23 November. Online <http://www.bruno-latour.fr/sites/default/files/downloads/REPORTERRE-11-15-GB_0.pdf> (accessed 20 September 2018).

—. 2017. *Facing Gaia: Eight Lectures on the New Climatic Regime*. Trans. Cathy Porter. Cambridge: Polity Press.

— and Steve Woolgar. 1979. *Laboratory Life*. Princeton: Princeton University Press.

Leahy, D. G. 1994. *Novitas Mundi: Perception of the History of Being*. Albany: State University of New York Press.

Lenoir, Frédéric. 2003. *Les Métamorphoses de Dieu*. Paris: Plon.

Lertzman, Renee Aron. 2013. 'The Myth of Apathy: Psychoanalytic Explorations of Environmental Subjectivity'. In *Engaging with Climate Change: Psychoanalytic and Interdisciplinary Perspectives*, pp. 117–33. Ed. Sally. Weintrobe. New York: Routledge.

Lévy-Bruhl, Lucien. 1926. *How Natives Think*. Trans. Lilian A. Clare. London: G. Allen and Unwin.

Lonergan, Bernard. 1957. *Insight: A Study in Human Understanding*. Fifth edition. Ed. Frederick E. Crowe and Robert M. Doran. Toronto: University of Toronto Press, 1992.

—. 1971. *Method in Theology*. Toronto: University of Toronto Press.

—. 1990. *Understanding and Being: The Halifax Lectures on Insight*. Ed. Elizabeth A. Morelli and Mark D. Morelli. Toronto: University of Toronto Press.

Lovelock, James. 1979. *Gaia: A New Look at Life on Earth*. Oxford: Oxford University Press, 1995.

—. 2006. *The Revenge of Gaia: Earth's Climate in Crisis and the Fate of Humanity*. New York: Basic Books.

Löwith, Karl. 1949. *Meaning in History: The Theological Implications of the Philosophy of History*. Chicago: University of Chicago Press.

Luther, Martin. 1516. *Lecture on Romans*. Trans. Walter G. Tillmanns and Jacob A. O. Preuss. *Luther's Works, Vol. 25*. Saint Louis: Concordia University Press, 1972.

—. 1518. 'Heidelberg Disputation'. In *Luther's Works, Vol. 31: Career of the Reformer*, pp. 39–58. Ed. Harold J. Grimm and Helmut T. Lehmann. Augsburg: Fortress Press, 1957.

Magee, Glenn Alexander. 2001. *Hegel and the Hermetic Tradition*. Ithaca: Cornell University Press.

Maritain, Jacques, 1940. *Scholasticism and Politics*. Trans. Mortimer J. Adler. London: Geoffrey Bles.

McGinn, Bernard, trans. and ed. 1981. *Meister Eckhart: The Essential Sermons, Commentaries, Treatises, and Defense*. New York: Paulist Press.

—. 1986. *Meister Eckhart: Teacher and Preacher*. Trans. Bernard McGinn. New York: Paulist Press.

McGrath, Sean J. 2003. 'Toward a Technology that Allows the Beautiful to Occur'. *Animus*, 8, 11–20. Online <http://www2.swgc.mun.ca/animus/Articles/Volume%208/mcgrath8.pdf> (accessed 20 September 2018).

—. 2006. *The Early Heidegger and Medieval Philosophy: Phenomenology for the Godforsaken*. Washington, DC: Catholic University of America Press.

—. 2008a. *Heidegger: A (Very) Critical Introduction*. Grand Rapids: Eerdmans.

—. 2008b. 'Heidegger and Medieval German Mysticism'. *Heinrich-Seuse-Jahrbuch*, 1, 71–102.

—. 2012. *The Dark Ground of Spirit: Schelling and the Unconscious*. London: Routledge.

—. 2013. 'The Logic of Indirection in Heidegger and Aquinas'. *Heythrop Journal*, 54:2, 268–80.

—. 2014a. 'The Question Concerning Nature'. In *Interpreting Nature: The Emerging Field of Environmental Hermeneutics*, pp. 211–24. Ed. Brian Treanor and Forrest Clingerman. New York: Fordham University Press.

—. 2014b. 'Melancholy, Death, and the Longing for Being in Schelling's *Clara*'. In *Melancholia: The Disease of the Soul*, ed. Dariusz Skorczewski and Andrzej Wiercinski. Catholic University of Lublin.

—. 2014c. 'The Theology of Consumerism'. *Analecta Hermeneutica*, 6.

—. 2018a. 'In Defense of the Human Difference'. *Environmental Philosophy*, 15:1, 101–15.

—. 2018b. 'Friedrich Christoph Oetinger's Speculative Pietism'. *Kabiri*, 1, 175-92.

McKibben, Bill. 1989. *The End of Nature*. New York: Random House.

McLuhan, Marshall. 1962. *The Guttenberg Galaxy: The Making of Typographic Man*. Toronto: University of Toronto Press.

Merchant, Carolyn, 1980. *The Death of Nature: Women, Ecology, and the Scientific Revolution*. New York: HarperCollins.

Merton, Thomas. 1961. *New Seeds of Contemplation*. New York: New Directions.

Mills, Stephanie. 2008. 'Going Back to Nature When Nature's All But Gone'. *Environmental Philosophy*, 5, 1–8.

Molloy, Michael. 2006. *Experiencing the World's Religions: Tradition, Challenge, and Change*. New York: McGraw-Hill Education.

Moltmann, Jürgen, 1967. *Theology of Hope: On the Ground and the Implications of a Christian Eschatology*. Trans. James W. Leitch. New York: Harper and Row.

—. 1980. *The Trinity and the Kingdom*. Trans. Margaret Kohl. Minneapolis: Fortress Press.

Morton, Timothy. 2007. *Ecology Without Nature.* Cambridge, MA: Harvard University Press.

—. 2010a. *The Ecological Thought.* Cambridge, MA: Harvard University Press.

—. 2010b. 'Thinking Ecology: The Mesh, the Strange Stranger, and the Beautiful Soul'. *Collapse,* 6, 195–223.

—. 2013. *Hyperobjects: Philosophy and Ecology after the End of the World.* Minneapolis: University of Minnesota Press.

Naess, Arne. 1977. 'Spinoza and Ecology'. *Philosophia,* 7, 45–54.

Nagel, Thomas. 2012. *Mind and Cosmos: Why the Materialist Neo-Darwinian Conception of Nature Is Almost Certainly False.* Oxford: Oxford University Press.

Nietzsche, Friedrich. 1882a. *The Gay Science.* Trans. and ed. Walter Kaufmann. New York: Vintage, 1974.

—. 1882b. *Thus Spoke Zarathustra.* Trans. Walter Kaufmann. New York: Penguin Books, 1966.

Oetinger, Friedrich Christoph. 1776. *Biblisches und Emblematisches Wörterbuch.* Ed. Gerhard Schäfer. In two parts. In *Texte zur Geschichte des Pietismus.* Ed. Gerhard Schäfer. Abteil VII, Band 3. Berlin: Walter De Gruyter, 1999.

O'Regan, Cyril. 1994. *The Heterodox Hegel.* Albany: State University of New York Press.

Otto, Rudolph. 1917. *The Idea of the Holy.* Oxford: Oxford University Press, 1950.

Pachauri, Rajendra K., et al. 2015. *Climate Change 2014: Synthesis Report.* Intergovernmental Panel on Climate Change. New York: Cambridge University Press.

Paracelsus, Theophrastus. *Alchemical Catechism.* Trans. A.E. Waite. Online <http://www.sacred-texts.com/alc/tschoudy.htm> (accessed 20 September 2018).

Peirce, C. S. 1955. 'Evolutionary Love'. In *Philosophical Writings of Peirce,* pp. 361–74. Ed. Justus Buchler. New York: Dover.

Pieper, Josef. 1953. *The Silence of St Thomas.* South Bend: St Augustine's Press, 1999.

Plato. *Complete Works.* Ed. John M. Cooper and D. S. Hutchinson. Indianapolis: Hackett Publishing, 1997.

Pound, Marcus. 2008. *Žižek: A (Very) Critical Introduction.* Grand Rapids: Eerdmans.

Randall, Rosemary, and Andy Brown. 2015. *In Time for Tomorrow? The Carbon Conversations Handbook.* Cambridge: Surefoot Effect.

Reeves, Marjorie. 1976. *Joachim of Fiore and the Prophetic Future: A Medieval Study in Historical Thinking.* Stroud: Sutton.

Ricoeur, Paul, 1967. *The Symbolism of Evil.* Trans. Emerson Buchanan. Boston: Beacon Press, 1969.

—. 1970. *Freud and Philosophy: An Essay on Interpretation.* Trans. Denis Savage. New Haven: Yale University Press.

Rubin, Jeff. 2012. *The End of Growth.* New York: Random House.

Schelling, F. W. J. 1797. 'Ideas on a Philosophy of Nature as an Introduction to This Science'. Trans. Priscilla Hayden-Roy. In *Philosophy of German Idealism,* pp. 167–202. The German Library, Vol. 23. Ed. Ernst Behler. New York: Continuum, 1987.

—. 1798. *Von der Weltseele. Eine Hypothese der höheren Physik.* Schelling Sämtliche Werke, Vol. 2, pp. 345–584. Ed. K.F.A. Schelling. Stuttgart: J. Cotta, 1861.

—. 1799. *First Outline of a System of the Philosophy of Nature.* Trans. Keith R. Peterson. Albany: State University of New York Press, 2004.

—. 1800. *System of Transcendental Idealism.* Trans. Peter Heath. Charlottesville: University Press of Virginia, 1978.

—. 1802–3. *The Philosophy of Art.* Ed. and trans. Douglas Scott. Minneapolis: University of Minnesota Press, 1989.

—. 1809. *Philosophical Inquiries into the Essence of Human Freedom.* Trans. Jeff Love and Johannes Schmidt. Albany: State University of New York Press, 2006.

—. 1831. *Urfassung der Philosophie der Offenbarung.* Ed. Walter E. Ehrhardt. Frankfurt: Meiner, 1992.

—. 1833. *On the History of Modern Philosophy*. Trans. Andrew Bowie. Cambridge: Cambridge University Press, 1994.

—. 1842. *Historical-Critical Introduction to the Philosophy of Mythology*. Schelling Sämtliche Werke, Vol. 11, pp. 1–252. Trans. Mason Richey and Markus Zisselsberger. Albany: State University of New York Press, 2007.

—. 1854. *Einleitung in die Philosophie der Mythologie (Darstellung der reinrationalen Philosophie)*. Schelling Sämtliche Werke, Vol. 11, pp. 253–572. Ed. K. F. A. Schelling. Stuttgart: J. G. Cotta, 1861.

Schleiermacher, Friedrich. 1799. *On Religion: Speeches to Its Cultured Despisers*. Trans. Richard Crouter. Cambridge: Cambridge University Press, 1996.

Schumacher, E.F. 1973. *Small is Beautiful: A Study of Economics as if People Mattered*. Vintage Books, 1993.

Schweitzer, Albert. 1931. *Out of My Life and Thought: An Autobiography*. Trans. Antje Bultmann Lemke. Baltimore: Johns Hopkins University Press, 2009.

Seidler, Victor. 1986. *Kant, Respect, and Injustice: The Limits of Liberal Moral Theory*. Abington: Routledge.

Serres, Michel. 1995. *The Natural Contract*. Trans. Elizabeth MacArthur and William Paulson. Ann Arbor: University of Michigan Press.

Smith, Anthony Paul. 2013. *A Non-Philosophy of Nature: Ecologies of Thought*. London: Palgrave Macmillan.

Spinoza, Benedict. 1883. *The Chief Works of Benedict de Spinoza*. Trans. R. H. M. Elwes. New York: Dover, 1955.

Sullivan, Robert. 1998a. *The Meadowlands: Wilderness Adventures at the Edge of a City*. New York: Scribner.

—. 1998b. 'I Sing the Meadowlands.' *New York Times Magazine*. Online <https://www.nytimes.com/1998/02/15/magazine/i-sing-the-meadowlands.html> (accessed 17 October 2018).

Taubes, Jacob. 1947. *Occidental Eschatology*. Trans. David Ratmoko. Stanford: Stanford University Press, 2009.

—. 2004. *The Political Theology of Paul*. Trans. Dana Hollander. Stanford: Stanford University Press.

Taylor, Charles, 2007. *A Secular Age*. Cambridge, MA: Harvard University Press.

Tillich, Paul. 1967. *Systematic Theology*. Three volumes in one. Chicago: University of Chicago Press.

—. 1999. *The Essential Tillich: An Anthology of the Writings of Paul Tillich*. Ed. F. Forrester Church. Chicago: University of Chicago Press.

Toadvine, Ted. 2017. 'Our Monstrous Futures: Global Sustainability and Eco-Eschatology'. *Symposium*, 21:1, 219–30.

Tobler, Georg Christoph. 1783. 'Nature: Aphorisms by Goethe'. *Nature*, 1, 9–11 (4 November 1869). Online <http://www.nature.com/nature/about/first/aphorisms.html> (accessed 20 September 2018).

Tritten, Tyler. 2014. 'Christ as Copula: On the Incarnation and the Possibility of Religious Exclusivism'. *Analecta Hermeneutica*, 6.

Vater, Michael, 1978. Introduction to F. W. J. Schelling's *System of Transcendental Idealism*, pp. xi–xxvi . Charlottesville: University of Virginia Press.

Walshe, Maurice O'C. 2009. *The Complete Mystical Works of Meister Eckhart*. New York: Crossroad.

Weber, Max. 1905. *The Protestant Ethic and the Spirit of Capitalism*. Trans. Talcott Parsons. New York: Charles Scribner's Sons, 1958.

—. 1922. *The Vocation Lectures: Science as a Vocation/Politics as a Vocation*. Ed. Tracy B. Strong. Trans. Rodney Livingstone. Indianapolis: Hackett, 2004.

Weeks, Andrew. 1996. *Paracelsus: Speculative Theory and the Crisis of the Early Reformation*. Albany: State University of New York Press.

White, Lynn, Jr. 1967. 'The Historical Roots of Our Environmental Crisis'. *Science*, 155 (issue 3767, 10 March), 1203–7.

Williams, Mark, Jan Zalasiewicz, P. K. Haff, Christian Schwägerl, Anthony D. Barnosky and Erle C. Eills. 2015. 'The Anthropocene Biosphere'. *Anthropocene Review*, 2:3, 196–219.

Wright, N. T. 2008. *Surprised by Hope: Rethinking Heaven, the Resurrection, and the Mission of the Church*. San Francisco: Harper One.

—. 2017. *Paul: A Biography*. San Francisco: Harper One.

Yates, Frances. 1964. *Giordano Bruno and the Hermetic Tradition*. Chicago: University of Chicago Press.

—. 1979. *The Occult Philosophy in the Elizabethan Age*. London: Routledge.

Zaehner, R. C. 1938. *Hindu Scriptures*. Translated and introduced by R. C. Zaehner. New York: Alfred A. Knopf, 1992.

Žižek, Slavoj. 1996. *The Indivisible Remainder: On Schelling and Related Matters*. London: Verso.

—. 2000. *The Fragile Absolute – Or Why the Christian Legacy Is Worth Fighting For*. London: Verso.

—. 2008. 'Nature and Its Discontents'. *SubStance*, issue 117 (37:3), 37–72.

Index